Climbing Free

Climbing Free

My Life in the Vertical World

Lynn Hill
with Greg Child

Foreword by John Long

W. W. NORTON & COMPANY
NEW YORK   LONDON

Frontispiece: Negotiating the crux on Calippo in the Dolomites,
Italy (5.13b). (BETH WALD)

For information about permission to reproduce selections from this book, write to
Permissions, W. W. Norton & Company, Inc., 500 Fifth Avenue, New York, NY 10110

The text of this book is composed in Sabon with the display set in Univers and Industrial
Composition by Gina Webster
Manufacturing by Quebecor Fairfield
Book design by Lovedog Studios
Production manager: Julia Druskin

ISBN 0-393-04981-7

W. W. Norton & Company, Inc., 500 Fifth Avenue, New York, N.Y. 10110
www.wwnorton.com

W. W. Norton & Company Ltd., Castle House, 75/76 Wells Street, London W1T 3QT

1 2 3 4 5 6 7 8 9 0

To my mother and father,
who took all seven of us on many camping trips across
the country and instilled in me a deep love for and
appreciation of nature.

And to those who introduced me to the world of climbing:
my sister Kathy, my brother Bob, and
Chuck Bludworth (1954–1980).

Contents

Foreword

I first saw Lynn Hill at Trash Can Rock, in Joshua Tree National Monument, in 1975. She wore a sassy little Grand Prix driver's hat, gym shorts, a bikini top, and looked about twelve years old (she was fourteen). Her older brother Bob, and her sister's fiancée, Chuck, were slip-sliding all over a little slab climb and eventually gave up. They reluctantly let Lynn tie into the rope and she danced up the slab in about fifteen seconds. On top, she looked like she'd just been crowned queen of some exotic land. The boys seemed unimpressed by her flagrant delight. *Girl's got a future*, I remember thinking.

Maybe three years later, also out at Joshua Tree, John Bachar (at the time one of the world's greatest free climbers) and I were trying to scratch up the overhanging side of a ten-foot boulder. Rumor had it that some Frenchman had climbed it the previous week, but we didn't believe any such thing, since neither of us could even get started. Then who should walk around the corner but Lynn Hill. She wasn't a girl anymore. She smiled, then proceeded to climb straight up that boulder, on her first try. We couldn't have been more amazed had a giraffe pranced by on its front legs. Lynn down-climbed the back side of the boulder and joined us on the front. "That hurt my fingers," she said, not a trace of cunning in her voice. I clasped the first razor-blade holds and still couldn't pull my feet off the ground. Neither could John. I never did climb the damn thing, though not for lack of trying.

Perhaps a year later, Lynn and I were an item and, along with Richard Harrison, were attempting a new climb at Red Rocks, an adventurous sandstone area twenty miles outside Las Vegas, Nevada. Lynn was working up the first pitch, ratcheting up a bottomless chimney that pinched off after about 60 feet, forcing her out onto the steep face to the right. After barely a body length on the face, a hold broke and she was plummeting though the air—and kept plummeting for about 50 feet before a nut finally arrested her fall, leaving her dangling upside down, in midair, about 10 feet off the deck.

"Jesus!" Richard yelled. "You okay?"

I was too stunned to talk. Bar none, that was the most spectacular airball "whipper" we'd ever seen. And a mighty close shave at that. Another 10 feet and she'd have left the cliffside in a black bag.

"I'm fine," she said, slightly annoyed. Straightaway she squeezed back up the chimney, climbed out onto the face, and without hesitation, cranked up to a ledge about 30 feet above.

I mention these anecdotes because they illustrate several traits that remain hallmarks of Lynn's character: enjoyment, excellence without guile, tenacity in fearful situations, and naked boldness. These certainly factored into the success of the five-foot, one-hundred-pound dynamo (and don't believe her if she claims to be bigger) who would soon come to dominate the "greatest sport in the world."

By and large, Lynn Hill was (and still is, when she wants to be) as good as the very best male climbers, which, considering her size, is miraculous. Many climbs favor masculine dimensions, such as wide fist cracks and steep faces obliging a long reach. Lynn comes up to the middle of my chest, and I swear she can slot her fist inside a walnut shell. Yet even on those wide cracks and reachy face climbs she can hold her own. God knows how. On climbs that favor Lynn's stature, especially small hold routes or tricky balance problems, Lynn is untouchable.

Almost from the first days when "Little Lynnie" tied into a rope, the common refrain was, "Who the hell is that girl?!" The macho ones among us—and I marched point for that group—were left to watch and weep as Lynn breezed over what often had cost us several layers of skin and a few of our nine lives. We normally would have growled like wolves at having our male luster dimmed by a woman. But Lynn shattered the gender barrier so thoroughly that no one could put the pieces back together again. So after the initial shock of it all, the bone-deep chauvinism most of us had unconsciously embraced soon melted away like fat off a holiday ham. Guys no longer begged her onto their rope because she was pleasing to the eye, which is reason enough when you're twenty or fifty, but rather because when you tied in with Lynn, you could get up any damn climb. What the hell? Why not cash in while the going's good, meaning so long as you could inveigle Lynn onto the same cord. We all did. Repeatedly. We all wanted our name on a new climb that would stand forever.

Unlike other sports, a climber's deeds are literally fixed in stone. Barring features (such as hand- and footholds) that occasionally break off, a climbing route forever remains the same climbing route, with a difficulty rating arrived at through consensus. Comparing past and present routes, and performances on these routes, is fairly straightforward. The routes Lynn did, many for the first time, remain at the top of anyone's "A" list.

Her greatest triumphs are ghastly hard "free" climbs, a term and deed the lay public often mistakes for "free soloing," which is climbing without a rope. Basically, free climbing is anything using your own body—hands, feet, gams, et al.—for upward progress. Free "routes" are specific paths up given cliffs and usually follow prominent features such as cracks, arêtes, lines of holds or pockets, and so forth. Because severe routes are hit-and-miss even for world-class climbers, falls are frequent and expected. A rope and attending gear are used to safeguard the fall.

When the tackle is used for upward progress, or to hang on to rest after a fall (standard practice), the climber is no longer free climbing, rather "aid" climbing—that is, using the gear as an "aid" to fight gravity. On titanic rock walls, like the blank, overhanging palisades of El Capitan in Yosemite Valley, cracks and features tend to run out—meaning there is nothing for the free climber to clasp—and aid climbing is often the only way up. Here, experienced teams might take a week to scale the 3,000-foot cliffside, slowly, precariously building a ladder of pitons and other gear up the sheer granite ramparts. These two forms, free and aid climbing, are distinctive arts; to Lynn's credit, she excels at both. But it is in her free climbing, often performed on the grandest possible scale, where Lynn Hill made history.

Her first free ascent in 1993 of the Nose route on El Capitan, the most sought-after pure rock climb in the world, remains a high-water mark in a sport where the technical tide rises by the week. It is difficult for a nonclimber to grasp the significance of this effort. Insiders well know how good she was—and still is. But even to authorities in more traditional, media-driven sports, Lynn Hill remains a curiosity who, to my knowledge, has never been contrasted with other great female athletes of her era. Suffice it to say that I am not alone in thinking that throughout the eighties and nineties, Lynn Hill was quite possibly the best female athlete in the world. El Capitan rises in bold testament to this claim.

We all know that "great" men or women are often lousy people, that the Napoleons of the world often advance over the backs of others. We also know how high achievements are often traceable to the love of acclaim. Lynn is the exception to both rules. She would climb anything with most anyone, putting so little emphasis on her stature that it seemed as unreal as watching her walk on water, figuratively speaking. The end result is that many climbers of our era came to call Lynn a close friend, and have the memories to prove it.

Can I take the measure of Lynn's humility and humanity? I won't even try. I trust both will shine through in this engaging book. But in closing, I want to touch on the reasons why I believe Lynn's conquests reach beyond a person scratching up rock walls from Montana to Madagascar.

Mastery is admirable in any field. But when this mastery plays out by slaying gender stereotypes, embracing primal terrors (always a factor in climbing), having the vision and chops to do long-established things in novel ways, fighting through injuries, slim wages, and one's own doubts and insecurities, and growing more modest in the process, a mere rock climb becomes a victory for the human spirit. Through choice or temperament, most of us are followers. Greatness, on the other hand, is almost always a path leading into the unknown and unproven. And Lynn walked that path like a giant.

I have been all over the world and have had the fortune of doing things with many special people, some famous, some anonymous. But the biggest little hero I've ever known is Lynn Hill. The rest of us are just holding her rope.

—John Long
Venice, California
August 2001

Acknowledgments

I started recording anecdotes about my life over ten years ago, but it took me until now, at the age of forty, to finally finish writing this book. The story in these pages is by no means a thorough representation of climbing history, nor even a complete account of my life. My intent has been to describe the experiences that have most shaped my life and love for climbing. I've been extremely fortunate to have had the chance to follow my passion for climbing for over twenty-six years, and to have been part of such a wide spectrum of the climbing community across the world. Because I started climbing in the 1970s, my career bridged the gap between the great pioneers of previous generations and the sport climbing champions of today. Although I've seen enormous changes in the sport, I realize that no matter what generation we are from or what style of climbing we pursue—from sport climbing to big walls to high-altitude expeditions—we all share a spirit of adventure, curiosity, and a love of playing in a beautiful natural environment with our friends.

This book would not have happened without the efforts and encouragement of a great many people. I'd like to thank Greg Child, whose superb writing skills and friendship helped make this book a reality. I'd also like to thank my editor, Helen Whybrow, who helped guide me through this entire process, and my agent, Susan Golomb, whose sincere interest and encouragement helped motivate me to carry through to the end.

I would like to express my deepest gratitude to all my friends and family who have listened to me talk about this book for years and who have given me plenty of inspiration and thoughtful advice along the way. The list would be too long to thank everyone, but I'd like to acknowledge the following friends and colleagues: Shaoshana Alexander, John Bachar, Giulia Baciocco, Anna Biller-Collier, Jamie Bludworth, Jim Bridwell, Russ Clune, Ed Connor, Maria Cranor, Pietro Dal Pra, Robyn Erbesfield-Raboutou, Dean Fidelman, Margaret Foster, Brad Fuller, Rolando Garibotti, Mari Gingery, Sallie Greenwood, Linda Gunnerson, Aaron Huey, Steven Kaup, Susan Krawitz, Mike Lechlinski, John Long, Brad Lynch, Roy McClenahan, Jean Milgram, Simon Nadin, Salley Oberlin, Alison Osius, Bob Palais, Russ Raffa, Rick Ridgeway, Mark Robinson, Brooke Sandahl, Isabelle Sandberg, Susan Schwartz, Paul Sibley, Gene and Laura Smith, Antonella Strano, Steve Sutton, Steve Van Meter, Beth Wald, Jean Weiss, Elliot Williams, John and Bridget Winsor, Eva Yablonsky, and all my sponsors who have helped support me in sharing my passion for climbing with others.

I also owe a big thank you to all of the photographers who have generously provided such beautiful images: John Bachar, Thomas Ballenberger, Chris Bonington, Jim Bridwell, Simon Carter, Greg Child, Greg Epperson, Dean Fidelman, Philippe Fragnol, Tom Frost, Oliver Grünewald, Tilmann Hepp, Bob Hill, Mike Hoover, Michael Kennedy, John McDonald, Chris Noble, Jessica Perrin-Larrabee, Philippe Poulet, Brian Rennie, Rick Ridgeway, Mark Robinson, Charlie Row, Brooke Sandahl, Marco Scolaris, Sandy Stewart, Pascal Tournaire, Jorge Urioste, Beth Wald, and Heinz Zak.

Climbing Free

Chapter 1

The Perfect Fall

Deep in the countryside of southern France, nestled in a canyon of limestone cliffs the color of soft blue velvet, lies the village of Buoux. It is a sleepy hamlet of old stone-block farmhouses, rambling vineyards, and glades of twisted oaks in which old men and their cherished pigs roam in search of that curiously local delicacy, the truffle. Higher up, on the rocks above the village, are the water-worn ruins of steps, aqueducts, chambers, and battlements, chiseled long ago by medieval cliff dwellers looking for places of refuge during the various religious wars.

The air is quiet at Buoux, save for the grinding song of cicadas or the occasional call of a climber shouting, "Off belay," to a partner on the ground. For Buoux is among the most famous rock climbing destinations in Europe. It is also the place where I almost lost my life.

The day was May 9, 1989, and as I hiked the fifteen-minute walk up the trail to the cliff, I was thinking about my life and how smoothly it seemed to be running. I was twenty-eight years old, an American traveling through France, earning a living as a professional rock climber. I only had to turn my head and look down the hill to see the brand-new car—a compact metallic blue Ford—that I had just won in a climbing competition in Munich, Germany.

It seemed incredible, strange, even a little perverse, that I could win cars and cash and be touted as a star in magazines and on TV for rock climbing—a sport that remained a complete mystery to most people. But I had the knack for winning, consistently, the climbing competitions that were the current rage throughout Europe, and I was ranked as the number one woman in the sport climbing competition circuit. These competitions challenged the contestants to scale an artificial cliff with a difficult course set with adjustable finger and toe grips made of plastic resin that are supposed to simulate the natural features of rock. The contests were held inside sports stadiums, and the walls, lit by floodlights and made of steel scaffolding, plywood, and resin, were shaped like abstract castles. These man-made walls were quite different from the natural cliffs I had learned on, and I found the challenge of competition exhilarating. To be making a living at something that I found so personally gratifying felt too good to be true.

Those were my thoughts that day as I hiked to the base of the cliff with Russ Raffa, my husband of seven months. At the base of the gray-blue wall I dumped my small rucksack on a platform of knotted tree roots and shifted my thinking to the routine of getting ready to climb.

Who knows how many thousands of times I had gone through the motions of launching up from the ground, engaging my fingers and toes with the rock for the hundred feet or so of a route, then clipping my rope into a set of steel "anchors" and being lowered back to the ground by my partner? The routine was as second nature as riding a bicycle or starting a car. It was so intuitive that I barely gave it a thought.

The cliff we were heading toward is called the Styx Wall, after the river in the Hades of Greek mythology over which the souls of the dead must cross. And the name of the route itself was Buffet Froid, which in French means "Cold Buffet." All climbs have a name, and for some quirky reason the climbers who had first ascended this one named it after the cold lunch that is served following a funeral.

Neither of those names registered in my thoughts that day as portents of ill luck, and why should they? It was a cool, blue-skied afternoon, Russ and I had spent a languid morning sleeping in and breakfasting at an auberge—a country inn—back down the winding road that links Buoux to Apt, and Buffet Froid was an easy climb on which we planned to loosen up. Russ decided to lead the first warm-up route of the day. He would set the rope for me from above and I would then "follow" the pitch. A pitch refers to the section of a climb between belay stations, and can be no longer than the length of a rope. In this case, one pitch would get me to the top of the cliff.

Russ prepared to climb. He uncoiled our 165-foot-long climbing rope and lay it in a neat heap on the ground. He buckled his climbing harness around his waist and tied the rope into it. Then he laced up his climbing shoes and finally he left the ground, moving gracefully upward by poising his fingers and toes against ripples and pockets in the rock. Along the way, about every 10 to 15 feet, he passed a steel bolt drilled into the rock.

The idea behind sport climbing is to make a safe path up a cliff so the climber can enjoy the gymnastic play between the human body and steep stone. The bolts on Buffet Froid were outposts of safety, inserted into the rock for climbers to clip their rope into as they passed. The intent of the bolt is not for the climber to use it for aid in getting up the cliff. The bolt is there to catch any accidental falls. So at each bolt, Russ unclipped from his harness a quickdraw—a short sling with a carabiner at either end—and attached it to the bolt. He then clipped the other end of the quickdraw to the rope. Now, if he slipped, he could not fall far beyond that bolt before the rope arrested him.

Standing on the ground, my job as his belayer was to hold the other end of the rope, which was threaded through a small gadget called a belay device. In the event of a fall, my quick reaction and the belay device, which was clipped to my harness, would save the day by pinching the rope tightly and bringing Russ to a stop when his rope came snug against the bolt he had just clipped.

Russ took about ten minutes to climb up Buffet Froid. At the top he came to a pair of immensely strong steel rings, also drilled into the rock. Here he rearranged the system by anchoring himself momentarily, untying from the rope and threading it through the rings. He then tied back into the rope again and let his body weight come onto the rope—and, therefore, onto me—and I lowered him down. Back on the ground he untied and handed me the end of the rope.

"Your turn now, Lynnie," Russ said.

The rope now went up from the ground, where Russ controlled it through his belay device, through the rings at the top of the climb, and back down to me. Thus, for my ascent of Buffet Froid I had the added safety of the rope being above me. Technically, if I fell I would drop barely any distance at all.

During Russ's climb my thoughts had drifted to my next competition, which would be held in Leeds, England. This would be the very first international World Cup contest in which many of the top-ranked men and women climbers would compete. The competition would be fierce. To win, I'd have to be in top mental and physical shape. But these thoughts were like casual mental flotsam. I was relaxed and content—perhaps too much so.

I began by threading the finger-thick nylon strand of rope through my harness with the intention of tying a knot called a bowline, a maritime knot which sailors prize for its strength. But instead of finishing my knot, I decided to walk over to where I left my climbing shoes on the ground about twenty feet away. My shoes happened to be sitting near a Japanese woman who was preparing to climb a route beside Buffet Froid.

"Hi, are you having a good time climbing here in Buoux?" I asked as I laced up my climbing shoes.

"Yes, yes," the Japanese girl had replied, nodding enthusiastically.

When I returned to the base of the climb, I noticed that Russ had already put me on belay. The thought occurred to me that there was something I needed to do before climbing. I asked myself, *Should I take my jacket off?* But I figured since this was a warm-up climb, my jacket wouldn't be a problem, so I dismissed this thought, wiped the dirt off the soles of my shoes, and began climbing.

"Okay, climbing," I said to Russ, using the simple verbal signal all climbers use to tell their partner they are setting off.

But this time the system had a glitch in it: pilot error. I had poked the rope into the loop in my harness, but, distracted by the actions of fetching my rock shoes and chatting with the Japanese girl, I had not tied the knot. The end of the rope hung at my waist, hidden underneath my jacket, like a ticking time bomb. Neither I nor anyone else at the cliff noticed my potentially fatal mistake.

For a confident, expert climber, Buffet Froid poses little challenge. Its rating on the French scale of difficulty is 6b+. On the U.S. scale that's 5.11, which is no pushover, but for a climber used to a diet of 5.13 routes, it's relatively easy. For me, executing its moves would be like a slow warm-up lap in the pool or a gentle bicycle ride over the flats.

I latched on to the first holds, two limestone flakes no wider than matchbooks. Arching my fingers like grappling hooks, I bore my weight onto the flakes, spreading the force across my torso. I then raised a toe up onto a smooth bump on the wall and pressed down with my hands and feet. Lifting myself off the ground, I reached up with my other hand, directing my fingers to a grape-sized pocket denting the wall. I burrowed a fingertip into the hole, shifted my weight onto it, and climbed higher. This basic sequence was repeated foot after foot, yet, I should say, no two moves were alike. That is part of the beauty of

Free climbing in France. (PHILIPE FRAGNOL)

rock climbing: no two moves are ever the same. That rule applies to all climbs, whether they are easy or hard, because the rock holds infinite variations and possibilities.

At any point in the 72 feet of Buffet Froid's steep face, the rope could have slipped out of my harness and snaked down the cliff through the carabiners to land in a pile on the ground.

It would have been embarrassing to have made such a blunder, but in fact it would have been no big deal to become unattached from the rope while I climbed, because this was a fairly easy climb for me and I knew there was little chance of falling. Sure, the sight of the rope slipping out of my harness and falling down the cliff would have produced a tingling shock wave up my spine. I probably would have had a chance to practice my French by exclaiming, *"Merde!"* Russ would have shouted, "Oh, my God!" and the Japanese girl and other climbers at the cliff would have uttered exclamations in a half dozen languages. But I probably would have solved the problem by either climbing up a few feet or down a few feet, to grab one of the quickdraws clipped to the bolts. I would then have clipped my harness into one of these and hung safely until Russ, who would have found another climber to belay him, climbed up to me with our rope.

But the rope did not detach from my harness and Russ did not get the opportunity to come scampering up the rock to rescue me. Had that happened, we would have engaged in one of those caring-yet-chiding husband-wife tiffs that end in laughter. Doubtless, we'd have retreated down the trail to have a glass of wine in the auberge in the valley. No sense in pushing the odds when the gods of the odds are going against you.

I climbed on.

Over the next five minutes there must have been a dozen more opportunities for the rope to drop from my waist. Only the barest friction of the rope being pressed through a narrow webbing loop on my harness held it in place. It should have fallen out whenever I shifted my weight to the side or whenever Russ pulled down on the rope to take in the slack as I climbed up.

And then I reached the end of the climb, about 72 feet above the ground. That's about the height of a seven-floor apartment building. In front of me were the two steel bolts and the threaded rope: a rig strong enough to hang a car from. To descend safely, I only had to lean back and Russ would hold me, carefully letting the rope slide through his belay device, controlling my speed of descent with his hand. I would descend as if in an elevator and land gently back down on the ground.

Here was the last chance for my mistake to reveal itself before disaster struck. When I yelled to Russ that I had completed the climb, I expected to feel the rope tight against my waist so he could lower me. I glanced down and noticed Russ was talking to someone, so I grabbed the rope with both hands to pull in the slack. I leaned back, expecting the rope to hold me.

Instead, I felt the rush of air against my cheek.

Climbers at the cliff and in the valley that day described a "bloodcurdling scream" that echoed off the walls. My scream—an involuntary shout of horror—was even heard by Pierre, the mayor of Buoux, who sat in the library of his house half a mile away. Looking toward the source of the scream, climbers on neighboring routes saw a figure free-falling down the cliff, carving an outward arc through the sky. All told, I covered the 72 feet in less than two seconds. As fast as that may be, the sight of anyone falling leaves an imprint on a person's memory as sharp as a photographic image etched into a frame of film.

Parachutists talk of the "ground rush effect" in which the rapid approach of the earth getting closer and closer becomes so powerfully mesmerizing that some unfortunate jumpers have forgotten to open their chutes. As I fell backward I waved my arms frantically in a circular motion to keep myself from landing on my head. Instincts dating back to my days as a gymnast must have resurfaced from deep in my subconscious: *Look for a landing*, some inner voice instructed me. I veered toward the leaves of a tree to my left and saw Russ, getting closer, his mouth gaping in confusion and shock. Then I felt the slap of leaves and branches.

It is not true that in a fall one sees one's life flash before one's eyes. There is not enough time for even a single formed thought. But survival instincts are wired on a faster pathway than any other mental process, and when I saw the approaching tree I knew instinctively that my best chance to live was to land in it. If it could be said that I aimed myself at any landing zone, it was toward that short, stunted green oak tree.

Speeding toward it, I tucked my body into a ball, blasted through its branches, then my left buttock slammed into a lattice of tree roots sprawling on the ground. The impact jarred the senses out of me.

Jennifer Cole, an American climber at the cliff that day, said that when I hit I bounced three feet into the air like a rubber ball, then I released my tuck with a flail of arms and smacked onto the ground, face first into the limey dirt.

The next thing I remember was the throb and ring of my brain as my consciousness partially returned. When I opened my eyes, Russ was wiping dirt from my face, my head resting in his lap.

"What happened?" I asked.

"I don't know," replied Russ.

Even if someone had explained that I had not finished tying my knot and had plunged from the top of the cliff, I may not have been able to grasp the meaning of the words. I was stunned, and was now flushed with the unfamiliar processes of shock and injury. I repeated the question.

A crowd of people was forming a circle around me. I heard a mix of languages—English, French, Italian, Polish, Japanese—and I picked up on a conversation about how to get me out of there. Though still in a semi-conscious state, I saw myself more clearly now, and I took stock of my injuries. Most of the pain was in my left arm, which was twisted in an unnatural position. It appeared broken. My jacket was ripped at the chest, and blood leaked through the hole. My butt ached as if a car had hit it.

"What happened?" I repeated. No one seemed to answer.

By now I knew I had done something stupid, and, ridiculously, I felt embarrassed. I stared up at the faces of those huddled around me. Estelle, the mayor's daughter, hovered over me. Her eyes had tears in them and her dark straight hair hung toward me like vines. Russ, still cradling my head, looked ashen. Other climbers seemed to come and go from my field of vision as they scurried back and forth. Already the wheels of a rescue were in motion, but I lay there understanding only one thing: I needed to concentrate on relaxing in order to better cope with the buzzing sensations of pain and confusion.

Sometime around late evening, in a fleeting spell of awareness, I saw that more people had arrived at the cliff: rescue people, dressed in bright orange-colored overalls. I groaned as I felt myself lifted up and placed onto a metal basket-shaped litter. Then I heard the creak of ropes and pulleys as a crew winched me to the top of the Styx Wall, where a helicopter was waiting to airlift me to a hospital more quickly. I saw hands holding the rails of the stretcher, and felt the bump and movement of being carried through some trees and into a field. Finally, there was the din and wind of the chopper, and inside it a rocking sensation that lulled me into a trancelike state.

The next thing I remember clearly was the emergency room in a hospital in Marseilles. Three women in white gowns stood with their backs to me, chatting in French—a language that at the time I could not speak or understand. I began making noises, asking for something for the acute pain in my elbow. But they seemed to ignore me, until all at once they turned around and began cleaning dried blood from my nose and from the thumb-deep stab wound in my pectoral muscle, which a tree root had pierced. Then, just as I was about to complain that I didn't care about a bit of dried blood on my nose, that their attentions were hurting me, I smelled a chemical odor and felt a rush of relief as an opiate shut out the hurt.

Twelve hours later I woke from a dreamless sleep. I lay on my back in a hospital bed. Daylight streamed through the curtained window. Sounds of people moving through the corridor and the mayhem of French traffic on the street outside filtered through the walls. Piece by piece I recollected the events of the previous day. I knew I had fallen from the top of the Styx Wall, though I still was not sure what had gone wrong in a system I considered to be foolproof. Then I saw Russ coming toward me from a corner of the room.

"Thank God you're alive," he said. "You're so lucky. You can't imagine what it was like to see you fall from that high up. I had no idea what happened—I thought you were dead when I turned you over on the ground. You crashed through a small tree, then landed on the ground right between two big boulders. How are you feeling now?"

"I feel like a truck ran over me. What went wrong?"

"I think you forgot to tie your knot."

I felt a sense of embarrassment to have made such a stupid mistake. Ironically, earlier in the week, I had noticed that Russ had forgotten to double-back his harness and I reminded him to do so twice. Then the very next day I forgot to tie my own knot!

It was all coming back to me. I remembered the events leading up to my fall, then the helicopter flight, the nurses in the hospital, and the moment sometime in the dead of night when I had briefly regained consciousness to find myself in a darkened room with my arm dangling over the side of the bed, holding on to a large bucket of water strapped to my wrist. No sooner did I note this as being odd than the doctor who was standing over me told me to let go of the bucket. At that point my muscles were ready for the next maneuver; the next thing I knew, the doctor took my arm and gave it a sudden tug and a twist. There was a searing pain as the elbow joint slipped back into its correct alignment. Then I had returned to the oblivion of sleep.

My arm now lay propped on a pillow, cradled in a three-quarter-length plaster cast. An IV tube protruded from the other arm and I was lying in a crooked position so as to relieve the pain I felt in my left buttock. Although I was grateful to know that my arm was not broken, only dislocated, still I wondered what permanent nerve or ligament damage I might have suffered. The strength in my arms was my lifeblood; without that power I could not climb. What I could see through the gauze and plaster surrounding my arm was swollen blue flesh. I thought about trying to wriggle my fingers, but there was too much pain and inflammation to even consider it.

As more and more thoughts broke through the haze of the painkiller, I noticed I was seeing through swollen, squinting eyes. Easing myself over the edge of the bed, I held my arm in the cast and shuffled toward the bathroom. When I switched on the light and saw my reflection in the mirror, I let out a groan of revulsion. My eyes were blackened, my cheeks swollen, my hair matted in a clump.

The sight of my beat-up face jarred my thoughts toward reality. I was lucky to be alive, but this would also mean that I would not be competing at the first World Cup competition in the history of the sport.

Disappointment overwhelmed me. I staggered away from the mirror and its ugly reflection. Limping back to my bed, I lay down. How well things had been going until this blunder. I felt I had a good shot at winning the competition in Leeds and I was climbing harder than any woman ever had. Now, so far as I knew, my elbow may never heal well enough to climb at that level again. My life as a competition climber could be over. I'm not the type given to crying, but my eyes grew wet as I realized what I had always known—that nothing in life is guaranteed. Just when everything seems to be going along smoothly, some unexpected crisis always seems to happen.

As I stared at the white ceiling, my mind filled with the kind of questions that come up after a brush with death. How did I survive such a fall? What did this fall mean? This incident brought up the obvious question of fate and my purpose in life. Climbing had defined my life, it was in my blood, yet when people asked me why I did it, I struggled for words to explain. I couldn't imagine my life without climbing, but where was I headed on that journey? Having nearly lost my life in a moment of absentmindedness, I realized that I needed to pay more attention.

Suddenly everything in my existence had a question mark looming over it. I realized it was time for Lynn to have a close look at Lynn.

Then I reentered the refuge of sleep.

Chapter 2

Early Days

I believe that every event in life happens for a reason. The consequences of my carelessness on the rock that day were like an unexpected slap to the face: stinging but enlightening. In the weeks following the fall at Buoux I came to see my brush with death as an awakening. It was time to pay attention not just to how I climbed, but to how I lived.

That new sense of awareness began the morning after that first day in the hospital in Marseilles. I woke with a clear head. Gone were the gloomy clouds of disappointment that had closed around me when I had seen the extent of my injuries. It was as if during my sleeping hours I had told myself, *I know my body—I'll recover from these injuries.*

There was no one to blame for my accident except myself, and it was my responsibility to drag myself down the road to recovery. That road began in the hospital with a series of X rays and electrical tests that revealed no head injuries and no broken bones other than a hairline fracture in my foot.

My elbow, though, had been wrenched sideways and dislocated when I smashed through the tree. Although the French doctor had popped it back into place, my elbow ligaments, tendons, and cartilage had been painfully torn and stretched. The elbow is one of the most sensitive joints of the body, and to climb again I would have to work hard to restore its strength and flexibility.

But my body was not the only part of me in need of rebuilding. Lying in that stark white ward, I thought about my life of the past few years. My primary focus had been to climb my absolute best, and I had shaped my world around that desire. The result was a whirlwind of travel and rock climbing and physical training. This was precisely the life I wanted, but by letting climbing take precedence, I had let many important things slip to the back of my mind. I found myself thinking about the relationships with family and friends that had helped form the person I had become. I began to realize that my intense focus on climbing had prevented me from confronting imbalances in my personal life. If my life had not flashed before me during my fall, it ran through my thoughts in that French hospital.

My life began in Detroit, Michigan, in 1961. I was the fifth-born in a family of seven blue-eyed children. My father, James Alan Hill, and my mother, Suzanne Biddy, both came from small Catholic families. My father was a descendant of European immigrants who had come to the promised land of America in the late 1800s.

In 1895, my great-grandfather, John Fucentese, moved to Michigan from a small village in southern Italy, changed his last name to Hill, and married a woman of German descent from Baden-Baden named Anna Krauth. Their son Frank worked for Lawyers Title Insurance Company in Detroit and married a Scottish woman, Ruth Gilchrist, whose family owned coal mines in West Virginia near the cliffs of the New River Gorge. Perhaps I inherited my wanderlust from my ninety-four-year-old Scottish grandmother, a woman who describes herself as having "hot feet," and whose home is crammed with souvenirs from her world travels.

It is just as likely that I acquired my adventurous spirit from my maternal grandfather of Irish descent, although I never had the chance to meet him. My mother lost her father when she was only six months old. It was the Great Depression and Ralph Biddy was earning $100 a week—more than many folks made in a month—making films and writing stories for the newsreels that played in cinemas. One fateful day Ralph was flying in a small biplane, filming a new streamline train called the Lincoln Zephyr. When the "barnstormer" pilot edged the plane too close to the train, they were sucked into the vacuum behind the speeding engine and crashed.

I recall little of the suburb of Detroit where my family's roots took hold, although when I returned there during a family trip at the age of eleven, I was shocked to see a place of urban decay. I began to imagine my parents growing up amid boarded-up buildings and rampant crime, but apparently Detroit wasn't so bad when they were children. It was only after we moved that it deteriorated into a place fraught with riots and unemployment from the faltering car industry. In 1962 we moved from Detroit to Columbus, Ohio, where Dad was working toward a Ph.D. in flight mechanics at Ohio State University.

The Hill family, clockwise from left: Bob, me (with the cat), Michael, Trish, Kathy, Tom, and Jim.
(LYNN HILL COLLECTION)

Both of my parents were twenty years old, married just a year, when they had their first child, in 1956. Then, nearly each year thereafter they produced a new baby, until by 1964 we formed a family of nine. I can only imagine the chaos involved in keeping tabs on so many children. According to family lore, the year we moved from Detroit to Ohio—I was an infant at the time—the family was standing around the loaded station wagon, saying good-bye to friends. When the car took off, there was a shout of, "Hold on, don't forget the baby!" I had been inadvertently left behind in the arms of a neighbor.

A few years later we moved to southern California, where my father got a job working for North American Rockwell as an engineer in the aerospace division. We stayed in Fullerton, in Orange County, throughout the rest of my childhood. Our house sat on a hill, and from the end of the street we could look toward Anaheim and see fireworks light the sky at night above the magic kingdom of Disneyland. When I think of the landscape of our quintessentially American suburb, I think of rows of track houses with double garages, wide streets, shopping malls, and occasional oil derricks, their steel arms and wheels grinding like mechanical monsters, silently pumping oil out of the ground.

We rode bikes everywhere, and a short ride from the house brought us to the neighborhood tar pit, a site full of mystery for local children. This tar pit wasn't far from the La Brea tar pits, the famed archeological site where prehistoric creatures like dinosaurs and mastodons had sunk into a tarry black muck and had in recent times been exhumed. We would run about on the black semi-liquid surface of the local tar pit, leaving imprints of our feet and sometimes even breaking through the skin into the oily ooze underneath. Whenever that happened, we'd scream and run off, lest we sink in and suffer the same fate as the mastodons. Twenty years later, when my sister Trish and I went back to visit our old neighborhood, we found that the fields where we had spent most of our free time were covered in tract homes, and our tar pit playground was surrounded by a high wire fence and posted with a sign:

DANGER
DO NOT ENTER
TOXIC WASTE SITE

Our tar pit playground, where we had imagined that ancient fossils lurked, was in fact a wasteland of industrial poisons dumped by a local oil company.

But not all the fields were so hazardous. Elsewhere in our suburban wilderness I spent hours building forts and hunting reptiles. My brother Tom and my childhood boyfriend Scott showed me how to catch snakes slumbering under old pieces of wood or cardboard. We'd keep them as pets in a glass aquarium at home, along with all the cats, dogs, chickens, turtles, and hamsters that shared our lively household. Unlike most of the girls I knew, I was drawn to the beautiful form, color, and texture of snakes, which I regarded as friendly creatures. But when it came time for the monthly ritual of placing a mouse in the snake cage, I felt sad watching the savage drama of the snake capturing and swallowing the poor mouse. Despite my compassion for all animals, I realized that this sacrifice was a natural part of the life cycle.

Like most dads, my father worked nine-to-five, five days a week, to support the ever-growing family while Mom took care of the home. My mother had studied dental hygiene in college, but being perpetually pregnant and busy caring for all of us, she had no time to work during those early years in California.

An aeronautical engineer with a gift for problem solving, Dad worked on the control panels of the early space shuttles. At home, he developed a knack for tuning out the noise of his family. I remember one day when I was about five I found him reading the newspaper. Not to be deterred, I bounced around in front of him shouting, "Hey, Dad!" The paper stood between us like a wall and no matter how much I shouted, he remained hidden and silent behind it, ignoring me. Time alone was elusive in our family, and as he read the day's news, he was determined to have five minutes without interruption. As a child it never occurred to me that he needed time to himself, because what I wanted most was his undivided attention. But the sheer size of our family made one-on-one parental attention a scarce commodity. Looking back on this period, I realize now how much I craved my father's attention. When he took to calling me Peanut Ears when I was about six years old, I cherished the nickname for no other reason than because it had come from him.

The Hill family comprised a diverse collection of personalities, yet it was age that determined the family pecking order. Kathy, Jim, and Bob were the "big kids," which meant, from my young perspective, that they got to stay up later at night and enjoy more privileges than us "little kids," who were Trish, me, Tom, and Michael. My sister Kathy was the oldest, and she assumed the role of chief administrator over the rest of us. Even outside the family she had a habit of taking charge. So much so that at the age of six she was reprimanded at school for telling other kids what to do in class. Bossiness aside, she was a helpful and dependable source of information for me on matters of growing up, which she was experiencing ahead of us. You could ask Kathy any question at all and she had a reply. Nothing stumped her. If she didn't know the real answer, she'd make one up.

After Kathy came my brothers Jim and Bob. Both of them inherited the red curly hair and freckles of our mother's Irish genes. Jim was the oldest boy and he took full advantage of his position of male seniority. While playacting a cowboy TV show called *The Roy Rogers and Dale Evans Show* that was popular at the time, Jim, the forceful personality of our troupe, would always assume the star role of Roy. Kathy played the lovely Dale Evans. And Bob, who was youngest in the line of "big kids," was left with the role of Cowboy Nothing. Nevertheless, he always played his role in a good-natured way. Like the rest of us, he learned to adapt to the rules of survival that govern a large family. One of our favorite family sayings was, "If you snooze, you lose." This meant that if there was a half gallon of ice cream in the freezer, you'd better get some before it disappeared. One day Bob thought he'd be clever and stash a Popsicle away in his drawer to eat later. He was disappointed when he discovered the Popsicle had melted all over his clothes.

My sister Trish was the leader of us "little kids." Though she was the middle child, she aspired to be one of the big kids. I was so far down the line that I had no other choice but to accept my rank as a little kid. Trish and I shared the same room throughout childhood. Much to my mother's annoyance we would chatter endlessly after lights-out time, which brought her to the door several times a night with a stern whisper to "Be quiet! Go to sleep!" To foil Mom, we devised a phone system made from two paper cups linked by a string; into these kid-phones we talked, bed to bed. Maybe it was because we had complementary personalities that the pair of us got along like best friends. While Kathy and I tended to be serious and pragmatic by nature, Trish had a more flirtatious approach to life. Cute, girlish charm was Trish's strong suit, and she knew how to use it on babysitters, teachers, or any boy she wanted to win over. In school, Trish seemed to have just the right blend of charisma and intelligence to excel. Though I did fine in school, I felt most in my element while playing outside.

My birth followed Trish's by fifteen months. One of the classic family stories about us relates to when I was about two years old. My Aunt Gale mentioned that I didn't speak much. Trish, who was three at the time, replied by saying, "She talks but nobody listens." Being heard in such a large family was never easy, so instead I learned to engage in my own world and to figure things out on my own. I can still hear my mother's words from those years: "If you want something done, do it yourself." I embraced her philosophy early and this approach has stayed with me ever since. Apparently, by age three I insisted on tying my own shoes. Whether by nature or by necessity, or a bit of both, I learned to be independent and self-sufficient.

As far as a presage to my career as a climber, there is a quote from my baby journal that reads, "Lynn climbs the monkey bars like a pro." Climbing movement seemed natural and alluring to me from the earliest days. By age twelve I had invented a method of climbing up the neighborhood light pole using a technique similar to that of a coconut tree climber. I wrapped my hands around the cement pole while clamping my bare feet against opposing sides and climbed up it for 25 feet. My technique for getting down involved sliding down the rough-textured pole like a fireman. The other kids in the neighborhood were impressed, but my mother looked on with bemused concern. Little did she know where this would lead.

Next in line after me came my brothers Tom and Michael. Tom was the hyperactive child of the family. When he was two, my mother had to lock the deadbolt on our front door because Tom had developed a nocturnal urge to explore the neighborhood. Like a pint-sized escape artist, he would wait until everyone was asleep, climb out of his crib, unlatch the door, and wander the surrounding streets and yards in the dead of night. Once my mother found Tom inside a chicken coop in our neighbor's front yard at six A.M., the hens huddled nervously at one end, and our naked and chicken-shit-covered Tom at the other. My mother used to call him Tom Terrific after a cartoon show about a young superboy and his wonder dog, both of whom found trouble everywhere.

At school, Tom had a hard time sitting still in class and was often sent to the principal's office for causing trouble. He even bit the principal once when he was being reprimanded. Whenever possible, I stuck up for "Yom," as I used to affectionately call him (he called me "Yinn"). One day when I was about eight years old, I saw that a particularly heavyweight neighborhood bully was picking on Tom, and I wasn't sure what to do. Later that night, I rehearsed the way I would defend him in the future. I sat on the counter in front of the bathroom mirror and pursed my lips and clenched my teeth, imitating Robert Redford's tough-guy look in *Butch Cassidy and the Sundance Kid*. I practiced my line: "Leave my little brother alone or I'll beat you up." Just as I finished saying this, I noticed my mother watching my performance in the hallway and we both burst out laughing.

Michael was the adorable baby of the family. As a toddler, if he didn't get his way, he would bang his head against the car window. For several months he had a large bump on his forehead. At that time I couldn't imagine what Michael would be like as a mature individual. But then again, as a young girl I couldn't imagine what it would be like to have a separate life outside my close-knit family. I'll never forget when this thought first occurred to me. We were on a family camping trip, traveling by night in our camping trailer. I was about nine years old and Jim was thirteen and we had crawled into a nest of sleeping bags and pillows in the overhead bunk, where Jim began reciting a song he'd made up about our family. Each of us was the subject of a mocking verse, which my talented brother punctuated with musical fart noises. I laughed until my stomach hurt. Then he suddenly stopped singing.

"You know, one day when we're all grown up, we'll have families of our own and we won't live together anymore," he said after a studied pause.

It saddened me to think that he was right, that someday the family would be scattered across the country and would no longer share our day-to-day lives. But for the moment our family seemed indestructibly happy, every bit the *Brady Bunch* model that American families seemed to aspire to. Our family was even selected to pose for a Kodak advertisement, and as the photographer had us all parade in front of our sub-

My parents, Sue and Jim, on one of our family trips to the beach. (LYNN HILL COLLEC-
TION)

urban home with our tricycles and toys, we were one big happy family
in glowing color. Little did I know then that there's no such thing as a
perfect family.

Those family camping trips were some of the best times of my childhood. When I was a toddler, we spent nearly every weekend waterski-
ing at nearby Lake Elsinore. Then came our sailing phase. First, Dad
bought a little sabot, then he worked up to a Hobie 14. Later he got
together with some friends and bought a twenty-four-foot sailboat.
When we attempted to sail the twenty-six miles from Newport Harbor
to Catalina Island on this small yacht, nearly everyone became seasick
except Dad and me; Mom was smart enough to stay home. So ill were
my siblings that halfway to Catalina we turned about and headed
home. That was our first and last major family sailing trip. After that
we reverted back to long trips by station wagon to the mountains,
deserts, or lakes, where we enjoyed the big-sky views of the western
states.

The year I turned thirteen, one of our drives took us north from LA,
past Bakersfield, and up the Merced River. As we rounded the last bend

coming out of the Wawona tunnel, the full view of Yosemite Valley stunned me like no other landscape before. Goose bumps raced across my body as I stared at the marbled walls of El Capitan. To its right I saw more cliffs and a waterfall cascading in a great arc, sending slow-moving waves of mist into the air. Half Dome, a huge semicircle of rock, crowned the end of the valley. I knew people climbed these cliffs—Kathy's new boyfriend, Chuck, had just graduated from a rock climbing course and had told me about Yosemite—but I couldn't imagine how anyone could climb a wall as sheer and as high as El Capitan.

When they weren't taking us on trips along America's scenic roads, my parents wisely immersed us in activities that harnessed our abundant physical energy. Since Dad dabbled in Californian pursuits like surfing and cross-country skiing, so did we. Skateboarding, roller-skating, softball, baseball, football, and summer camp were all activities we enjoyed. My mother juggled our complex sports schedules and shuttled everyone around from one activity to the next in our station wagon.

Dad busied himself with the boys' activities, coaching Jim and Bob's football and baseball teams and chaperoning Michael's Indian Guides group, an organization similar to Boy Scouts. One of the activities that Mom participated in with us girls was Bluebirds, the female version of Indian Guides. But instead of learning to make fire by rubbing two sticks together, as the boys did, we made wall hangings and other "feminine" homemaker-style crafts. I envied the fire makers and their camping trip to Joshua Tree and wondered why girls couldn't do it too.

It took me years to fully appreciate the meaning of my mother's words when she said that I "marched to the beat of a different drummer." But looking back now, I realize that I was never the type of girl who liked dressing up in uncomfortable clothes and wearing makeup. I felt better wearing blue jeans, climbing trees, and catching snakes and lizards in the fields near our neighborhood. Such unfeminine endeavors earned me the label "tomboy." Despite the negative stigma then attached to the term, this never deterred me from pursuing my own natural inclinations.

Everyone in the Hill family pursued their own interests outside the family, but the one activity that we all had in common was swimming. When my mother started part-time work as a dental hygienist, she would drop us all off at the Los Coyotes Country Club, where we trained and competed on the swim team. One experience stands out in my memory from those early days, and it concerns the last important race of the year. I was just seven years old, but already I had been promoted to the more advanced "all-star" level swim team. The night before the event, there was a party with music and dancing at the country club. My coach, whom I adored, picked me up and danced with me in his arms. When he asked me to do my best in this race, I felt a powerful motivation to win. For him. I was deep in puppy love with this man.

The morning of the race, while standing on the starting blocks waiting for the sound of the starting gun, I felt a ball of energy in my stomach. At the sound of the starting gun I exploded into a dive and hit the water. The race was a fifty-yard freestyle sprint, and on the final stretch I noticed a competitor in the neighboring lane closing in on my lead. Threatened with losing, I concentrated all my force to make one final stroke to the finish line. Barely grazing the tips of my fingers on the wall at the end of the pool, I emerged smiling, convinced I had won.

But the judges hadn't seen my fingertip finish and minutes after the race my coach broke the news to me that I had been disqualified. I felt a hollow sense of disappointment with myself. Though just a child, I realized that if I hadn't been so concerned about "winning," I might have followed my own natural rhythm and won anyway. This was a lesson that became imprinted on my memory: don't let the desire to win interfere with your performance.

Although swimming was an ideal activity for building a basic athletic foundation as a child, the training process of endlessly lapping a pool was unbearably monotonous. Fortunately, I soon found another interest to replace swimming. One day, going with my mother to pick up my brother at the YMCA, I caught sight of a full-fledged gymnasium for the first time. Fascinated by the sleek, honed bodies whirling around on the bars and rings and flipping around on the exercise mats, I suddenly found myself joining in by performing a few cartwheels. One of the guys watched me cartwheel past.

"Pretty good. Can you do a round-off?" he said.

"What's that?"

"I'll show you."

He demonstrated the move. A round-off is an advanced variation of the cartwheel, but instead of letting your legs circle around your body like the spokes of a wheel, they are brought together in midair so you can land on them solidly together, facing the direction you came from. After the gymnast demonstrated the move, he offered to show me other techniques. Learning how to perform acrobatic moves in a gym seemed more fun than anything I'd done before. While I learned tricks from the gymnast, my mother waited patiently outside in the car. This would mark the first of many trips to this place and the awakening of my lifetime passion of playing with the forces of gravity.

The YMCA gymnastics program was in an early stage of development when I joined. I was one of only two girls in the group. But over the next few years our growing team performed in exhibitions at local schools, did halftime shows at the Angels Baseball Stadium, and competed in gymnastics competitions all over southern California. Our afternoon practice sessions allowed me to explore the capacity of my body, as well as my mind and imagination. For the first time I understood that physical action isn't only physical, but has a mental component as well.

On the balance beam at the local YMCA. (LYNN HILL COLLECTION)

This essential element of performance dawned on me one day during practice when I had just broken through the mental barrier of being able to perform a round-off, backhand spring, and back flip all in sequence, without help from a "spotter"—someone to catch me if I made a mistake. As I waited for a ride home after practice, I sat alone in the gym thinking how confident I had felt performing this tumbling maneuver by myself. On an impulse I stood up and launched into the series of flips again.

Just as my legs began to circle around overhead, the thought flashed through my mind that perhaps this was a bad idea. If I hurt myself, no one would be there to help me. Suddenly I froze in midair. The next thing I knew, I was lying on my upper back and neck on the mat. I wasn't hurt, but this experience taught me not to let fear interrupt my concentration once I was committed to action. That element of gym philosophy would, in time, translate into an important part of climbing philosophy for me.

My coach, Scott Crouse, was a former competitive gymnast on the California State University at Fullerton gymnastics team, and week by week he taught me more complex maneuvers. One day he suggested that I try a double back flip. I had seen a few world-class gymnasts like Kathy Rigby execute such difficult moves, and while I had a mental image of what a double back flip looked like, I wasn't sure how to translate this visual information into action.

"Just concentrate on three simple steps: the initial jump, tucking into a ball, and the final landing on the ground," Scott explained.

The thought of attempting this very advanced movement was daunting, but I trusted Scott to spot me well. As I practiced the double back flip, I mentally replayed what the flip looked and felt like each time I performed it. I discovered that I could dismantle the movement and focus on each separate phase of it, as if it were a series of photographs. This method of learning, called "chunking," was an effective means of understanding the components of movement in simple steps. At the age of eleven, I had discovered a powerful learning tool for getting my body to follow whatever my mind imagined. Visual learning, I would later find, also had direct applications to rock climbing.

Scott also emphasized the importance of using proper technique and form in gymnastics. He urged me to pay attention to the precise execution of each movement and to practice as though I were performing in a competition. One of Scott's dictums that still resonates in my memory was, "Once a bad habit is reinforced through repetition, it's hard to change. The brain tends to imprint incorrect movement patterns just as well as it does correct ones."

"Keep your legs straight and your toes pointed," he'd remind me.

One day while watching a performance by Shelly Lewins, one of the best gymnasts in the region, I suddenly understood the interrelationship between form and function. Shelly moved her arms and legs in perfectly linear or circular paths of movement. When she performed a split-leap, she was able to achieve maximum amplitude and perfect symmetry in the air by thrusting her arms and legs at precisely the right moment. In making transitions from one position to another, her arms flowed in graceful curves, or, conversely, in explosive thrusts to create efficient movement and aesthetic beauty all at once. This kind of perfection in movement was inspiring and clearly an effort worth working toward.

But as an eager young girl, I was more interested in learning complex acrobatic maneuvers than focusing on pretty formalities. The cute poses, stylish hand gestures, and fake smiles I was expected to display while performing competitions went against my nature. They seemed contrived and artificial and I resisted them. I did my routines with strength and agility and I did them deadpan and with few flourishes. Judges were not entirely impressed. As gymnastics became more rigid and structured, I began to lose my motivation and enthusiasm for remaining on the team.

At that time, entering adolescence, I felt resistant to rules. My nonconformist attitude was probably a reflection of normal teenage uppityness, but perhaps I was also influenced by the socially turbulent environment around me. The Vietnam War had ended a few years before and kids of my era had been exposed to some of the rebelliousness of that time. My awareness of issues like women's rights and the struggle for racial freedom began to grow. In 1973, at the age of twelve, I decided I'd had enough of competitive gymnastics and I quit the YMCA team.

As a teenager, I began to question authority and the traditional role-playing that occurred within my own family. Around the house the division of chores between the boys and girls seemed unfair. The boys only had a few tasks they had to do, like take out the garbage and mow the lawn, each a weekly event. But washing dishes and cleaning the house— an endless drudgery—fell to the girls. When I heard the phrase "a woman's work is never done," I understood why. Looking at the newspaper or TV, I wondered why women did most of the practical work while men controlled most of the power and money. It took me years to understand how women have developed other sources of empowerment to balance out the inequalities in external power.

By the time I entered the optimistically named Sunny Hills High School at the age of fourteen, I was aware that not all the world resembled southern California. Our suburb of Hollywood was the epitome of wholesome, white-bread America. It seemed to me that everyone around me was following some version of the latest trend they had seen on TV, like caricatures of the movie sets a few miles away. As for my own fashion sense—so key to fitting into the teen social scene—Trish summed me up succinctly: "You were clueless." Moreover, I didn't care. I had just discovered the world of rock climbing and this was the environment and community that I could identify with.

My life took a fateful turn that summer of 1975 when I jumped into the back of my oldest sister's fiancée's truck and traveled to a small climbing area in southern California called Big Rock. In the front seat sat Kathy with her long-haired boyfriend, Chuck Bludworth. In the back were me, my sister Trish, and my brother Bob, who was Chuck's climbing partner. Neither Trish nor I had ever climbed, and I was still uncertain how climbers even "got the rope up there"—an innocent question, I would later learn, that is often posed by tourists. The back of Chuck's blue Ford pickup—a present for his sixteenth birthday from his adoring parents—was strewn with strange-looking climbing gadgets, such as hexagonal metal objects threaded with loops of brightly colored nylon rope. I had no idea how these objects could be used to climb a cliff. As our truck ambled through the endless sprawl of shopping malls, suburbs, and cement freeways of LA, and I flicked through Chuck's well-thumbed copy of *Basic Rock Craft*, by Royal Robbins, I became no wiser to this odd-looking sport. I saw pages full of confusing diagrams of burly, unshaven men executing rope stunts and tying complicated knots, and the text was filled with new words like "piton," "prusik," and "carabiner." But Chuck had frequently reminded me that "you'd be good at it since you're light and strong from gymnastics."

After driving an hour and a half from our home in Orange County to just outside Riverside and hiking thirty minutes over an arid hillside, we arrived at the base of a 300-foot-high white granite slab called Big Rock, inclined at the angle of a steep ski run. The hot air carried the sweet odor of sage and a fresh smell from nearby Lake Parris. We dumped our rucksacks at the foot of the cliff, and I watched Chuck methodically sort through his jangling array of gear. Lizards darted up the rock wall, skating lightly up the smooth face on their tiny claws. But to me, the face appeared to be devoid of holds.

"Why don't you girls start on this easy climb while Bob and I do another climb nearby?" Chuck suggested.

Kathy pointed to the route that Chuck had suggested we try. The Trough was its inauspicious name, and she set about gearing Trish up for action.

Kathy (right) in her usual position of command at the base of the cliff, with Gary Cox belaying. (LYNN HILL COLLECTION)

"Okay," Kathy said, "first comes the swami belt harness."

This was the era of climbing before comfortable and adjustable harnesses with leg loops and buckled waist belts became popular among climbers. She wrapped a long strand of one-inch-wide nylon webbing around Trish's waist and then rigged a loop around her legs. She knotted the ends together and tied the climbing rope into the whole affair.

"This stuff looks like nothing but an old seat belt salvaged off a car," I said distrustfully as she finished Trish's knot.

"Well, yeah, but if it's strong enough for a car, it's certainly strong enough to hold you," was Kathy's confident reply.

Then she demonstrated how to execute the dreaded "body belay." This was also before the advent of mechanical belay devices that automatically create friction on the rope to prevent it from slipping in the case of a fall.

"This is your brake hand," she said while gripping the rope in her right hand. "If the climber falls, you stop them like this," at which point she wrapped the rope tight around her buttock and hip.

It looked painful, bound to produce rope burn. I crinkled my nose at the thought of having to hold a fall.

"Never let go of the rope with your brake hand," Kathy added with a solemn tone.

"Why?" I asked.

"Because if you do, the climber will hit the deck. Now it's time for someone to lead the climb." Kathy spoke directly to Trish.

Trish and I rarely questioned Kathy's leadership, but I thought it odd that Kathy would hand the responsibility of leading over to her novice sister. Trish and I didn't know that even though Kathy was well grounded in the basics of climbing, she was terrified of the exposed feeling that leading up a route produces.

Trish shuffled toward the cliff, looking uncertain. She wore climbing shoes called RDs. The name was derived from the initials of the famous French mountaineer René Desmaison, who had designed them. On Trish they were oversized and oafish gumboots and the hard black rubber soles clunked like wooden clogs when she placed them against the rock. I started laughing at Trish's ungainly appearance.

"Shut up," she yelled, laughing back at me.

"Where do I go?" Trish then asked in a nervous tone.

"You see those metal bolts sticking out of the rock? Follow those and clip these carabiners into them. Then clip your rope through the carabiner," Kathy answered.

Our route was an easy 5.4 grade, yet for a beginner the first climb is always a mystery and an ordeal. Trish headed upward toward the first bolt, clipped it as instructed, then kept moving to the second bolt. I could hear her labored breathing growing louder. Her feet slipped about and her hands fondled the rock with uncertainty.

Thirty feet off the ground and with two bolts clipped, Trish then got lost by veering left from the natural line of handholds onto a sheet of rock that to her looked easier. But when she saw the consequences of her detour—she was now far away from the protection bolts and facing a big fall if she slipped—her voice grew higher in pitch.

"What do I do now?"

"You need to climb back to the right and clip into another bolt," Kathy replied.

"What would happen if she fell?" I posed this hypothetical question to Kathy while Trish fumbled, shook, and whimpered.

Kathy calmly explained the mechanism of the protection system: If Trish were to fall, she would fall the length of rope between where she stood and the last bolt she had clipped, plus that far again as she fell past the bolt. The rope, which is clipped through the carabiner and bolt, would then catch her, but there would also be a few added feet of fall due to the stretch in the rope and the inevitable slide through Kathy's hands. I thought about this and it appeared that Trish, who was now thirty-five feet above the ground, was so high above her last protection bolt that she would hit the ground before the rope would catch her. *This looks dangerous,* I thought.

Then Trish's legs started trembling violently.

"Why are her legs shaking like that?" I asked.

"Sewing machine leg," Kathy answered cryptically. Because Trish was poised on the edges of her feet and had all her weight bearing down on them, the nervous tension in the muscles was causing her legs to gyrate up and down, like the needle of a sewing machine.

Trish inched back over to the protection bolt. When she clipped the rope through the carabiner, she grabbed it with both hands and hung, panting.

"Can I come down now?"

Kathy lowered her. I didn't bother to ask Trish how she liked the climb. It was evident from watching her trembling hands untie the rope that she didn't enjoy it. In fact, it would be eighteen years before she tried the sport again with her two young sons, in the shelter of an indoor climbing facility in Salt Lake City.

"Okay, Lynn, your turn now," said Kathy with her usual authority. But rather than try the Trough again, Kathy decided I would lead another route nearby that turned out to be even harder.

Trish handed me the RD climbing shoes. A full size too big, they felt clumsy on my feet. Kathy helped me tie into the rope, handed me a bunch of carabiners, and sent me on my way. After climbing several moves, I looked over my shoulder to the ground. I understood right away why Trish had looked so alarmed. I looked back up and saw the bolt, a rusty outpost of alleged safety, still several feet above me. *What have I gotten myself into?* I thought. Unlike gymnastics, there was no spotter to keep me from falling to the ground. And instead of facing gym mats, I was looking down at a hard rocky landing.

"Try to friction your feet against the face," Kathy suggested.

I set my feet against the rock, latched my fingertips firmly around a couple of small flakes, then began moving upward. My feet held, as if glued to the cliff. As clutzy as those RDs looked, their smooth rubber soles were doing their job.

I felt a sense of relief when I arrived at the first bolt and clipped my rope into it. But as soon as I made a few moves past it, I felt a sting of adrenaline in my gut when I thought about the consequences of a fall. With each step upward, I felt more vulnerable as I moved farther away from the security of my protection bolt. But rather than looking down toward the ground, I decided to maintain my focus on the rock ahead.

"Just keep going," I said to myself as I continued up the wall, clipping into one bolt after another. This process of hanging and standing on small edges and bumps on the rock seemed much more delicate and insecure than I had imagined climbing would be. The farther I went, the more my muscles ached. When I arrived at what my sister called the anchor—the point at which I had completed the climb and could lower

back down to the ground—I felt an immediate sense of relief and satisfaction.

When I arrived back on the ground, a woman with a beaming smile
said to me, "Good job! Was that your first climb?"

Unbeknownst to me, the person speaking was Maria Cranor, one of
the few women climbing at a high level back then and someone with
whom I would form a lasting friendship. From the first day I met her,
she was a source of inspiration and encouragement to me, as she was
to all her friends and colleagues.

By the end of the day I knew I had been hooked on some new sensation. As we walked down the hill back to the car, I watched the late
afternoon sun turn the granite orange and highlight every nubbin and
detail on its surface. Already I began to associate the beautiful form
and texture of the rock with my desire to climb it. From that day on, I
never saw a cliff in exactly the same way again.

Chapter 3

First Contact

"Hey, Lynnie, you want the sharp end?" yelled Chuck from up on the cliff 25 feet above me, where he dangled at the end of the climbing rope. He had just fallen from the hardest section of a climb called Trespassers Will Be Violated at a climbing area in the Mojave Desert known as Joshua Tree.

"The what?" I answered, not knowing what the sharp end was.

Chuck laughed his braying, horsey laugh. "The sharp end is my end—the leader's end. I'm asking you if you want to lower me down to where you are and then you can come up here and try to lead this route. I can't see a way to climb past this section."

Only a few weeks had passed since Chuck and Kathy had introduced me to the world of climbing at Big Rock. I had led a few more routes since then. When I tagged along with Chuck and Bob, I followed behind

Chuck Bludworth (center), my brother Bob, and me gearing up for a day of climbing. (CHARLIE ROW)

on the safer "blunt end" of the rope, with Chuck secured to the rock, ready to catch me on the rope if I slipped. Even so, it had become apparent that I had a talent for drifting fairly easily up the climbs we did—sometimes more easily than Chuck, Bob, or Kathy.

I leaned my head out and looked up at the section of the climb where Chuck had slid off. Twice he had climbed out sideways from the first protection bolt, and twice he had become infected with sewing machine leg. One lesson I'd learned was that once sewing machine leg sets in, it is only a matter of seconds before the climber falls off. Sure enough, Chuck had come careening off the "crux"—the climb's hardest section—precisely on sewing machine leg schedule, and he had swung sideways for twenty feet by the time the rope, running through the carabiner and the piece of protection it was clipped to, arrested his fall. Belaying him at the other end of that rope, I was jerked up against the cliff by the impact. Chuck easily outweighed me by forty-five pounds, and I was feeling like a passenger in a car that had been repeatedly rear-ended.

"Sure, I'll try it."

At this point in my climbing career I knew little about the rating system that climbers use to differentiate between one climb that is easy and another that is harder. The rating scale as we know it today in the American system contains about twenty-five degrees of difficulty, from 5.0 at the beginning level to 5.15 at the top end. Like the belt system in martial arts, each number and letter grade indicates the relative degree of difficulty. In 1976, when I was tying into the sharp end of the rope to try Trespassers Will Be Violated, the top end of the rating scale was 5.11. The climb Chuck had talked me into leading was rated 5.10+ and it was also poorly protected, since there were only three bolts on the entire 80-foot climb. Diving into a climb as hard as that with my fledgling experience was a little like dropping into an expert "black diamond" chute when you'd just gotten past mastering the snowplow in skiing. In other words, it was potentially reckless. But I had no idea what I was getting into.

After I lowered Chuck down to the ground, we traded ends and I headed back up over the vertical terrain he had already covered. Around me sprawled Joshua Tree's surreal landscape. Thousands of blobs of rock between 50 and 200 feet tall dotted the desert floor for miles in every direction. Depending on your bent of imagination, it either resembled the aftermath of a meteor shower or a parade of giant desert tortoises, as each granite dome was distinctly carapace-shaped. Chuck, being a geology major, was always lecturing our climbing clan about the rocks we grappled with, and he identified the rock here as a type of granite called quartz monzonite. To me, it seemed like a coarse, granular type of rock, and as I traversed sideways to the point where Chuck had plummeted, I saw the reason he had fallen: this patch of granite had virtually no holds on it.

All I had to work with was a slabby surface of rock textured with crystals the size of grape seeds. Only if I could perch my toes and wrap my fingertips around these tiny, sharp clusters would the traverse in front of me be feasible. To move forward required a combination of brutish finger strength, balletlike toe pointing, and fluid balance. If I faltered along the traverse and stopped out of concern that I was getting too far away from my protection, then I'd slide off like Chuck. Although my range of climbing experience was minimal, I found I could look at the rock in front of me and analyze the situation as if it were an abstract problem: the rock features and my body were elements of the puzzle and the correct answer lay in me reaching the other end of the traverse. If I connected the moves accurately, getting my body in the most efficient position to continue moving fluidly, then I would solve the problem. Any single wrong move and I would lose my strength and fall.

"Okay, Chuck, here goes," I said as I set off.

As I moved sideways like a crab scuttling along the shoreline, I realized I had never climbed anything as demanding as this before. The combination of controlling every position of my body and of forcing my mind to shut out the ever-present urge to submit to the very real fear of falling created an interesting result: a feeling that I was simultaneously acutely aware of both everything and nothing. Everything, because twenty-five years later I still recall the kaleidoscope of crystal patterns in the rock in front of me as I moved over it, and nothing, because at the time I was so immersed in the passage of movement that I felt no sense of time, gravity or existence. The only sound I heard was the flow of my breathing.

I continued past the point where Chuck had fallen, moved several more feet across the grainy rock slab, and found myself eyeing a protection bolt an arm's reach away. All I had to do was clip the bolt with a carabiner and clip the rope into that and I would be home free. But my body was splayed across the rock like a starfish, and I felt that releasing one hand from the rock to grab a carabiner from the bandolier slung around my neck would cause me to peel off of the face.

"Keep it together Lynnie. You can do it," Chuck's voice rose up, barely registering with my thoughts.

But my momentum had stalled. Fear had set in. Sewing machine leg was building up in the ball of my foot. My forearms were bloating and aching as blood swelled the veins. I had to think fast. The options presented themselves. I could reach out quickly and wrap two of my fingers through the steel eye of the bolt and hang from one finger. But no, that would be as digit-friendly as grabbing a knife. Anyway, the rules of the game dictated that the bolt was there only to protect me, not to support my weight; if I grabbed it, I'd be guilty of bad free-climbing style. Option two then became clear: I had to calm my nerves and keep going past the bolt to a more secure place to stand. From there I could more easily clip the bolt.

I took a couple of deep breaths and climbed on. My gambit worked, and a second later I was clipping a carabiner to the bolt, feeling a tingle of new energy running through my body. Minutes later I reached the top of the dome and I was rigging an anchor, then pulling in rope and belaying Chuck up to me.

"Awesome, Lynn, awesome," he gasped when he reached me.

That night around the campfires at Joshua Tree the local expert climbers were sipping beers, talking about "the girl who'd led Trespassers." I didn't know it at the time, but the climb had a serious reputation and had scared several experienced climbers out of their wits.

If I could choose one person to call my first mentor of climbing, it would be my partner that day on Trespassers Will Be Violated. Chuck Bludworth opened my eyes to the world of climbing and taught me something about its heart and soul. Chuck encouraged me to get on the rock and do my best. He never fell prey to the insecurity of being outdone by a young, novice girl.

Chuck and my sister Kathy had been childhood sweethearts since their teens. They'd gone to the high school prom together, they began climbing together, and they would marry in 1977, when they were twenty-two and twenty-one, respectively. A photo of them together taken the night of the prom shows them dressed in formal attire, my sister with a corsage, and a bearded Chuck with a mane of blond, wavy locks that almost matched the length of Kathy's Rapunzel-like hair.

Chuck had initiated the climbing experiment for Kathy and my brother Bob, but while they merely saw it as an interesting weekend diversion, Chuck looked at climbing as a way of life. He regarded climbing as a thing of beauty and mystery. A sunset of red clouds against which the otherworldly forms of shaggy-leafed Joshua trees and rock domes were silhouetted in the twilight, viewed from the top of our last climb of the day, represented to Chuck a deep connection between himself and the land. He saw climbing as a kind of spiritual journey, not unlike the vision quests that Native Americans put themselves through. The ritual of preparing and planning for a climb, of embarking on the journey, of testing yourself with fear and exhaustion in a risky setting, all spoke to some part of Chuck's deeper self.

This was the period of the 1970s when the Brave New World of mind expansion through any means was hip, and the novels of Carlos Castaneda were in vogue. Those books were part of nearly every climber's book collection. *A Separate Reality* and *Tales of Power* described a mystical journey through Yaqui Indian sorcery, replete with encounters with spirits that were accessed by mind-controlling rituals with drugs like peyote. Climbing was a sacred vehicle that could lift these J-Tree aficionados out of the daily grind of life in the concrete jungle of LA and take them to another plane.

With his Merlin-like hair and his bent for the mystical, Chuck cut a striking swath through my teens. One day as I was strolling down a street with Chuck, we passed an unoccupied parked car and the radio suddenly turned itself on. Chuck immediately insinuated that this had happened because of his powerful magnetic presence. In some ways he was pulling my leg, yet in other ways there was a side to Chuck that believed exactly that.

Even more than rock climbing, Chuck idealized mountaineering in the high ranges as the epitome of the spiritual quest. Chuck's bookshelves were lined with volumes penned by famous alpinists of the day like Reinhold Messner and Walter Bonatti. Messner wrote with Germanic seriousness about climbing in the "death zone," a frigid realm somewhere above 26,000 feet. In one book Messner described his ordeals on the Himalayan peak Nanga Parbat, one of the fourteen peaks above 8000 meters (26,000 feet), on which he and his brother Günther had climbed a hard new route. On the climb back down the other side of the mountain an avalanche killed Günther, and Reinhold, alone and lost, suffered days of starvation and anguish. By the time native shepherds found him he was a mere rail of a man, with such severe frostbite that his toes had to be amputated. Astonishingly, a couple of years later Messner returned to the same face on which his brother had been crushed under tons of ice and climbed Nanga Parbat again—alone. On this ascent Messner wrote of ghosts, spirits, hallucinations, and of feeling a sense of closeness to the realm of death that the combination of high altitude, physical deprivation, and his own near-death experience had created.

Chuck aspired to such extremes of adventure. I, on the other hand, listened to such tales and never quite understood his attraction to the frozen realm. From a young age I saw the mountains as being cold, rugged, and unstable places. Though I could appreciate a kind of austere beauty in such high places, it was nothing like the type of climbing with which I had begun to bond. I felt a strong sense of belonging in Joshua Tree's sun-soaked landscape, with its tawny-red stone dappled with cactus-green. In this desert playground I felt a sense of harmony among the forms and shapes of nature.

Nevertheless, all climbing was exciting to me and Chuck easily persuaded me to visit the "mini-mountains" of the Sierra Nevada range. Temple Crag is a semi-alpine-style peak in the Palisades Range of the Sierras, and in the summer of 1976, when I was fifteen years old, we carried our backpacks over alpine meadows, shivered through the night

Chuck climbing in the Sierra Nevadas. (BOB HILL)

in our inadequate sleeping bags in a small tent, and then at first light set out up a scree slope toward the west face.

I had never climbed snow or ice. When we were confronted by a barrier of firm snow on a slope of about forty-five degrees, we had to kick steps into it to prevent our feet from sliding off. Of course, on a real alpine expedition the climbers would be wearing crampons over their stiff-soled, waterproof mountain boots, and they'd be swinging an ice ax into the snow slope. But Chuck and I wore sneakers for the approach to the climb, and the closest thing to an ice tool we had was a hammer, designed for driving in pitons, that sported a short, pointy pick on the other end of the hammerhead. It looked more like a gardening tool than an ice ax, and as it belonged to Chuck, he led the way, using it to cut steps in the hard snow.

When we stepped off the snowfield at the base of the summit tower, we tied the rope onto our harnesses and began climbing up a cliff comprised of shattered alpine granite. First I slotted my hips into a wide fissure and shimmied up; then, higher, we encountered pitches on which cube-shaped blocks the size of TV sets poised on ledges, looking ready to tumble off with the slightest brush of an elbow. While we climbed, pitch after pitch, slotting in nuts, Chuck, the geology expert, explained why the rock resembled a badly stacked china cabinet.

"It's because of the action of freeze and thaw," he explained. "During the day the snow slopes on top of the cliff melt and water trickles into the gaps between blocks. When the water freezes in the cold of night, the ice expands, acting like a crowbar that forces the rocks to fracture and break apart. The process takes eons, but it ensures that most mountain climbs are comprised of tottering rubble."

"Are the Himalayas and Andes loose like this?" I asked, having recently heard him talk in awe of those ranges.

"If anything, they are way worse," he replied. "The taller the peak, the more shattered the rock."

"That does it, I'm never going there. I'll stick to dry solid rock in the sun," I replied.

We didn't get to the summit of Temple Crag. A long ridge lay between us and the pointed top, and it looked like a dump truck had emptied a quarry-load of boulders all over it. There was no way I was going to paw my way over such life-threatening rubble just for the sake of getting to the top. We had climbed the route—ten pitches of 5.9—and that was good enough for me.

Thumbing through Chuck's library of alpine literature, I had absorbed one thing: that most mountaineering accidents occur on the descent. As we padded down the other side of Temple Crag, the terrain grew steeper and remained covered with delicately perched boulders. At a cliff we had to break out the rope and rappel for 200 feet. If done correctly, rappelling is a safe and easy method of getting down a cliff by hooking a rope through a metal device that is clipped to the harness, and which creates friction so one can slowly slide down the rope. But here, as the sun-cooked Sierra snows melted, small stones were being freed from the snow and were rolling off the slopes, whizzing by us like bullets.

"This is like a shooting gallery," I told Chuck with a sense of alarm.

He smiled as if he'd seen it all before and beckoned me down the rope. At the bottom of the cliff he stood on a narrow bridge of snow that spanned a gaping chasm. As I lowered myself to him, he reached out and grabbed my hand.

"Whatever you do, don't fall into the *bergschrund*," he instructed.

"The what?"

"*Bergschrund*. It's a German word. *Berg* means mountain, *schrund* refers to the gap. It's this void where the snow slope has melted away from the cliff."

"Why don't you just say 'snow gap'?"

"Because mountaineering started in Europe."

We pulled the rope back down from where it had been anchored for our rappel, then prepared to descend the last few hundred feet to the ground. At that point, our only choice of descent was either to climb down the steep exposed snow slope or chimney down between the rock and ice that formed the *bergschrund*. Chuck decided to climb down the snow slope using our only tool while I belayed him from above with no belay anchor. To secure myself from being pulled off in case Chuck should fall, I sat behind a hump of ice with my feet braced against this natural barrier.

Once Chuck arrived safely down to the ground, he shouted up, "Okay, Lynnie, come down."

Since Chuck had gone down first with our only hammer, I was left with no other choice but to climb down between a slippery wall of ice and the wet rock face, while straddling a three-foot-wide gap. Below me I saw darkness that led into the bowels of the mountain.

My hands and feet went numb as I carefully straddled the dark abyss, placing my bare hands and the smooth soles of my rubber climbing shoes against ice on one side and wet rock on the other. My mind kept flashing on horrifying images of falling into the cold, dark oblivion.

When I got down to where Chuck waited, he held up a hand.

"Watch your step. I fell into a hole just in front of you. I was lucky enough to have stopped on a snow bridge a few feet down, but if I hadn't stopped there, I would have gone down another sixty feet or so."

I felt more at ease when we stepped off the slippery snow onto the thick peaty soil of the meadow. On the hike back down the trail that led through the twisted claws of a pine forest, I marveled at a beautiful crystal I had found while descending the scree field from the top. I wondered how there could be such perfect natural order and beauty in the midst of the random chaos of this mountain environment. The crystal seemed to be a symbolic reminder of the duality of nature. True, the high dry Sierra air and the views of rolling thunderheads and distant peaks were sublime, but the mountains could also be a place of potentially harsh, life-threatening experiences. Though I was grateful to have had this experience of climbing in the mountains with Chuck, I realized that what I enjoyed most of all was rock climbing. Exploring a sense of movement on the rocks, without risking life and limb in the death zone, was where I placed my destiny. I didn't feel the need to court death in order to get meaning from climbing, I decided.

One form of climbing that suited my interests more closely was "bouldering." When Chuck introduced me to this form of climbing on the boulders that are scattered on the desert floor of Joshua Tree, I discovered the heart of free climbing movement in its purest form.

Surrounding the campgrounds were scores of boulders that offered mini-climbs just a few feet tall but of extreme difficulty. They were so short that no rope was needed. Clans of climbers would wander through these boulder fields, working on "problems," where they'd climb a few feet up a boulder, try a move, then jump or fall off. After a short rest they'd try the problem again, but this time they'd be armed with more information about the climb and would more efficiently swing into the sequence of moves they'd perfected on the last try, getting a little farther. I saw similarities between the choreographing of moves in bouldering and those I had been taught for performing gymnastic routines. Both disciplines even depended on a "spotter" to catch one's mistakes. But where gymnastics required a contrived, scripted form of grace, climbing was beautifully free-form and spontaneous, each movement being different from any other.

When I saw a photo of John Gill hanging from an overhanging face by his fingertips, I was amazed to see how he was able to transfer his gymnastics skills on the rock. Having been a competitive rope climber, Gill was as famous for his incredible strength and technique as he was for his acrobatic leaps up the rock. A visionary climber who was ahead of his times, Gill did the first ascents of many difficult boulder problems across the country back in the late fifties—some of which weren't repeated for twenty-five years and others that are still unrepeated.

In delving into bouldering, I found that it wasn't much help to me to watch the way other climbers solved a problem. Being small, with my own unique physical characteristics, I found that I often climbed completely differently from the men who surrounded me. To get up a boulder problem, I had to explore all the options and touch all the holds myself. One day, I quickly made it to the top of a boulder problem called the Stem Gem by spanning across the rock with my flexible hips. When I reached the top and looked down, I noticed a male climber had been watching me.

"Gee, I can't even do that," he said dismissively, and walked off in a huff.

As I watched him walk away through the desert, I wondered about his remark and found myself taking it negatively. He could have commended me on succeeding on a climb that he could not do, but instead he seemed to brush it off as a bit of beginner's luck on my part. His assumption seemed to be that as a man he should automatically be physically superior to a small girl, and he seemed put out to see the "weaker sex" outdo him.

I was often disappointed by sexist attitudes outside the climbing

Using pretzel logic on the Stem Gem boulder, Joshua Tree. (JIM BRIDWELL)

scene, but it made me even more annoyed to see them among climbers. Perhaps this was because I felt that climbing was the first truly egalitarian activity I had participated in: everyone was equal before the rocks, it seemed to me. The beauty of climbing is that each person is free to choreograph his or her own way of adapting to the rock.

In fact, the very first climb I did at Joshua Tree, with Kathy, had been a fiasco because of stereotypical role playing. In an echo of that first day at Big Rock, Chuck chose a climb for us—a very easy route called Southeast Corner on Intersection Rock—and headed off elsewhere to climb with Bob. He expected Kathy to lead me up the route, and she let him think she was comfortable with that. But as before, as soon as Chuck was out of sight, Kathy suggested I lead. She wanted no part of the scary job of going first, placing the gear and mastering the moves. It seemed to me that Kathy was just humoring Chuck when it came to climbing. It was clear to me that Kathy came along not because she loved to climb, but because that was how Chuck wanted to spend their weekends.

When Kathy handed me the rack of gear for Southeast Corner, I barely knew what to do with it. Jangling around my neck was an array of about twenty gadgets, each on a sling of rope or wire, and each connected to my equipment sling that I had looped around my neck and shoulders. There were stoppers, which were V-shaped tapered wedges in a range of sizes from as thick as a wallet to as thin as a car key. They slotted into tapering pockets or cracks. Harder to figure out were the hexentrics, six-sided tubes of aluminum that at their biggest were the size of a clenched fist, and which had to be fiddled into a crack with more precision. Kathy proceeded to explain where the route went.

"Just climb up this short face to that flake up there. Once you get there, you can put one of those chocks into the crack," she said.

"What crack?" I asked.

"It's behind the flake. You can't see it from here, but you'll see it once you get there."

As I started up the route, I felt like a student pilot who'd just signed up for flight school and was unexpectedly handed the controls of a plane. I padded up a low-angle slab of rock for several feet, then looked back down toward the ground. When I realized that a fall meant that I would land quite a long way down on some big boulders, I felt the sting of adrenaline in the pit of my stomach. Suddenly I felt completely ill-prepared to continue upward.

"How do I use these things anyway?" I said, referring to the collection of gear I was carrying.

"You just place them in the crack wherever there's a constriction. You'll see, they work really well."

"But what happens if I fall here?"

"I don't know. Just don't fall, okay?"

Chuck had a sort of mantra about climbing: "The leader never falls." This ethic was reminiscent of the early days in climbing, at a time when there were no stoppers or hexentrics at all, and if you did fall you'd probably be pulverized on the ground below. I knew that Chuck and everyone else did suffer falls from time to time, so I took it to mean that you can only afford to fall if you have properly placed protection in the rock.

I looked around me and realized that I was out of my league. Though I was eager to climb, I wasn't willing to run blindly into something I was clueless about.

"I'm not doing this. I'm coming back down," I said.

"All right, then, come down."

Kathy seemed glad. When I reversed my moves and stepped onto the ground, she happily packed up our gear and led the way back to camp. I, on the other hand, felt cheated out of a day of action on the rock and kept thinking about what I could have done to make the climb a success. When Kathy saw the look of disappointment on my face, she offered condolences.

"Oh, don't feel bad. I tell you what, let's just tell Chuck that we didn't do the climb because you felt sick."

My mouth gaped. Did we really need an excuse? Couldn't we tell the truth, which was that one of us didn't really want to climb because she only does it to humor her boyfriend, and the other is too clueless to lead? Kathy seemed to assume Chuck would be disappointed that we hadn't done a climb, and she didn't want to let him down. Exploiting some kind of feminine weakness—"the girl got sick, and you know how girls get sick"—was just a device to appease Chuck.

I had seen this sort of game before, with our parents. On a surfing weekend to Huntington Beach, an argument between Mom and Dad over some trivial matter had been settled by Mom when she quipped, "Okay, Jim, you're right." To her, it seemed less important whether she was right or wrong. What mattered more was to keep the peace, even if it meant capitulating to her husband. This attitude left me a little dumbfounded. Was this what women were expected to do?

But these were carefree days. I was competing on the high school gymnastics team, so my weekdays were taken up with training and school, while my weekends and school breaks were devoted to climbing. I thought about climbing day in and day out. At night as I lay in bed, I would envision myself on future climbs on the big walls of Yosemite, Joshua Tree, or Tahquitz Rock, and I would soon feel my palms sweating with excitement.

Then, in the fall of 1976, the solid foundation of our family that I had always taken for granted was shattered by a devastating event. I learned of this disaster one evening after dinner when my brother Jim and I were sitting along the edge of the brick walkway in front of the house. I didn't suspect anything was wrong, when all of a sudden Jim said, "Mom and Dad are having serious marital problems."

"What do you mean?"

"Dad has a girlfriend."

"How do you know that?"

"Dad told me."

I was stunned. I had no idea that anything was amiss in my parents' relationship. If anything, they seemed like the perfect couple. They'd been together for twenty years. Relatively young, physically and intellectually alive, they socialized with a group of friends in the neighborhood, and they appeared to be happy together. If they argued, they did it so that I barely noticed a word out of place between them. Later, as an adult, I understood how this could happen, but at this time I took the news with utter astonishment.

Jim revealed that Dad had taken each of the "big kids" to dinner, separately, to break the news. Jim, being the oldest son, had heard more details about the situation than anyone else had. Instead of sympathizing with his father, he had become quite upset. Us "little kids" learned of this shocking news from our older siblings.

"Who is she?" I asked, suddenly feeling as curious as I felt shocked.

I learned that my father's new love was half his age and that she lived in Texas and worked in a bar. They had met when Dad had gone to Houston on business. Further snippets of information that Jim and my other brothers and sisters would learn formed a rough picture: she had a southern accent; she studied architecture and French; she had a big smile.

"How do you think Mom is taking this?" I wanted to know.

"She's very upset and angry with him. But mostly she just wants him to think it over carefully and not do anything rash," Jim said.

During the next few weeks a strange, uncomfortable undercurrent ran through the Hill family. Dad remained part of the household, yet he was withdrawn. We all did our best to carry on with our daily lives, but no one dared to broach the issue directly with our parents. They issued few announcements regarding the status of their impending separation. Whatever I gleaned about it filtered in to me as if my senses were absorbing the news but my mind wasn't. All of us held on to the hope that Dad would change his mind and stay.

Mom held on stoically, though as time passed she shed a great deal of weight. One night, as my mother and I piled the dishes from the evening meal into the sink, I saw that she was staring abstractedly at the plates. Then she began to weep.

"Doesn't it bother you, what's going on?" she asked, wiping her eyes.

It bothered me immensely, yet I felt powerless to do anything about the situation. These matters had been shaped by adults and I was a teenager. I didn't know what to say or do other than to hug my mother and cry. I felt a terrible sadness for her, and was aware that she faced the prospect of beginning a new way of life as a single mother with four children still under the age of eighteen. The situation seemed like a nightmare that I hoped we would all wake from soon.

Then came the dark Christmas of 1976, the last Christmas my father spent with us all together. No one had planned that Dad should spend Christmas with us, but December came around and before we knew it a Christmas tree sat in our living room like an unwelcome guest. We went through the motions of exchanging gifts and cards, but no one's heart was in it. The tension between what we felt and what we were acting out pushed all the joy from the room. There was no longer any denying that our family had changed forever.

And then Dad was gone.

For me, it was a confusing period with much sadness and uncertainty. Gradually, the climbing life I was discovering supplanted the family life that was crumbling all around me. There was only one way to handle the meltdown of our family: by quietly accepting it as proof that nothing in life is permanent. I looked to my weekend excursions to Joshua Tree as a life raft, and the act of climbing as therapy. To this day, climbing is still one of the few activities that makes me feel good even when I'm feeling down.

Chapter 4

Joshua Tree

The band of residents who were establishing the routes at Joshua Tree kept to themselves and looked upon people outside their circle, like Chuck and our group, with skepticism. While Chuck respected the superior abilities of those climbers, he saw in them no small amount of arrogance. To this end, he and Bob called the good climbers the "Haughties," for their haughty attitude. Conveniently, the term sounded a lot like the "Hotties," and "hot"—or talented—they certainly were.

The origins of this name came from an encounter with one of the local "Haughties" in Joshua Tree one day. It concerned one of the best of that bunch, a ripped, blond Adonis named John Bachar. Bachar had developed a head for climbing routes of great difficulty without a rope—an activity known as free soloing. It was immensely exciting to watch a climber carefully yet confidently climb a route without a rope. Today I would say that soloing is a case of so much to lose, so little to gain, in that the fleeting sense of personal satisfaction in the experience must be outweighed by the risk of death or broken limbs if the climber falls to the ground. Yet Bachar was a solo maestro, and he never put the wrong foot forward when free soloing.

After watching Bachar solo a route rated 5.11 called Left Ski Track, Chuck, Bob, and I waited until he had scrambled down the easy descent. Chuck expressed his admiration by simply exclaiming, "That was hot!"

Bachar strode by, barely even looking at us, and as he sauntered off among the boulders he sniggered in mimicry of Chuck, "Yeah, hot! Real hot!"

Hence the "Haughties."

One day I unwittingly gave the Haughties a good show on a route called EBGB's, whose name is a pun on two things, one being the slang expression for your nerves when scared—the "heebie-jeebies"—and the other being a corruption of the famous New York nightclub CBGB's. Chuck had given the route a try but had failed to make it past the first hard move, so he handed the lead over to me. As I started up the route, I began to appreciate Chuck's old adage that "the leader never falls" because EBGB's involved long sections of hard climbing between the bolts. Unbeknownst to me, a few of the Haughties were watching from a distance to see if little Lynnie might "take a whipper."

I started out on the route strongly, quickly overcoming the move that had stumped Chuck. That move was easier for me due to my small size and flexibility. It involved a "mantel" move, which is best described by a mental vision: imagine the movements one's body would be put through if one had to climb up and stand on the mantelpiece over the living room fireplace. On EBGB's I was able pull up to chest height on a shelf of rock, then pivot my hands and elbows around and press down until both arms were in a straight-locked position. I then swung my foot up to waist level next to my hands and stood up. At that point I realized I had gotten in over my head.

The moves above me involved gripping tiny flakes with my fingertips, move after move, for fifty feet. "Crimping," as this sort of finger-bending climbing is known, creates a painful "pump," or buildup of fatigue in the forearms. The farther I went, the more I felt I might fly off backward. A high of adrenaline began to spur me on. As I eyed the last move onto the top of the dome, I thought, *Ahh, the top at last.* I began to make a high step onto a shallow, sloping depression on the face, and as I shifted my weight, my foot slipped off and I toppled over backward. Thirty feet later, I bounced onto the rope and hung upside down in my harness. Dazed but unscathed, I righted myself and lowered off. It would be a couple more years before I had the courage to try this climb again, but the show I had given the Haughties earned me an invitation.

Not long after, one of the most endearing of the Haughties visited our campsite at breakfast time. His name was John Long, and his nickname reflected his bodybuilder dimensions—*largo* being Spanish for "large." Largo hailed from Claremont, California, and was in the process of perfecting his own power-based style of climbing in which he

John Long on the Pinch Grip Overhang in Horsetooth Reservoir, Colorado. (MICHAEL KENNEDY)

would fling himself up difficult sections of rock by dynamically propelling his body upward with a mighty pull of his arms. But what set him apart was his blustering attitude and his mastery of the campfire scene, where he held court by telling jokes, impossibly tall tales, and even reciting self-penned poems in his loud baritone voice.

John had been on his way out to go climbing with his friends when he spotted me from across the campground and said, "Hold on. Let's ask that girl over there to come with us."

Then he jogged over to our campsite and promptly asked, "We're on our way out to try a new route called the Equinox today. Do you want to join us?"

Although I wasn't sure what I would be getting into, I didn't hesitate one minute to spend the day with a group of climbers who were, at the time, the best in the country.

Billy Westbay, Jim Bridwell, and John Long after the first one-day ascent of the Nose. (JIM BRIDWELL COLLECTION)

After that first day of climbing with John Long on the Equinox, I was accepted into the group of pranksters, eccentrics, and savants that I had previously known only as the Haughties. That day John coined his own nickname for me, "Little Herc," since he said I looked as strong as Hercules. What began as a small group of friends expanded into a community of people from all walks of life. Quite a few were students majoring in esoteric fields like astrophysics, math, and archaeology. There were also a lot of unemployed vagabonds, and even a few whose lives hovered on the fringe of legality. But most of the climbers I knew held down an array of jobs and careers from carpenters and construction workers to doctors, lawyers, scientists, actors, and shop managers. Climbing was the one passion we all shared in common.

Chief of the Haughties was Largo, with his blustering yet sweet omnipresence and his weight-training-fueled climbing strength. Largo had recently participated in one of the major events in American climbing: the first one-day ascent of the Nose route on El Capitan in Yosemite Valley. Normally, this 3,000-foot route took climbers several days to climb, but when Largo, Jim Bridwell, and Billy Westbay teamed up and blitzed it in a fifteen-hour marathon in the summer of 1975, it shattered the previous standards of athletic performance on the rock.

Largo was also a founding member of that unofficial clan of climbers known as the Stonemasters, a loose collective of incredibly fit, daring, and talented Californians who led the world in rock climbing during the seventies. The name said it all: mastery over the stone, and mastery over being stoned. It was an elite club that had no admission fees, charter, or secret handshake, but this clan was exclusively male and a ritual was required to join. Initiation as a Stonemaster came from making one of the first ten ascents of Valhalla, a particularly tricky and scary route on the granite cliff of Suicide Rocks in the San Jacinto Mountains above Idyllwild. The climb—first ascended by Bud "Ivan" Couch—had such an epic reputation with the young climbers of the day that mastery over it had become a rite of passage, a bit like the moment when a young Indian brings down his first buffalo.

Years later I heard the story about how Maria Cranor did an onsight ascent of Valhalla after her partners, Kevin Powell, Tim Powell, and Darrel Hensel, failed to lead the route. (An "on-sight" ascent is particularly impressive in that a climber free climbs the route without a fall, having never practiced or seen the moves before.) Meanwhile, Mari Gingery and John Long were at the top of Insomnia Crack watching as she cruised up the first two pitches. When Maria arrived at the belay before the last pitch and said she wanted to descend, John shouted to her, "No, you must keep going!" So Maria continued up and made not only the first ascent by a woman but she made a perfect on-sight ascent, back in 1978!

Nearly everyone in the climbing scene sported a nickname. Russ Walling, the Fish, was so named because he liked to fake flipping, twitching epileptic fits in front of tourists. Out of this he got pity, spare change, or, if he grossed out the tourists and they abandoned their picnic, he got a crack at their sandwiches. Bullwinkle, a.k.a. Dean Fidelman, was, and remains today, a photographer. For two decades Dean has documented many classic moments out at the crags through his black-and-white photography.

Dave Neilson, Too Tall, at nearly six feet four inches, could easily reach holds on climbs that most of us had to jump to. Tobin Sorenson had no particular nickname, but he had a presence. A modest person, he bundled within his climbing persona a weird blend of skill and clumsiness, athletic drive and recklessness, boldness and Christianity. He was polite, and painfully shy around women. When most climbers would scream, "Oh, shit," in terror whenever they fell off, Tobin would demurely quip, "Oh, biscuit," and he fell regularly and far because he was into pushing his limits in order to push the frontier of climbing. His fearlessness seemed in part born out of a religious background. After he disappeared from the climbing scene for a few months, he returned with tales of smuggling Bibles into communist Bulgaria. Later, after he had immersed himself in mountaineering, I saw a grinning magazine photo of him on Switzerland's dangerous Eiger North Wall. On his helmet he had written "One Way" with an arrow pointing heavenward.

By day we climbed, by night we played. The maze of canyons and boulders around Joshua Tree provided a fine natural playground for après-climb activities. Moonlight ascents were among our favorite pastimes. On these nocturnal excursions we'd wander out through the desert to some easy dome of rock, dodging cholla cactus and the spiny bayonets of yucca trees as we came on them in the dark. Then, as agile as raccoons, we'd scamper up and down under the lunar light. On those moonlit nights coyotes would howl crazily in the distance. On darker nights we watched shooting stars, and distant pinpoints of light that were probably military missions flying around the Twenty-nine Palms Marine base. And J-Tree was reminiscent of the mysterious site called Area 51, where supermarket tabloids and TV shows had claimed for three decades that an alien spacecraft had crashed. Such stories postulated that a top-secret desert lab was trying to replicate the craft and master the art of flying it. Such fantastic stuff appealed to us and we'd study each speck of light, imagining it to be a spaceship coming to take us on the ultimate adventure. Always there to ground us back to reality was the pulsing orb of Los Angeles not far beyond the horizon.

Among the more outrageous of my new friends was John Yablonsky. Going by the nickname of Yabo, this twenty-year-old had recently dropped out of high school and left his unhappy home to become a denizen of Joshua Tree by winter and Yosemite Valley by summer. He had little shape to his life except what climbing offered it, yet in that arena he excelled. Otherwise he was rarely employed, more rarely washed, and perpetually penniless. With an untidy mop of dark blond hair, Yabo resembled the Artful Dodger in Charles Dickens's *Oliver Twist*. He went by numerous other titles: the Yarbarian was one. A loner by nature, he liked to joke that he was the sole member of a one-man tribe, and that tribe he dubbed the Yabaho Tribe. Though I found it strange to be around him when he uttered his nervous, staccato laugh and began hammering on an empty tin can to produce the bongo-driven, ritual-sounding chant of the Yabaho Tribe, I nevertheless felt a sense of compassion for Yabo.

One night the crowd put down a stake of $5 to dare Yabo to make a nude moonlight solo of a route named North Overhang. The route is rated 5.9, and its trickiest section requires one to climb a section of a crack splitting through a nearly horizontal ceiling of rock. Not having a penny to his name, Yabo unhesitatingly took the meager bet, stripped, and set off up the climb clad only in rock shoes, a chalk bag, and a wool cap. Those on the ground heckled him as he swung baboonlike through the roof, and we shone our flashlights onto his bare, untanned rump. When he finished the climb, he down-climbed the other side of the overhang and returned to the ground, only to find that his clothes had been snatched and hidden by one of his friends. We laughed while he wandered stark naked in the cold desert air for a few minutes, but then he reached under a rock and pulled out another set of trousers, socks, and a sweater.

"I might be crazy, but I'm no fool," he said, cackling the deranged laugh I would grow to know well in the coming years. Yabo had predicted his scurrilous companions would take advantage of him and spirit his clothes away, so he'd quietly stashed a spare set just in case.

More often than not, campfires were dominated by Largo's boisterous tale-telling. While flames animated our shadows against a backdrop of Volkswagen vans and rusting jalopies, Largo would recount fabulous stories that were half true and half a cocktail of imagination. He was a born raconteur with not a trace of shyness in him, and Largo's 205-pound frame roved the fringe of the campfire as if it were a stage and he the main event. The most memorable tale I heard him tell concerned a hair-raising experience during a day when he was soloing routes at J-Tree, trying to keep up with John Bachar. Largo was a formidable climber in his own right, but he held Bachar's free soloing ability in high esteem.

"All climbs are easy for Bachar," he said. "He completely dominates the cliff with his grace and confidence. He never rattles, never loses control."

Bachar and a few others had developed a sort of high-stakes cult in which they would solo route after route, sometimes at levels as demanding as 5.12. The subsport of soloing rock climbs even hit the media's radar when in the early eighties *Newsweek* ran a story about Bachar's ropeless exploits.

Largo's tale began with him arriving in J-Tree during a spring break from college. A meeting with Bachar leads to a darelike invitation to embark on a soloing tour. Being the host, Bachar offers Largo a choice: they could have an "El Cap day" or a "Half Dome day." El Cap is 3,000 feet tall, which translates into climbing about thirty pitches. Half Dome is 2,000 feet, which equals about twenty pitches. All unroped. Largo wisely chooses the Half Dome option.

"In a wink Bachar was booted up and he set off," Largo told the campfire crowd. "He climbed flawlessly, then it was my turn to solo up behind him. I was nervous as hell. Shaking. As if jackals were running up and down my spine."

**John Bachar free solo-
ing Leave It To Beaver
(5.12).** (JOHN BACHAR COL-
LECTION)

Their method was to climb a hard route on a particular formation
about 150 feet tall, then they'd descend via a different, easy route. After
three hours they'd disposed of a dozen climbs.

"We felt invincible," Largo decreed. "Then we upped the ante from
easy 5.9 to a stiff 5.10. Now we were in expert terrain. We slowed
down, but by early afternoon we'd climbed our twenty pitches. Half
Dome was history."

But there was still daylight and Bachar suggested they solo a 5.11—
a tough feat even for Bachar. Listening to Largo describe what came
next left me slack-mouthed and awed.

Largo described how Bachar escorted him to Intersection Rock, to
the climb where Chuck, Bob, and I had watched Bachar free solo Left
Ski Track. Scores of climbers from all over the world "froze like stat-
ues" when Bachar started up unroped.

"He moved with flawless precision, plugging his fingertips into shallow pockets in the hundred-and-five-degree wall. I scrutinized his moves, making mental notes on the intricate sequence. He paused at 50 feet, directly below the crux bulge. Splaying his left foot out onto a slanting edge, he pinched a tiny rib and pulled through to a gigantic bucket hold. Then he walked up the last 100 feet of vertical rock like a kid climbing a staircase. From the summit Bachar flashed down that sly, candid snicker."

Largo told how he headed up.

"The first bit passed quickly. Everything was clicking along, severe but steady. Then I glided into the coffin zone," he said.

This sinister-sounding zone was a bit of Largo-speak, like Messner's "death zone" in the Himalayas. Simply put, it represented the point on a solo climb above 50 feet. Fall from there, and you'd probably end up in a wooden box.

Largo now had the campfire crowd in the palm of his hand. He turned up the drama, describing in animated detail how he bungled a sequence of moves while deep in the coffin zone.

"Man, my hands were too low to reach up for the big 'Thank God' bucket hold just above me, and my puny power was going fast. My foot started vibrating and I was instantly desperate, wondering if and when my body would plummet. There was no reversing any of this because you can't down-climb truly hard rock any more than a hurdler can run the one-ten 'highs' backward. The only way off was up. A montage of black images flooded my brain."

As Largo described the climb of his life, flickering campfire flames enhanced his stage movements. He contorted himself into the position that he had climbed himself into on that route—a position that he could not move out of.

"I was stuck, terrified, my whole existence focused down to a pinpoint, a single move. Arms shot, legs wobbling, head on fire. Then my fear overwhelmed itself and a little voice calmly intoned, 'At least die trying.'"

Largo then demonstrated to the crowd the muscle-twisting maneuver he pulled off to get himself out of the jam he was in. A nanosecond before his strength evaporated and he would free-fall to oblivion, he summoned all his remaining adrenaline and heaved through a do-or-die maneuver. When he grabbed the bucket hold and pulled onto the easier climbing above it, he stood quaking on the rock. He didn't want to go any higher—"I'd rather yank my wisdom teeth with Vise-Grips than continue up," he said. But he had to keep going. As he clawed up the last hundred feet, dancing black orbs dotted his vision, a residue from the onslaught of fear and adrenaline. On top Bachar snickered and told Largo that he had "looked a little shaky."

"The next day I didn't climb," Largo confessed. "Instead I wandered listlessly through dark desert corridors, scouting for turtles, making garlands of wildflowers, relishing the skyscape, doing all those things a person does on borrowed time."

Years later he would pen the story of this climb and call it "The Only Blasphemy." It would become one of the classics of climbing writing. In that tale, of the pivotal moment of risk recognition when he was poised between life and death, he wrote: "Shamefully I understood that the only blasphemy was to willfully jeopardize my own existence."

Most campfire yarns portrayed brinkmanship as a virtue. They were exciting, scary, and funny. They always ended on a happy I-made-it-by-the-skin-of-my-teeth note. We were all still young back then and mortality had yet to track us down.

Another riotous Largo campfire thriller, later published as a story called "Three Little Fish," concerned Tobin's first ascent of a climb at Tahquitz Rock, a climb named the Green Arch. This climb was the focus of several attempts by the Stonemasters, but every time they tried its smooth wall and its leaning open-book-shaped corner, they would be spat out. Only Largo had gotten high enough in the corner to gingerly touch the rounded mushroom-shaped knobs of dark rock on the wall above. He pronounced them as being ungrippable and he continued shuffling across the leaning arch until fatigue made him sag onto a piton he had laboriously hammered into the crack. Largo lowered back to the ground. It was now Tobin's turn to try. He immediately climbed up to the ungrippable knobs.

"No, those knobs don't go anywhere," Largo yelled, but it was too late.

"Understand that Tobin was a born-again Christian, that he'd smuggled Bibles into Bulgaria risking twenty-five years on a Balkan rock pile, that he'd studied God at a fundamentalist university," Largo explained. "And understand that Tobin was perfectly mad. Out on the sharp end he ignored all consequences. He even mocked them. Once, at Joshua Tree, I saw him climb a difficult crack with a noose tied around his neck. But most horrifying was his capacity to charge at a climb pell-mell."

Largo described how on straightforward routes Tobin's charge was an impressive display, but on routes requiring patience and cunning he was a disaster and he would climb into the most grievous predicaments.

"Against all my advice, Tobin clawed his way up to that sea of knobs. Just as I predicted, it was a dead end and he was stuck. The full impact of his folly hit him like a wrecking ball. He panicked and wailed and nearly wept," said Largo.

Tobin was 25 feet from the piton, so if he fell he would fall that distance, plus the 25 feet past the piton. There would be rope stretch and slack in the belay to add another 10 feet. But, as Largo pointed out, the chances were that the lousy blade-shaped piton he had bashed into the crack under the roof would rip out under the force of a fall. He would then drop a further 20 feet to the next piece of gear, making for an 80-foot fall. Largo worried that Tobin would end up crashing into the ground.

"As Tobin wobbled far overhead, who should lumber up to our little group but his very father—a minister, and a quiet, retiring, imperturbable gentleman who hacked and huffed from his long march up to the cliff. After hearing so much about climbing from Tobin, he'd finally come to see his son in action."

The sweat-soaked, mustached pastor "squinted up at the fruit of his loins." Tobin's knees knocked like castanets and he sobbed pitifully at the prospect of his fall. Then he suddenly screamed down to Largo, "I'm gonna jump."

"Jump off?"

"Yes!"

"No!" Largo screamed.

"You can do it, son," the pastor put in.

Inspired by his father's urging, Tobin groped at the holds above, but his fate was sealed. A second later he came flying off the wall. The top piton ripped out with a pinging sound. He screamed. His arms flailed as he cartwheeled through the air. Then the lower piton caught him and he jolted to a stop. Largo lowered him to the ground, where he lay motionless, moaning softly.

"He had a lump the size of a pot roast over one eye. Then he wobbled to his feet," said Largo.

"I'll get it next time," Tobin grumbled.

"There ain't gonna be a next time," declared Richard.

"Give the boy a chance," the pastor put in, thumping Tobin on the back.

This proved to Largo that both father and son were mad, and they withdrew for the day. The first ascent of the Green Arch finally came four years later, when Rick Accomazzo led it in a bold brilliant stroke. Largo and Tobin followed on the rope. Tobin went on to the European Alps to solo the north face of the Matterhorn, the Walker Spur, and the Shroud on the Grandes Jorasses, and he made the first alpine-style ascent of the direct route on the Eiger. I had read of these climbs in Chuck's apartment, particularly the latter, on which the American climber John Harlin had fallen thousands of feet to his death after a rope snapped. Tobin's list of solo mountain climbs grew as the years rolled on, and he became one of America's most famous alpinists. Then he met his end in the Canadian Rockies in 1980.

Largo wrote something of an obituary for his friend and in it he said, "I've never since experienced the electricity of watching Tobin out there on the quick of the long plank, clawing for the promised land. He finally found it while attempting a solo ascent of Mount Alberta's north face. His death was a tragedy. But I sometimes wonder if God himself could no longer bear the strain of watching Tobin wobbling and lunging way out there on the sharp end of the rope, and finally just drew him into the fold."

During my last year in high school, I found myself examining the concrete jungle of our LA environment with a sense of detachment. More and more I came to believe that my sense of belonging was with the imperfect family of friends I was meeting in the climbing scene. From that point on, I drifted away from climbing with Chuck, Kathy, and Bob. The change came as a natural transition for all of us. It was as if we each had our own separate paths to follow. I was reminded of the poignant prediction my brother Jim had made on our family outing years earlier: "You know, one day when we're all grown up, we'll have

Bachar trying to impress us with his long-jumping skills, in camp at J-Tree. From left to right, Mari Gingery, Jessica Perrin, Roy McClenahan, Rick Cashner, John Long, me (hidden), and John Bachar. (DEAN FIDELMAN)

families of our own and we won't live together anymore." Chuck's jaunts to Joshua Tree became fewer as his interests shifted more to mountaineering and less to rock climbing. As for Kathy, she became immersed in her pharmacology studies at the University of Southern California and in working part-time. Bob continued to climb easy routes in the mountains with Chuck, but his outings on the rock became less frequent as his time was taken up with work and studying psychology at Fullerton Junior College. As for me, I felt a calling coming from the rocky places like Joshua Tree. There, I felt as if I were a welcome figure in a familiar landscape.

Chapter 5

White Wind

Kathy tells a story about the moment in January 1980 when she had a premonition that Chuck had died. She was winter camping in Yosemite and a blizzard was raging outside the tent. All through the night she and her tent mate had to dig their tent out from a growing weight of snow to keep it from collapsing. Kathy lay in the tent shivering, drifting in and out of a troubled sleep. A sense of Chuck filled her thoughts. In those images he was in dire trouble. In reality, Chuck was, at that moment, fighting for his life somewhere around 22,000 feet on Aconcagua, the tallest peak on the South American continent. A month earlier he had followed his own mountaineering dream and had joined an expedition to attempt the first American ascent of the mountain's enormous and dangerous south face.

Chuck and Kathy had married in August 1977, after an eight-year courtship. Initially the marriage had gone well, but Chuck's decision to stop teaching high school geography and devote his time to being in the mountains meant he saw less of Kathy and they began to drift apart. By the middle of 1979 they were separated, and Chuck took the split badly. I remember a weekend when I found myself in Yosemite Valley at the same time as Chuck, and I chanced upon him sitting in his car, tearfully writing a letter to Kathy. Chuck was quietly devastated by the failure of his marriage, yet, perhaps strangely, after he moved out of the apartment that he and Kathy had shared, he maintained his link to the Hill family by moving into my brother Bob's apartment in Fullerton. As is often the case with men who climb and who have suffered an emotional trauma like a marital breakup, he found solace by devoting himself to climbing more seriously than ever before. Perhaps he was casting off the last shred of stability that a mate provides by plunging into the uncertainty of adventure.

Aconcagua is an ancient volcano 22,834 feet high in the Andes of southern Argentina. Though gigantic, from most views it is an unattractive peak, a hump, really, made of a dirty jumble of ash-smeared glaciers and decaying rock. If not for the fact that it is the highest point in South America, few people would bother to trudge up its gently angled north and east flanks. But Aconcagua's status as the highest on the continent gives it enough caché to attract hundreds of mountaineers from all over the world each year. It is even likely that ancient Incans climbed the mountain; a mummy was dug up at 17,800 feet. The first Westerners to climb it came in 1897, under the guiding eye of the Swiss mountaineer Matthias Zurbriggen. That ascent was from the north.

Ascents of the northern or eastern sides require only high-altitude walking. As of today, mountain bikes and dogs have even made it to the summit via the northern route, but nevertheless by 1979 some two hundred climbers had died while trying to get up, or down, those "easy" routes. High-altitude cerebral edema and pulmonary edema accounted for a good share of those deaths, but the real killer on Aconcagua is the wind. Known as El Viento Blanco, or the White Wind, it is a maelstrom that originates in Antarctica, races across the southern oceans and the Argentinean pampas, and slams into the exposed heights of Aconcagua at speeds in excess of a hundred miles per hour. In the arid cold found at the tallest reaches, El Viento Blanco produces temperatures capable of freezing flesh or inducing hypothermia in minutes. Such a wind can pin a climber to the mountainside and make movement impossible. If it blows fast enough, it can even suck the atmosphere from around the mountain and leave pockets where there is barely enough oxygen to breathe. The trick to surviving such hostile elements is to climb the mountain as fast as possible. This makes the easy north and east flanks the most viable gamble.

But it was not the easy way up that Chuck and his companions had in mind. From the south, Aconcagua presents an entirely different picture. Rising from the Horcones Glacier, the south face is a 10,000-foot precipice of rotten rock towers, gaping cold chimneys, and collapsing ice cliffs. The first party to climb it, in 1954, was a six-man French expedition led by René Ferlet. The climbers worked on their route for a month, weaving a path around steep rock towers and ice cliffs that frequently avalanched. During that month they set up a series of well-supplied camps linked together with thousands of feet of rope. When they were within striking distance of the summit, they set out for a final climb that ended up lasting seven days. On the last day a storm battered them, nearly freezing them to the face. They continued up, but by the time they descended from the summit, all of the climbers had frostbite. Back in France, only one of the climbers avoided amputations of fingers and toes. Ever after, the south face of Aconcagua—an ancient Incan word meaning "sentinel of stone"—has been shrouded in notoriety among climbers.

Between the French expedition and 1979, a mere six expeditions had claimed success over this intimidating wall. None of the victors were American. That distinction attracted the leader of Chuck's expedition, thirty-seven-year-old Ed Connor, a civil engineer and builder of golf courses who lived in Palm Springs, California. The kudos of having a tough "first" under one's belt is an integral part of the climbing experience, and Aconcagua from the south was a worthy objective to satisfy such an ambition. Connor started climbing comparatively late in life, when he was thirty. He had extensive experience on hard ice climbs and multiday rock climbs and had climbed a few mountains, but most of what he had done was in the league of high-altitude, nontechnical snow climbs. He made an ascent of Mount McKinley (20,320 feet) in 1973 and Mount Orizaba (18,700 feet) in Mexico in 1977. His most ambitious attempt on a mountain came in 1978, when he joined an expedition to Annapurna III (24,787 feet) in Nepal. Although this seven-man team was unsuccessful in their attempt to climb a new route, the experience proved to be valuable on Aconcagua.

For Aconcagua, Connor asked along his partner from Annapurna, twenty-year-old Guy Andrews, a San Diego travel agent. Andrews, a bachelor, was a lean, physically strong youth with a natural climbing talent. In his Aconcagua diary Connor wrote glowingly of his protégé: "Guy will be one of the best. I can't even describe to him what is in store for him if he continues at his present pace. Ideal job, good physical attributes. Good mental attitude. I only hope to contribute to his development. He can be the Jack Nicklaus of climbing in a few years. Another Messner."

Chuck appeared to be the odd man out on the team. He didn't really know Connor or Andrews and he had never been higher than 14,000 feet on a mountain. He had heard through a mutual friend in their local climbing community, Steve Van Meter, that Connor was financing everything but air travel on an expedition to Aconcagua and that a third member was needed, so he went to meet the other men at Connor's house in Palm Springs. After a few practice climbs in nearby Yosemite to test their compatibility, Connor invited Chuck to join the expedition. Chuck was eager and willing to go, and he had the money. Now that he was a bachelor again, he had the time. What he lacked was high-altitude climbing experience.

Connor took on a paternal role in his leadership of the expedition, calling Chuck and Guy his "boys." While in Santiago, Chile, on their way to the mountains, Connor wrote in his journal, "I'd forgotten what it was like to be young and impatient. Chuck and Guy are just two forces of light energy bursting at the seams. Focusing intense bursts on the nearest female shape, their rock and roll cassette tapes, each other and their aged leader. It's difficult at times to get a moment of peace and Mozart around their energy belts."

Connor's journal would become the only record of Chuck's last days.

Connor and his team planned to tackle the south face in highly ambitious style. Ever since the French, all the teams that had succeeded on the south face—Argentinean, Chilean, Austrian (a team that included Reinhold Messner), and Japanese—had used the tactic known variously as "expedition style" or "siege style." This method of going up and down a mountain repeatedly to secure the route with thousands of feet of rope creates a "safe" highway that can aid in either a head start when it comes time to sprint to the summit or a speedy escape route to lower camps when the weather turns bad. Along the way, tent camps stocked with food and supplies are placed at strategic intervals. This time-honored but heavy-handed mode of ascent involves a large team with lots of gear and requires weeks of preparation before a summit team can be sent up.

Connor didn't want to climb Aconcagua that way. He and the boys wanted to dispense with the path of ropes and in-situ camps and make a bare-bones ascent, going from the bottom to the top in one fast push, camping on the face wherever night fell, carrying only what they could cram into their backpacks. Incredibly, they would even go so light as to not take a tent, reasoning that there would be few places to pitch a tent on the steep south face. Instead, they'd sit on ledges in their sleeping bags.

This was "alpine-style" climbing at its boldest. This way of climbing mountains had become the more respected style of mountaineering in the 1970s, largely due to the example of Reinhold Messner, a brilliant climber who espoused climbing mountains "by fair means." Messner pooh-poohed the grand old style of big expeditions. Confronting the mountains in this lightweight manner was more adventuresome and more spiritually connected to the mountain, yet more risky and less certain of success. It was a style befitting only elite climbers.

The team landed in Santiago on December 15 and headed to Mendoza. They got along well from the start. "We really felt we were taking on a significant first; there was a real sense of adventure," Connor told an interviewer after the climb. "We felt pretty special. There was a lot of camaraderie. It showed. At the airports. At dinner together. We were a pretty close group."

A bus ride took the climbers and their six hundred pounds of supplies to Mendoza. The bulk of their gear jammed the bus, crowding the Argentine passengers, who jokingly called them *gringos locos*. To the local people it must have seemed strange that they had come so far for a holiday on frigid Aconcagua. From Mendoza another bus took them another hundred miles to the Puente del Inca ski hut at the end of the road. They rented mules to carry their loads and headed toward the mountain. Connor recorded in his journal their first view of the mountain:

> The Andes have the majestic allure of the Himalayas without the tropical climate at lower elevations. This tends to make the trekking much more pleasurable. The Horcones Valley has a stark beauty and grandeur I was unprepared for. Huge tilted strata of ancient sandstone stacked row upon row for your viewing pleasure. Because I now get away only once or twice a year or so, I think each experience is more enriching to me. The South Face is magnificent. One-and-a-half-times the face of the Eiger, four times Half Dome, with ice and altitude thrown in. Two-and-a-half-times El Cap. The scale is astonishing. There stands 10,000 feet of steep ice and rock and no American has climbed it! Unbelievable!

They placed a base camp at 13,000 feet and set about acclimatizing for the next twelve days. Connor, an amateur medical buff, monitored everyone's blood pressure, pulse rate, and lung capacity. He also tended to Chuck, who had developed serious diarrhea that they suspected was dysentery. After treatment with Lomotil and tetracycline antibiotics, Chuck felt better and joined Connor and Guy on short training climbs onto the lower ramparts of the mountain.

Timing of the ascent was a critical factor. After about a week in base camp to acclimate to the 12,000-foot elevation and venturing to around 16,000 feet on neighboring ridges during training with no ill effects, the team became concerned that the superb weather they had experienced might soon deteriorate.

Connor had directed a fair amount of attention to timing the size and location of the avalanches that seemed constantly to rack the face, adding to its menace. Connor wrote, "About 2:00 AM on the morning of Dec 30 a huge earthquake shook the area. Being from California, we all three knew at once what was happening. Our camp was safely away from any danger, but I stuck my head out of the tent in time to witness a spectacle never equaled in my experience. The entire 9 kilometer wide and 3 kilometer high South Face under a full moon started moving all at once in slow motion, as the Face shed millions of tons of unconsolidated snow and ice. It was mesmerizing to be standing within a mile of this event and to be so transfixed by it that thoughts of danger or fleeing didn't really occur to us. The spindrift settled to the bottom with a muffled roar that eventually cast a mild snow cloud over our camp with a gentle rustling of fabric. After the excitement subsided, we realized this was the sign we'd been waiting for. With the removal of all this unconsolidated material, we reckoned the avalanche danger would never be less than in the days following then earthquake."

So on New Year's Eve the three set off at four-thirty A.M. to start the climb. In each man's pack they carried gear and supplies weighing fifty pounds. That included food for six days. "There was an element of unpredictability about the climb," Connor said later. "We knew we were sticking our necks out farther than we ever had before. It intrigued us and gave us spirit to think that we could do the climb while realizing there was a possibility we couldn't. That's exactly where you want to be on a climb. If you were so certain of success, the spirit of adventure would be removed and you probably wouldn't even go to the effort."

The first day the trio strapped crampons to their boots and climbed 2,300 feet of snow to the bottom of a landmark on the face called the Broken Towers. To get there they had run a gauntlet of snowslides triggered by the morning sun, which warmed the slopes and set off avalanches. Higher up, bands of vertical ice cliffs, known as seracs, would also bust loose when warmed by the sun, sending tons of ice exploding down the mountain. The climbing route followed a winding path that narrowly avoided these hazards. At the Broken Towers their lives started getting difficult.

Wrote Connor, "We are on a knife-edge at 6:15 PM with no good bivouac ledges in sight. So we decide to find a better place to sleep. Chuck did a magnificent lead to get to the bivy but we lose! No ledge and no place to cook or lie flat. We bivy in an ice-filled chimney of rotten rock hanging in harnesses, unable to cook or sleep. The price we pay in loss of energy is at least a day."

When I learned that Chuck and his partners had stood upright all night, clipped to their harnesses to prevent them from slipping off the face, shivering, thirsty, and hungry because they could not set up a shelter or cook, it was obvious to me that from the very first day the odds were stacking up against them. To me, enduring such punishment and then continuing on up was hard to imagine. But carry on they did.

Again from Connor's journal: "Only reluctantly did the Towers release their hold on us. The last 20 feet we had to tiptoe on a knife edge arête with packs on and no belay. I just swallowed my apple, waiting for a death fall. My greatest fear now is that someone will make a tired mistake and we will have an accident."

After four hours of "struggling fearsomely," according to Connor, they reached the top of the Broken Towers. There they stopped to cook and rest. They didn't climb much farther, but stopped at a section known as the Sandstone Band. At the base of this 1,000-foot cliff they used their ice axes to chop out a ledge in the ice field and spent the night.

According to Connors, "I estimated we had surmounted the first third of the face (granted not the most difficult third). Although we did not find a great bivy site, the weather was good and we were not terribly uncomfortable. There was never any question of not continuing at this point. We were very fit and once we got some more snow melted at the top of the Broken Towers, we felt strong and confident."

The summit was visible above them. But how far above them they were unsure, as Connor couldn't be certain if his altimeter was reading the altitude correctly. It read 17,000 feet, yet he was certain they had climbed higher. But if the altimeter was right, they had nearly 6,000 feet remaining. Of his confusion over this Connor jotted down, "Nothing makes sense at this altitude . . . Surely we must be on Mars or at least the Moon, I feel mountain lassitude today. Dull, insipid thought patterns."

On day three they climbed with difficulty into the sandstone band, then an afternoon storm pelted them with snow. Connor took the lead and scurried about the rocky slope looking for a ledge they could squeeze their bodies onto for the night. Wrote Connor, "I promised Guy a flat place to lay down and so it shall be. I stamp out a flat place in the snow and bring the boys up. Both near hypothermia. We get settled about 9:00 PM. Dead tired and needing liquid and food badly. Force ourselves to cook and melt snow. Without liquid we will be wasted for the next day."

His journal records how the increased altitude made it hard to stomach their freeze-dried meal of shrimp creole, though they were famished. Then he wrote, "Guy develops a bad headache and numb feet. Chuck got snow-blind sometime this afternoon so we have to watch him. He is in great pain. Evening views from this space platform over the Central Andes are incredible. Unfortunately we were too concerned with survival to appreciate them."

Day four dawned fairly clear, but the drama, as carefully recorded by Connor, continued: "I lead off heading for a snow ramp and boom! My right leg disappears into a void. I look down into an evil hole about 10 feet wide with no bottom. I'm suspended by a rotten snow bridge. With Guy pulling me backward and a frantic ice axe arrest I'm able to roll back out of it. It does block the path to the ramp however, so I'm forced to do some rather desperate moves over a steep ice wall to get back onto the ramp. Very hard with a pack on!"

They camped in a small gully at the base of a section known as the French Rib. They were cooking dinner and trying to recover from the efforts of the day when a massive cliff of ice above them collapsed and set off an avalanche "big enough to bury 10 people." It missed them by 150 feet. "We are too tired to celebrate our good fortune," wrote Connor.

From this bivouac they hoped to get to the summit in one more day, but as it turned out, it took them three. They woke sluggish from altitude and from having been deluged by blowing spindrift, or powdery wind-blown snow that washes around the mountain like water. After taking a couple of hours to inventory their food and supplies and repack gear, they set off at ten-thirty A.M. Soon thereafter, Chuck stepped through a snowbridge partway into a crevasse and had to be pulled out. Connor was expecting to find somewhere on the rib above them an easy walk-off that headed over to the less steep summit plateau. But they found no escape route, only tricky rock pitches, all at around 20,500 feet.

"Chuck ignores his bout with snow blindness to push the lead about 60 or 70 feet," Connor wrote. "He gets stuck and Guy goes up to finish the pitch. In his haste to find us a decent bivy, Guy does not take enough gear and ends up getting stuck about 50 feet above Chuck. I holler for a retreat to the stance I'm on but they feel a good ledge is above."

Connor headed up toward them and realized quickly that they had a problem: both Guy and Chuck had left their packs with him and Connor could not drag three heavy packs up the wall. Darkness was falling and the wind building. Connor's journal then hinted at the stress that Chuck must have been feeling: "Chuck gets panicky and drops a glove which heightens his anxiety (and mine) . . . I pass him one of my own along with a sharp order for both men to GET DOWN NOW!!!"

Connor headed back down a few dozen feet to his belay ledge and began to chop at the ice to make a space for a bivouac. He ordered Guy to help Chuck get down, and he described Chuck as being "quite blown out by this time and I half expect to see him just plummet in his state of anxiety."

So Guy rappelled down the rope to Chuck and helped him regain his composure. The two of them descended to the three-by-four-foot ledge that Connor had been hacking away at. Said Connor later, "I would have hated to have seen Chuck try to come down without Guy's help because he was pretty panicked at this point. Sometimes you have to slap a guy and say, 'Hey, if you don't move from there you're gonna die.'"

In the middle of the night the dreaded El Viento Blanco rammed into them like a freight train. The three of them sat on a one-man ledge without a tent, with no room to even get in their sleeping bags, bearing the brunt of the freezing wind. Soon their feet began to grow colder and colder. Connor and Chuck stuck their feet in each other's crotches in an effort to unlace each other's boots, as the cold was causing their frozen leather boots to swell and press in on their feet, cutting off circulation. But their fingers went numb the moment they touched the laces. Frostbite was now almost guaranteed.

Wrote Connor, "We knew that if we didn't get those boots undone we were going to lose our toes. We worked at it maybe half an hour, but finally we just said, 'Screw it, Let 'em freeze.' That's pretty remarkable. We were not people of low willpower, and to just sit there and say, 'Well, I guess I'm going to give up my toes because I'm too tired to get my boots off,' is hard to imagine."

The altitude and its lack of oxygen, the cold and their state of fatigue, conspired to create a potentially fatal state of apathy in them all. Yet thoughts of rappelling down the south face were, in their assessment, out of the question. They felt that to try to head down with only loose rock and snow to anchor the ropes to would be suicide. The way out of this mess was to climb up to the top and descend the other side. So they waited for the next twelve hours, huddled on the ledge, a knot of arms and legs clinging to the edges of the sleeping bags they had blanketed themselves with to fend off the wind.

By the sixth day they were able to move. "The thing that really startles me is how we were able to get up and climb," said Connor. "I think you realize you have no choice. You can't stop there and you can't go down. In a way it's even kind of a mental relief for everything to be immaterial but one goal. You have to climb, and you have to do it yourself. You have to get to the top, and you have to keep from falling."

Connor had endured the wind a little better than Chuck or Guy, so he took the lead up the ridge in front of them for the next few pitches. Of this pitch Connor wrote, "I led a very steep snow covered rock pitch that seemed like climbing styrofoam peanuts on a steep glass wall."

Any fall would have been deadly, as the protection and belays they rigged along the way would have ripped out under any weight. When his "boys came up looking a bit weary" he continued leading the ridge, which became narrow as a knife edge.

They made a sixth bivouac below a rock outcrop at around 21,500 feet. This one was much more comfortable than the previous night. They cooked a large meal and drank two quarts of liquid each as they settled down in their bags. They discussed the likelihood of frostbite damage to their toes. "When numbness is a constant companion as it was for the entire day, we knew there was tissue damage. In our precarious position, we couldn't afford to attempt treatment or therapy. We had to get over and off this mountain as quickly as possible and worry about the damage when we were safely off the mountain." Connor cautioned both Guy and Chuck not to remove their boots under any circumstances. They could loosen the laces for circulation, but if they removed their boots, their feet would swell hugely, dooming their escape from the peak.

The next morning Connor continued leading his team forward till they reached the end of the hard climbing and were on a huge, almost flat plateau that exited the south face and joined the top of the Polish route. The remainder of the climb was a hike, and so they decided to discard their ropes to save weight. For four hours they trudged over ridges, expecting the summit to appear, but another ridge always awaited them over each rise. Their energy and physical state were by now critical. By then, they knew they had frostbite on their toes and fingers. Around five P.M. they encountered what appeared to be the final obstacle to the summit—a very steep ridge of broken rock. Climbing it would be like walking a tightrope. With thousands of feet of exposure dropping off to either side, to fall would be to die.

They lingered here in a quandary, because night was coming on and El Viento Blanco was building up again. They were concerned about the ridge not leading directly to the summit and getting stranded in an even more exposed position for the night. The wind was already strong enough to knock them off their feet and they had to hold on to rocks to keep from being blown off the ridge. Chuck was now staggering, increasingly helpless with each hour. Judging Chuck to be nearly broken down from exhaustion, Connor told Guy, "We can't take him over right now," so they crouched together in a huddle and bivouacked again, for a seventh night, at around 22,500 feet.

"We bivied in the boulders," wrote Connor, "and spent a very unpleasant night as El Viento Blanco visited us again. The ridge above this platform looked even more exposed and we knew the summit would be very exposed with little snow to dig into."

It was another night in which they could not light the stove and melt water or cook. By morning the wind was still howling. Again they had to wait. Connor still was holding his own against the elements, and he told the boys to wait while he set off down the mountain a short way to look for a more sheltered spot. His six-two, 180-pound body and his mental maturity seemed to sustain him. He found a spot and waved them down, but Chuck and Guy stumbled down without taking their packs. Connor went back up and dragged the packs down. There they spent their eighth night on Aconcagua.

Connor had by this time ceased keeping his journal, but he later told a reporter, "The guys had done a magnificent climb . . . Nobody should be up there for nearly two days after they've done a six-day, 10,000-foot face and gone through what we went through. Nobody should have to put up with that. Nobody should have survived it."

Clear skies and little wind met them on the ninth morning. All three were by then suffering from the altitude and frostbite. "We were think-ing strictly of survival at this point," said Connor. "We abandoned all our gear, cut our loads to the bare minimum; just sleeping bags, a bivouac sack and a couple candy bars each. Didn't even carry ice axes."

They were counting on the route being easy, and they knew that on the way down the north side they would find huts and maybe even other climbers. They simply had to keep it together to get over the final hump. Connor claimed the boys were able to function well enough to pack their backpacks and eat and drink the three quarts of water Connor painstakingly melted and poured into their cups. He talked to them about the final section to the top and he instructed them to pace themselves by taking sets of five steps, then breathing deeply, and then taking another set of five steps. He would go ahead to break the trail, telling them to follow.

Connor described this critical moment later in a letter to me: "I told them if we lost visual contact, I would wait a while on the summit, and if I didn't see them there, I would meet them at the first hut on the trail back down. It seemed totally innocent. With the wind in a lull, a full meal in their stomachs, there was not the sense of desperation we had felt the previous day. They understood and acknowledged my instruc-tions with no sign of the erratic response that typifies diminished capacity at altitude. 'Fine,' they said. As we started off, I glanced over at Guy and Chuck and we gave each other a thumbs up as they were helping each other tighten straps and head out." Then Connor headed on. He would never see them again.

Without the gale-force wind the final ridge was not difficult. Connor reached the summit in just over an hour. He realized with frustration that they had sat an entire day at a point just under 300 feet from the top. He waited on top for over an hour but saw no sign of his compan-ions. Once he tried to reverse his tracks to look for them, but exhaus-tion overtook him and he feared for his own survival: "I took a few steps back down the route and my knees buckled. It was only then I realized the surge of adrenaline that got me up the last few meters had passed and I was dangerously weak from the ordeal of the past week. This was the first time my internal red flags went up. I could see about half the route back to the bivouac and they should have been in sight by now. The summit was a flat exposed plateau about an acre in size. There was a summit marker consisting of some tent poles tied together with wire and some loose tent poles scattered about nearby. I spotted what looked like the descent route to the Berlin Hut, which was visible directly below me. Closer inspection revealed this route to be much more technical than the descriptions we had studied, so I kept looking to the west side of the summit plateau. Here I found the Canoleta, a wide sloping gully that we had read about as being the final feature below the summit from that side. I fashioned a large arrow on the ground from two of the loose aluminum tent poles pointing to the Canoleta in the event they became confused on the summit."

Finally, feeling the wind rise again, he turned and headed down a foot-worn trail through the rubble.

Some twenty years later, Connor described to me the details of his descent alone. He was so tired he was reduced to sliding on his rear and dragging his ice ax over the rocks behind him to make downward progress. It took him three to four hours to reach the hut, which was nothing more than four walls. The roof had blown off years earlier. He collapsed into his sleeping bag and dozed. Three more hours passed. He had expected Chuck and Guy to appear within an hour. Then it got dark. At that point Connor knew the boys would never arrive; another night spent in the open would kill them.

El Viento Blanco blew its hundred-mile-per-hour anger all that night. "I don't think I've ever had a worse night mentally," Connor said later. "I was truly anxious for the first time about something other than technical difficulties. I knew I was dangerously weak and barely able to organize my thoughts about the options available to me. I kept rationalizing they would be along any second. There wasn't a damned thing I could do but sit there and listen to the wind howl. In total exhaustion and despair, I cried myself to sleep fearing the worst for the first time."

Next day—his tenth on Aconcagua—Connor reached a hut and met three Venezuelan climbers. One of them ran down to alert a rescue party, while the others helped Connor to the base of the mountain. But the wind and storm conditions prevented any search for four more days. When rescuers reached the summit, they found no one. At the bivouac where Connor had last seen the boys there was only one ice ax—Guy's. Gear lay strewn about. Guy's boots lay abandoned in the snow. Rescuers noticed that the heels had been sliced open with a knife. That last morning his feet had been so badly swollen that he had put on a pair of tennis shoes that Connor had been carrying in his pack. Prior to that he had been forced to cut his boots open to accommodate his painfully bloated feet. Connor had hoped to use these tennis shoes for the walk back to base camp. The only other object the rescuers found was a talisman that Guy's mother had given him before the climb.

A few days after this sad incident—on Sunday, January 13—a friend of Kathy's was reading a newspaper in Los Angeles and came across an article that read "Two U.S. Mountain Climbers Found Frozen to Death on Aconcagua." The story named Chuck and Guy as being "presumed

Chuck doing what he loved most. (BOB HILL)

dead," and reported that the army had found the bodies and Connor near the summit. Almost simultaneously, Trish was in a restaurant and read the same story. The headline was erroneous—no bodies had been found. But the news was shocking nonetheless. A flurry of phone calls between members of the families led them to contact the U.S. embassy in Argentina, where some of the details of the incident were confirmed. From the hospital in Mendoza, Connor called Steve Van Meter and asked him to pass on a message to the families saying that it was true that the two men were missing. After Connor returned to the United States, he "spent a tearful couple of hours with Guy Andrews' father at a public park." But he never spoke to Guy's mother or the Bludworths because he was told that they would be "too upset" to visit with him in person.

Those of us who were close to Chuck lived in a confused world for several days in which we believed against all reason that this was a muddle and that Chuck would phone to say he was alive and would be home soon. But gradually it sank in that Chuck was dead. And we learned that during the time of Chuck's darkest hours strange things had happened to some of us. There was Kathy's premonition in the snowbound tent in Yosemite. And while sitting in my room, Tom saw the framed poster of the famous climber Willi Unsoeld suddenly fall off the wall for no reason. "No goal is too high if we climb with care and confidence," were the words inscribed on the poster.

One night I lay in my bed thinking of Chuck, struggling to accept he would never return. I said into the darkness, "Okay, Chuck, if you are dead, come to see me now." Maybe I imagined it, but I felt that his presence entered my room.

Then I was certain he was gone from us forever.

To this day, the bodies of Chuck Bludworth and Guy Andrews have not been found.

I already knew long before Chuck's death that I would never be a mountaineer. I was never drawn to that realm of ice and altitude, nor was my body suited to the cold or for carrying loads that weighed nearly as much as I. Chuck's or anyone's fascination with high-altitude climbing remained mysterious to me. I imagined that climbing with ice axes, crampons, and other sharp devices in cold, oxygen-starved places would create a barrier between the climber and the climb. I loved the touch and feel of the rock, and the intimacy between climber and cliff. That, to me, was beauty.

But even more alien to me was the idea of expeditions. So often, expeditions I have heard about seemed comprised of people who share nothing but an ambition to climb a mountain, to accomplish a "first," or to plant a flag. I did not understand how Chuck could set out on an expedition on which life itself was at stake with people with whom he had barely ever climbed and hardly knew.

Although the experience of losing Chuck affected me deeply, there was no question in my mind that I would continue climbing after he passed away. Our shared passion for climbing and the experiences we lived together will always remain a part of me.

Chapter 6

Yosemite Days

In the early 1980s climbers from all over America and the world congregated in Yosemite Valley. They ensconced themselves there in a seasonal tent village named Camp Four, where many lived like a ragged occupying army, annoying park rangers by eluding camp fees, overstaying their welcome, and comporting themselves like gypsies. In the mornings, we climbers gathered in the now-defunct parking lot beside the lodge and the Four Seasons Restaurant, an eatery we dubbed the Foul Seasons, Foul Regions, or Foul Squeezin's, depending on the state of your digestive system after a meal there. The parking lot had been irreverently renamed the Arcing Plot by some climber as a commentary on the electric vibe emanating from the climbing crowd. This field of blacktop served as our de facto town square where, in between games of Hacky Sack, climbing plans were hatched and the long-haired luminaries of the scene held court. This was our neighborhood and these people created the community that gave me a sense of belonging.

Long before Yosemite Valley became a mecca to climbers, it was a place of inspiration to the Ahwahnee Tribe, who lived there for centuries. In the late 1800s explorers like John Muir wrote of the grandeur of thunderstorms rolling over the valley rim from the High Sierras, and later Ansel Adams communicated the same natural drama through his camera lens. When climbers began showing up in Yosemite in the post–World War II years, they found that the sun-bathed rock was impeccably solid, with cracks and features that made it a joy to dance over. With cliffs of every dimension—from house-sized rocks with short boulder problems of ferocious difficulty to 100-foot cliffs split by perfect cracks to immense walls that may take two weeks to ascend— Yosemite earned its reputation as the one of the very finest places on earth to climb.

Glaciers had gouged this canyon out of Sierra Nevada bedrock eons ago. When the Ice Age was over and the ice caps had melted, a 3,000-foot-deep, five-mile-wide corridor of rocky turrets and buttresses was revealed. In the highest reaches of the valley are the solid granite mountains of Half Dome and Mount Watkins, facing each other with walls so smooth they look as if a knife had slashed through the sky, slicing the timeworn, rounded domes in half. Downstream along the Merced River stand great portals of rock like Washington Column, the spear-pointed Lost Arrow Spire with thundering Yosemite Falls beside it, and the dark-faced tombstone of Sentinel Rock. Farther downstream still, amid grassy meadows and stands of huge sequoias, are other spectacular formations: the Leaning Tower, Middle Cathedral Rock, and the mightiest stone of all, El Capitan, which rises abruptly on the south flank of the valley in a clean, tawny sweep for 3,000 feet. If you take the secular view of existence, then Yosemite is a wonderfully sculpted geologic accident; if you believe in a cosmic master plan, then it is among the Creator's greatest works, a natural wonder of the world.

My visits to Yosemite in my teen years—from ages sixteen to nineteen—were always wedged between going to school and various part-time jobs like teaching gymnastics at Cal State University at Fullerton or flipping burgers in fast-food joints. Yet improving my skills on rock and living in the midst of Yosemite's walls to learn about the adventures of those climbers who had been there before me seemed, to me, as important as anything school had to offer. And with a climbing legend written in every wall, Yosemite was like a library of America's vertical history.

One of the legends that inspired my great respect and admiration for the early pioneers of Yosemite climbing concerned the Lost Arrow Spire, one of the most striking of all Yosemite towers. This 200-foot spire of rock sticks out like a thumb from the main wall from a point 1,200 feet above the ground. The year was 1946, a time when none of the major walls in Yosemite had been climbed, and the man of the moment was a Swiss-born blacksmith and vegetarian named John Salathè.

As is so often the case in climbing, it was a piece of equipment that shaped the destiny of the sport, and in the case of the Lost Arrow Spire, it was a piton. After World War II, the only pitons available were made of soft steel. Though these suited the soft limestone rock of Europe

Chuck relaxing on top of the Lost Arrow Spire while Bob makes his way across the spectacular Tyrolean traverse. (BOB HILL COLLECTION)

where they were manufactured, they were too malleable to use on hard Yosemite granite. Salathè learned this the hard way, while trying to be the first climber to reach the pointy tip of the Lost Arrow. On that attempt his soft pitons bent and deformed when he hammered them into cracks, and he'd ended up with a mangled, unusable pile of metal. Even though he was close to the top he had no choice but to retreat, because he was dependent on hanging directly from each piton. This was the accepted tactic back then: rather than free climb steep rock, one hammered in a ladder of pitons, a method we still call "aid climbing."

Bent pitons didn't deter Salathè. Turning to his blacksmith skills, he fired up his forge at home and took to the axle of a salvaged Model-A Ford, heating up slivers he'd cut from it until they glowed white-hot, and pounding them into a new type of piton. Made of carbon steel, his new designs were stronger and more durable than the old iron pitons, and they were better shaped to fit the cracks of Yosemite. They even resembled the shape of the Lost Arrow Spire, and climbers quickly began referring to them as exactly that—Lost Arrows. To help his ascent of the Lost Arrow, Salathè also fashioned a claw-shaped device that resembled a grappling hook, which he draped over the edges of flakes on the rock face and hung from. Today, climbers on El Cap carry such devices—called skyhooks—on most major big-wall aid routes. Salathè also took his bolt drills and tempered them with heat so the hard Yosemite rock would not blunt them. Finally, he refined the rope tactics he used, devising a system that is similar to that used today. Salathè caught my attention not only because of these technical breakthroughs, but also for his mental outlook: he had the faith in himself to try things no one had tried before.

John Salathè, teamed up with Anton Nelson, had already made the first ascent of the southwest face of Half Dome, in a twenty-four-hour push. That was probably the hardest climb in America at the time, but when the pair turned to the Lost Arrow Spire and began climbing a deep fissure splitting the wall behind the spire, they entered for the first time an even harder realm—the realm of true "big-wall climbing," ascents of huge cliffs that may take several days and nights to climb. Knowing their route would take longer than Half Dome, and that they would not be able to carry enough water for their multiday ascent, they conditioned themselves on other climbs to drink sparingly. Several weeks of this camellike training prepared them for a thirsty five-day climb of the Lost Arrow Chimney. Salathè's last stroke of genius came in July 1950, when he and Allen Steck—who was still making appearances in Camp Four when I was in Yosemite—climbed the north face of Sentinel Rock over four and a half days. Climbers still regard that route as a strenuous challenge.

Thirty years later, when my Yosemite career began, the gear, standards, and mental attitudes about climbing had come a long way. Instead of having only steel pitons, we also had nuts and cams that gently and easily slotted into cracks. We had better climbing shoes, stronger ropes, and more efficient devices to fulfill nearly every need on a wall. In addition, our more athletic style of training and the balletlike free climbing movements we had perfected allowed us to dance on our fingers and toes over many sections of rock that Salathè would have aid-climbed. Yet though we were climbing harder routes, I doubt we were climbing with more boldness or vision than Salathè, for nothing can compare with the demands of confronting the unknown.

In the summer of 1979 I stood in the Arcing Plot racking up a pile of climbing gear for an ascent of that most famous of all Yosemite routes, the Nose of El Capitan. The route, established in 1958, had been the first line up El Capitan. Days before the first climbers began work on the Nose, the steep north face of Half Dome had fallen to Royal Robbins, Jerry Gallwas, and Mike Sherrick. El Cap, towering at the opposite end of the valley from Half Dome, was the next frontier to explore. Nothing like it had ever been climbed before. The time, energy, and persistence required to do the first ascent of such a huge wall of rock was an adventure on a par with the race to the South Pole.

The biggest, steepest, most technical rock climb ever attempted caught the public eye more than any climb in America before it. Several climbers worked on the Nose, going up and down on fixed ropes on several attempts spread between July 4, 1957, and November 12, 1958. The sight of the climbers dangling on the wall had caused traffic jams in the valley below, and at one point a ranger had stood in the meadow shouting to a climber through a bullhorn, "Get your ass down from there!" The Park Service didn't warm to the vertical shenanigans going on above them and they initially banned the climb, but finally they relented, letting the climbers continue to push the route higher as long as they agreed to climb during the off-season in Yosemite—after Labor Day and before Memorial Day. These restrictions, the still-primitive gear, and the slow-moving nature of aid climbing almost the entire route contributed to the huge number of climbing days spent on the wall: forty-five, spread over a period of nearly eighteen months.

The mastermind of the Nose's first ascent, and the only man part of it from beginning to end during those intensive months, was a climbing visionary named Warren Harding. Harding later wrote a strange book called *Downward Bound* in which he chronicled in comic form the Yosemite scene of the 1960s, poking fun at the vanities and conceits of every climber, including himself, whom he painted as a wine-swilling maverick. In the book he constantly referred to himself by his nick-name, Batso, which was derived from his batty outlook on life, his bat-like habit of living on cliffs, and also a collection of angular facial features and a slicked-back, vampiresque hairline. Wine jug in hand, an older, more stoop-shouldered version of Harding strolled through Camp Four occasionally while I was camping there. He still climbed, but he seemed to avoid the Arcing Plot with its younger, more hippie-looking crowd. Just as I would come to feel some day in the future, Harding felt that his heyday in Yosemite had passed, but he still loved the place and couldn't get it out of his system.

My partners on the Nose were to be two Joshua Tree regulars, Mari Gingery and Dean Fidelman. By this stage, I had already climbed a few big-wall routes like the Regular and Direct routes on Half Dome, the south face of Mount Watkins, and other one-day wall routes like the Rostrum and Sentinel Rock. But I had done these climbs with people who had experience superior to mine, and I had to some extent relied on their know-how to get us up. On the Nose, the partnership would be more equally aligned. The Nose would be steeper and longer than anything I had previously climbed, and it involved a lot of aid climbing, something at which none of us was very experienced. For each of us, the Nose was to be a great learning opportunity.

Dean, a member of the J-Tree scene, felt like family, so when he expressed a desire to come along on the Nose, I figured his good humor and endless supply of wisecracks would come in handy. Mari, a soft-spoken research biologist specializing in electron microscopy in LA, felt like family too. She had become a regular partner of mine over many weekend jaunts to the southern California cliffs. On those weekends we had often been the only women in a sea of coarse-talking, hard-cranking men. We had found a sisterhood in figuring out our own methods of getting up sections of routes the guys simply muscled through. Since I was always the smallest person around, I had to use the strength and flexibility I had developed through gymnastics to get past sections where taller people could reach a hold. Born to a German-American father and a Japanese mother, raven-haired Mari has a slight build too, though she is several inches taller than me. Gifted with a balletlike climbing style, she was able to use sensitivity and technique to pass difficult sections. We shared a love of free climbing, and a big part of our devotion came from the joy of figuring out our own unique choreography of movement using the natural features of the rock.

On some of those weekends at Joshua Tree, I remember how Mari and I would lose track of time, like children playing, as we roamed the desert from one boulder to another, climbing until our skin burned from the sharp rock and we couldn't hang onto the holds any longer. At such times we'd examine our chalk-white hands with their callused skin and frayed nails and cuticles, and we'd joke about needing a manicure.

Loitering around us in the Arcing Plot that day, as we sorted gear and packed our haulbags with enough food and water for three days on the Nose, were several men and, in far lesser numbers, the women who comprised the hard core of the Yosemite climbing scene. Shirts off to soak up the morning sun, the men had bodies honed from a thousand strenuous rock climbs, and the sunlight beaming in over the north rim of the valley highlighted the ridges and troughs of their muscles. As paunchy middle-aged tourists strolled by on their way to breakfast or to sightseeing tours, they cast openmouthed glances at this living statuary of enviably fit young people. "They must be the climbers," tourists could be heard whispering.

Most of the usual Joshua Tree crowd had moved into Yosemite that summer. Largo, Yabo, Mike Lechlinski, Bachar, and others were standing in clusters around the van-choked parking lot, talking to Yosemite habitués like Jim Bridwell, Ron Kauk, Dale Bard, Mark Chapman,

The Joshua Tree gang. Left to right—back row: Yabo, Mari Gingery, Mike Lechlinski, Randy Vogal; middle row: Dave Evans, Maria Cranor, Largo, Charles Cole, Dean Fidelman, Jim Angione, Craig Fry; front: Brian Rennie. (BRIAN RENNIE)

Werner Braun, and Kevin Worrall. Collectively, this group represented some of the top American climbers of the day. Occasionally they offered advice on what we should take, or loaned us an item of gear we were lacking. "Racking up" is part of the ritual for a big-wall climb, and neatly laying out on the ground one's arsenal of gear and supplies is like arraying the ranks of one's army before charging into the foe. For the Nose we had assembled an array of hexentrics and stoppers for sticking in cracks; a few pitons; fifty carabiners clipped into a long, silvery chain; jumars and aid slings for ascending the rope; three hefty leading and hauling ropes; a pulley to make it easier to drag the haulbag up the wall; six gallon jugs of water; a stuff sack crammed with bagels, canned tuna, candy bars, and dried fruit; sleeping bags and foam pads.

While we sorted through this mounting pile, a distorting pair of car speakers blared a Jimi Hendrix riff over the distant roar of Yosemite

Falls. This provided dramatic mood music to a tale that Jim Bridwell, a.k.a. the Bird or the Admiral, was telling, about a death-defying aid pitch he had led on a new route that he and Kim Schmitz had recently completed on Half Dome. The route was called Zenith, and it climbed a patch of granite so steep that raindrops had never touched the 2,000-foot face. The pitch had an airy name: the Space Flake.

Bridwell was the undisputed leader of the climbing scene in Yosemite Valley at this time, and when he spoke, people listened. Tall, dusty-haired, leather-faced, muscle-bound, and sporting a droopy and seditious-looking Che Guevara mustache, he had, at age thirty-six, been climbing longer than some of us had been alive. He had also mastered many of the hardest, tallest routes in Yosemite. As John Long once jokingly remarked, Bridwell was old enough "to have known the Unknown Soldier and who shot him. In a manner, a rope ran from him back to the very beginnings of the sport." Moreover, he was also highly supportive of my climbing goals almost from the moment I met him.

"We are fifteen hundred feet off the deck and the wall overhangs thirty degrees beyond the vertical," Bridwell was saying of his climb up Zenith. "We get to this flake. It looks like a guillotine blade, only it's a hundred feet long, and it hangs over our heads like a death sentence. Schmitz says, 'No way, this thing is too dangerous, one tap of the hammer and it'll cleave us off the wall.' So we sit there for a long time, looking at it before I get the balls to start up."

Bridwell holds the young crowd's attention as he relates his tale. He describes with a mechanic's knack for technical detail the tricky ways he made each piece of his gear wedge into the gaping mouth of the flake. Bridwell's description is so vivid I can almost hear the flake vibrate like a gong as he drives pitons behind it with his hammer. He makes us feel that for every piece of gear he placed in that hundred heart-stopping feet there was an exact number of taps of the hammer to make it stick. One tap too few and the piece would rip out when he was hanging from it, creating a zipperlike fall that would send him careening like a wrecking ball into Schmitz. One tap too many and the tension of the flake would be broken, and hundreds of tons of razor-edged flake would snap off into Bridwell's lap, slicing off his legs, cutting the rope, and wiping Schmitz off the wall with him. Bridwell's ability to know precisely how many hammer blows to make and not kill himself seemed less guesswork and more testimony to his reputation as being a Zen master of big-wall climbing.

Jim Bridwell was not the only climber doing new routes in Yosemite back then, but for three decades beginning in the mid-1960s (culminating with his heyday of new climbs in the late 1970s), he was the king of Yosemite climbing. Bridwell's devotion to climbing typified a growing attitude of many climbers at the time: rather than follow the path of career, job, and secure future, he realized that the only way to climb well was to devote all one's time to the activity. Odd jobs and infrequent work sufficed to keep him going in between his demanding climbs. But he reaped great rewards from his adventures.

Jim had been born in 1944 in San Antonio, Texas. His father was a war hero and officer in the Army Air Corps, so he had moved about from one air base to another in classic army-brat style. As a teenager he displayed a talent for delivering fastballs for his high school baseball team, but another family move pulled him away from organized sports. The Bridwells moved to San Mateo, California, where Jim took up more solitary activities like hiking in the redwoods and falconry. In fact, his interest in visiting steep places was sparked by his curiosity to examine the nests of birds of prey. A visit to Yosemite sealed his fate as a climber, and he left school at age nineteen and headed to the valley. Quite quickly, Bridwell teamed up with an intense, energetic man some considered another demigod of Yosemite climbing, Frank Sacherer.

Bridwell's natural athleticism translated well into the brawny nature of 1960s free climbing that Sacherer espoused. These were the early days of the free climbing revolution, when climbers were just starting to realize the beauty of free climbing up the rock unaided by equipment. Yet it was still long before the invention of the easy-to-place spring-loaded camming devices that we take for granted today, let alone the ultrastrong bolts of millennium-era sport climbing. Pitons were the main form of protection and consequently most routes followed cracks. This meant that the climber led with a twenty-pound rack of steel pitons slung around his neck, and a hammer in a holster at his waist. The climber would lead up a few feet, then hang one-armed from a likely hold, fiddle a piton off one of the carabiners that stored it, slot the piton into the crack, then pound it in with the hammer. It was a strenuous, ungainly technique, more like being a steelworker than a climber. It also forced the lead climber to climb with daring. Because it was so strenuous to dangle one-handed to hammer in a piton, the leader frequently "ran it out" for long distances before finding a spot to hammer a piton in for protection. It was dangerous, but there was no other way; the equipment that was available governed the method. This need to accept risk in order to free climb a route created a culture of climbing that embraced and admired boldness. This tactic also gave birth to some ground rules of climbing that would last for many years before they were rethought.

The main rules were as follows:

Rule One: All climbs started on the ground. If you inspected a route from above by rappelling down a fixed rope, or if you placed protection on the route from above by this method, you had failed on the climb and you had cheated.

Rule Two: If you fell while leading, you had to immediately lower back down to the ground and start again. If you hung from any protection along the route, you had also failed and cheated.

These rules became commandments for us during the 1970s and 1980s, and when some climbers began to deviate from these tactics in later years, there were great controversies, fiery letters to the editors of many magazines, and even fistfights. Eventually, though, by the late 1980s, these philosophies would be almost entirely tossed out of the rule book of climbing. Not only did the equipment evolve, but also the vision and methods of free climbing changed, and these rules became virtually obsolete. The emphasis veered away from the mountaineering heritage of climbing in which risk and danger were considered integral to the experience, and toward making routes with rappel-placed bolts on which new levels of difficulty could be safely explored. But when I started climbing, these rules were law.

Embracing the doctrine of boldness, Sacherer and his protégé Bridwell climbed many famous routes together: Ahab (5.10), Crack of Doom (5.10d), and the first free ascent of a two-day route called the North Buttress of Middle Cathedral Rock (5.10a) were all on the tick-lists of Yosemite aspirants when I first arrived. When I met Bridwell, he was, in the manner of a tribal elder, passing on to us youngsters the bold lessons he had gleaned from Sacherer. Those lessons, passed on like a religion, included throwing oneself at routes with abandon, stepping over the line of commitment to give one's all, physically and mentally, even if it sometimes meant getting into dangerous situations. Sacherer left Yosemite in 1966 to work in Europe as a physicist. In the late 1970s he was climbing in the French Alps, on an ice route called the Shroud on the Grandes Jorasses, when lightning struck and killed him. Said Bridwell of his mentor's place in climbing history, "He had free climbed routes that the best climbers of the day said couldn't be done free. He had climbed routes in a day they said couldn't be done in a day. In the 1960s Sacherer did more to advance free climbing as we know it today than any other single person."

After Sacherer, Bridwell became the leader of the pack, surrounding

Jumaring up the first pitch of the Nose in 1979. (JESSICA PERRIN-LARRABEE)

himself like a Roman general with talented young warrior-climbers with whom he could team up to pluck off the scores of new routes that awaited the bold. The soaring hand-jamming cracks of Outer Limits (5.10c) and New Dimensions (5.11a) were some of his best free climbs of the early 1970s, and they taught me much about the art of climbing steep cracks. But no lessons were more keenly felt than those I learned on my first time up the Nose of El Capitan.

Vertigo, fear of heights, exposure—call it what you will, but the sense of adrenaline, or excitement, that we feel when standing on the edge of a huge cliff is part of our internal mechanism. Someday, I suspect, geneticists will unravel a part of our DNA to find a gene that governs the way we each react to heights, and parents will be able to test their children to determine whether they'll be BASE jumpers who leap off cliffs, or people who shiver with horror when gazing over a lookout. As Mari, Dean, and I got higher and higher on the airy, soaring Nose that first day of climbing, it became apparent which of us had the fear-of-heights gene and which of us didn't.

I could tell that something was wrong with Dean when his sense of humor vanished on the first day. His attitude suddenly became serious when he had to lead a pitch that required him to perform a maneuver called a pendulum. By that time we were 500 feet off the ground, high enough that we could look straight down onto the tips of the towering pines of Yosemite Valley. From our vantage point they resembled so many pencils jammed into the earth. We had begun the climb planning to share the leads, meaning that each person would lead every third pitch. But after Dean finished his pitch, he turned pale, jittery, and serious. He had just gotten through hanging at the end of the rope and running back and forth across the wall, swinging like a clock pendulum, until he gained enough momentum to dive at a crack 40 feet to his right. It was a rough-and-tumble maneuver, certain to terrify anyone prone to a fear of heights.

"I think I'll just hand over the leading to you girls," he said when I ascended the rope and hung next to him on a ledgeless patch of the wall.

"What? Don't you want to lead the next bit? It's a great-looking pitch," Mari said.

"It's okay, you can take it."

"No, really, go for it Dean, you'll have fun."

"No way, I don't want to lead anymore."

"Oh, go on, take the rack and—"

"Goddammit, I said no. I'm staying here. I'll jumar up behind you," he snapped back with a characteristic "Bullwinkle crinkle" in his brow.

Mari and I exchanged a look as if to say, *Okay, we'll take over the lead*. We all realized that at this point the only way down for Dean was up—behind us. For the rest of the day Dean hugged close to the rock as he ascended the ropes in our wake. I could tell from his rapid, nervy breathing and the beads of sweat pearling on his brow that he was not comfortable at this height. Perhaps the way Mari and I reveled in the verticality of El Cap—leaning back into the air in our harnesses, standing with our toes on the edge of ledges and peering down into the void—made him even more nervous. Years later, when I found myself feeling uneasy on a steep snowfield in the mountains of Kyrgyzstan I could relate to what Dean must have felt. Snow, I discovered, is a medium of the steep with which I have no affinity other than for skiing or snowboarding.

The Nose route goes right up the center of El Capitan, following a prominent prow that juts forward—just like a beak. Splitting this protrusion of rock is a crack system that is, by a quirk of geology, just the right size for a human to securely jam his or her fingers, hands, or body into. With only occasional blank spots, this 3,000-foot fissure forms a vertical highway to the summit of El Capitan.

Alternating leads, Mari and I moved steadily up, clipping into old pitons, and placing our own jangling cord-threaded nuts and hexagons into the crack as well. Sometimes we free climbed, up to 5.10 in difficulty, and sometimes we hung our bodies from the gear and aid climbed. Meanwhile, Dean climbed up behind us, ascending the ropes on his jumars, which are clamps with a handgrip; a jumar slides up a rope, but it locks on to the rope when one pulls down on it. Jumars are a Swiss invention, and they have had such an impact on climbing that the verb "jumar" has become part of the climbing lexicon.

About 700 feet up we came to a 500-foot-long section of unusually wide crack called the Stovelegs. The story of the way the first ascent team climbed this section in 1958 is another of those moments in climbing where necessity was the mother of invention. The question of how Harding and his crew would get themselves up the Stovelegs had been debated around Camp Four for weeks, as no one had ever invented protection to climb such a wide crack before. Although Salathè was beating out his custom-made Lost Arrows on his anvil as fast as climbers could hammer them into cracks, no one was making wide pitons, so therefore there was no equipment available for anyone to climb a feature like the Stovelegs. But when Harding's friend Frank Tarver found an old wood-burning stove while scavenging through the Berkeley city dump, he realized that the prettily enameled angle-iron legs of the stove could provide the solution to this section of the climb. Armed with the four heavy nine-inch-long legs, Harding reached the Stovelegs crack on July 8, 1957. Hammering the legs into the crack and clipping their rope around them for protection, the team leapfrogged them upward for several hundred feet to get to a point just below a prominent, flat-topped landmark now known as Dolt Tower. At that point, with their stove legs beaten and bent, and the Park Service shouting at them to descend, they retreated to the valley floor.

In more recent years climbers had found that it was no great problem to free climb the Stovelegs, and Mari and I inserted our hands into the crack and squeezed our fists into balls, using a special technique called jamming. Each hand jam was almost as secure as gripping the rung of a ladder. We moved up in this fashion, with our feet walking up the crack in a ladderlike lockstep. This went on for four pitches. The crack ended at Dolt Tower, named after Bill Feurer, a.k.a. Dolt, one of Harding's partners.

On this ledge, a few historical moments played out during the first ascent. While Wally Reed was prusiking up the team's fixed ropes, using a technique to ascend that preceded the invention of the jumar, he noticed that the ropes were beginning to show signs of wear. The next thing he knew, he found himself plummeting earthward. The rope had abraded through and he was lucky enough to land on the ledge a short distance below. But perhaps one of the least effective experiments in gear technology was the Dolt Cart. Feurer was an aeronautical engineer, and he came up with an idea for Harding and the rest of them to more easily haul the huge weight of gear, food, and water up the wall for their protracted siege of the Nose. He bolted to the cliff a large steel frame on which was mounted a big pulley—the Dolt Winch. A rope went through this and down to the ground, where it was attached to the most insane-looking bit of climbing gear ever created: the Dolt Cart. This was a cart replete with inflatable bicycle tires onto which the team would lash a fifty-pound haulbag. Harding called the Dolt Cart "a grand sight" as it rolled slowly up the wall on its 1,200-foot journey to Dolt Tower, but the contraption tipped over frequently and got stuck under protrusions of rock. Besides, it took four men to operate the winch and cart. Eventually, after the climbers had wasted several days with this device, it broke down entirely and they resumed the bruising task of dragging haulbags up the slabby wall using pure muscle power. As for us, we hauled our sixty-pound haulbag up each pitch using a small pulley, sweating and grunting under the sun and labor.

Our first bivouac on the Nose was spent on the spacious ledge of El Cap Tower. We laid out our ensolite pads on the flat but hard surface, then snuggled into our sleeping bags. We slept still wearing our harnesses, the rope tying us to the bolt anchors in the wall above the ledge—just in case someone rolled overboard or went sleepwalking. Once we were inside our bags, water jugs and the food sack were pulled from the haulbag and we began devouring our dinner. As Sierra alpenglow saturated the valley in hues of pink, an aerial animal show above our heads changed shifts. The swallows that had been swooping and chattering all day flew at breakneck velocity at the rock face, broke their speed at the last second, and disappeared into the cracks where they nested. Taking their place came the bats, which emerged from dark recesses and entered the night air to hunt for insects.

Tucked into his sleeping bag and positioned as far from the cliff edge as possible, Dean rediscovered his sense of humor. He opened a can with a Swiss army knife and passed it to Mari with the aplomb of a waiter in a ritzy restaurant.

"Madam, would care for some fruit cocktail?" he asked, and he catered to us the rest of the night, passing cookies and chunks of pemmican bar, and passing the water jug as if it were a bottle of fine wine.

The next day we rose early. As the sun brightened the valley, I saw a haze of smog lingering at car level. Above us, on a wildly steep patch of El Cap slightly to our east, a golden light kissed the wall. This was the final section of another of Harding's famous routes, the Dawn

Wall, also called the Wall of Early Morning Light. On this climb, completed in 1970, Harding and Dean Caldwell had spent twenty-seven days climbing and hanging in hammocklike "bat tents," to make the first ascent. This was nearly twice as long as anyone had ever spent continuously living on a wall. The ascent was, in the parlance of climbing, an "epic." The pair had set out on this highly technical aid climb with five haulbags weighing a total of three hundred pounds, plus eighty pounds of hardware (mostly pitons), twelve gallons of water, and several jugs of Christian Brothers wine. (The winery eventually used an image of Harding on the wall, tippling a glass of their finest, in an ad campaign.)

The climbers moved slowly, finding that they had to laboriously drill bolts and rivets to get through huge blank sections. They struck a hand-held drill handle with the hammer, every bolt hole requiring several hundred blows to drill out. A four-day rainstorm drenched the pair when they were about one-third of the way up, and their cocoonlike bat tents filled with rainwater. When the storm cleared, it was the fifteenth day of an intended fifteen-day climb. But they didn't give up, rationing food and water instead. They'd share half a can of fruit for breakfast

The visionary Warren Harding in 1968. (GALEN ROWELL)

and half a can of sardines for dinner. After twenty-three days the Park Service mounted a rescue and an Air Force helicopter circled in front of them, while a climber was lowered from the rim on a rope. "We attacked the rescuer . . . with a torrent of profanity and drove him back up the wall," wrote Harding in his book. They would not be rescued, and when they pulled over the top on November 19, they were greeted by more than a hundred reporters and observers who had become intrigued at this determined pair.

On the Nose, we had to climb ten pitches from El Cap Tower to reach our next bivouac ledge, a spot known as Camp Five. With Dean now figuratively "in the haulbag," all leading fell to Mari and me. Getting to Camp Five involved climbing up Boot Flake, a wafer of rock that seems to float on the wall and which will surely fall off one day soon—soon being, in geologic terms, sometime between next week and ten thousand years. From the top of Boot Flake, we had to make a giant pendulum called the King Swing, across a large blank face to another crack system 35 feet over to our left. Five pitches after Boot Flake, we stood below the Great Roof. This feature loomed over our heads like a mounting tidal wave. At the time, no climber in the world imagined that such a feature could be free climbed. Fifteen years later climbers would recant that belief but would find the Great Roof to be one of the hardest sections to free climb on the entire route.

"There are still two pitches before our bivy, and the sun is pretty low," I shouted to Mari, urging her to hurry through the aid climbing that lay ahead of her.

"Yeah, I know," she said, moving methodically from piece to piece. Even on aid climbing—something I consider ungainly and only a necessary evil when free climbing methods fail—Mari moved with precision and grace.

Forty minutes after she started the Great Roof pitch, she was nearing the belay, 120 feet above me. Mari shouted down that to speed our progress I should jumar up the rope she had just led on, "cleaning the pitch," or, in layman's terms, removing the gear she had placed. This would leave Dean to jumar up on our other rope, which would be secured to the belay at the end of the Great Roof. This rope hung out away from the rock and about 40 feet to the side. Though it was completely safe to clip one's jumars onto it and swing out, the idea of dangling around, spinning slowly and dizzyingly above the valley floor while trying to ascend, caused Dean's eyes to boggle.

"I prefer following the pitch rather than jumaring out in space," he said to me flatly.

"No, it'll take too long for you to clean this pitch. Just swing out. It's totally safe."

"No, Lynnie, it's too dangerous," he said urgently. "The rope could get cut up there if I swing out. Remember what happened to Chris Robbins?" he protested, referring to a young climber who, not long before, had been jumaring a dangling rope on an El Cap route called the Tangerine Trip and had fallen to his death when his rope had been severed by rubbing against a sharp edge. But Mari had been careful to check that no such hazard existed in Dean's case.

He carped at me to trade places—for me to jumar the dangling rope while he cleaned Mari's pitch. If night hadn't been approaching, I would have consented, but in my own anxiety to get up to our bivy ledge before dark, my patience was wearing thin. I replied sternly, "We can't afford to wait an extra hour for you to clean this pitch. We don't even have enough daylight left to reach Camp Five."

He moaned, muttered, then sat back and awaited his fate.

"Ready to haul," Mari shouted from the end of the pitch, and I sent the haulbag out into space. Then it was time to send Dean on his way.

"I hate this," he said.

"It will be fine," I tried to reassure him. "Here, I'll hold the end of the rope and slowly lower you out. That way you won't swing so much." I felt bad. Dean looked like a scared cat.

I lowered him out using what slack remained in the rope that he hung from. His unease at leaving the security of the belay ledge showed immediately as he displayed a textbook case of fear of heights. His feet pedaled in the air, and his eyes grew wide and white-rimmed. Then the end of the rope came tight in my hands. At that point I had to let go of it, letting Dean swing violently outward in a great arc that would be more exciting than an E ticket ride at Disneyland.

"No, Lynn, wait . . ." Dean pleaded when he saw the last few inches of rope in my hand. Below him was a drop of 2,000 feet to the toe of El Capitan.

"Sorry, Dean, there's no more rope. I gotta let go."

Just before I let Dean swing out into space, he looked me straight in the eye and said earnestly, "Tell Jessica I love her." Jessica was his girl-friend. Half scared out of his wits, half having the time of his life and looking for a quip to make us laugh, Dean would later repeat this melo-dramatic phrase on a daily basis.

When the rope left my fingers, Dean flew out into the air, screamed, grasped desperately at his jumars, and started to sprint up the rope like a man running from a tiger. I looked up at Mari, 120 feet above me, and we both burst out laughing.

I set about sliding my own jumars up the rope, pausing at the tiny stoppers Mari had placed, giving each one an upward tug till it popped out. All the way up the Great Roof pitch I found myself instinctually feeling the narrow crack with my fingers, trying to imagine what it would be like to free climb through this remarkable piece of natural architecture. Climbers like John Bachar and Ron Kauk had been try-ing to free climb different sections of the Nose in recent years, but everyone was unanimous that the Great Roof would always remain an aid pitch.

"Think it'll ever go free?" Mari asked me when I reached her.

"I don't know," I replied. "The crack is so thin I can hardly get my fingertips into it and the face is as smooth as a mirror." It was my lead next and I quickly began climbing up a golden-colored sliver of rock that looked as if it had been slapped to the wall. This was pitch num-ber twenty-three, the Pancake Flake.

By the time I was ready to lead toward Camp Five, it was pitch-dark. Being novices at the big-wall climbing game none of us even possessed a headlamp. What little moon there was that night hovered behind El Capitan, so the blackness was nearly total.

"Now what?" Dean asked.

"Well, we can't stay here. We'd be standing up all night; we'd never sleep," Mari replied.

"Dean, hand over your cigarette lighter. Maybe I can see the crack well enough with that," I said.

"Whatever you do, don't drop it. If I have to go through this without my smokes, I'll be an even bigger nervous wreck than I am now, believe me."

Dean's deadpan kibitzing got us laughing again. He handed me a Bic lighter. I flicked it on. The flame illuminated a circle of about two feet in front of me, but after a few seconds it got so hot I had to shut it off.

"Better than nothing," I said.

"Don't use up all the butane; it's my only lighter," Dean cautioned as I set off up the pitch.

The pitch that leads to Camp Five is rated 5.11, but most ascents aid climb the entire pitch. At that point in my climbing career, that was nearly as hard as anything I had ever led. Every couple of feet I would pause to light the path with Dean's Bic. The yellow glow would reveal a flash of information—the size of the crack in front of me, a foothold to the right—then I'd let the flame flicker out. I would grope up in the dark a few feet until I got into unknown ground again, then I'd pause again to light up another patch of rock. The crack opened into a V-shaped flare that swallowed my body. I shuffled and groveled. The process became hypnotic. It was neither pleasant nor unpleasant, calming nor terrifying, fun nor drudgery. It was just necessary, and I was simply there, like a bug on the wall, moving inexorably up out of instinct and need. My sense of time evaporated.

When I reached the welcome ledge of Camp Five, it was nearly midnight. I had been climbing by Braille for an hour and a half. As I methodically set up a belay anchor on the ledge, anchored the ropes for Mari and Dean to jumar up, then hauled the bag to the ledge, I had time to think about the altered mental state I had attained during my nocturnal climb. I began to truly see the meaning behind big-wall climbing. The wall was like some living entity that was testing our mettle by throwing up new challenges, new unknowns, that we had to overcome. This was the essence of what guys like Harding and Bridwell were talking about when they described some crazy stunt they were forced to perform during a climb. Because up here there was no turning back and no room for panic. Dealing with a space flake that was about to break off the wall and squash you, or making it through a pitch in the inky dark, were all parts of a journey of self-discovery and self-reliance.

I winched the haulbag onto the ledge just as my partners arrived. As we began securing ourselves into the anchor and trying to lay our sleeping bags out on the ledge to get some sleep, we crisscrossed the ropes into a rat's nest of a tangle. A few bites of food, a gulp of water, and I closed my eyes and entered a deep sleep.

When I woke next morning, I found myself cramped into a back-bending position, on the end of a ledge that was just wide enough for two people. Only my upper body lay on the rocky shelf we were sprawled on; my legs were draped over the edge of the cliff, resting on top of the haulbag. My head felt foggy from too little sleep and too much work. My hands immediately began throbbing; they were swollen and chafed from being stuffed into cracks, and blackened with metal oxides from gripping our carabiners. Worst of all, my tongue felt glued to the roof of my mouth. All I could think about was satiating my thirst.

I leaned over to unclip the water bottle hanging from the anchor, and in doing so I shifted my feet. Out of the corner of my eye I watched my feet kick the food bag out of the top of the haulbag. It was the only item not clipped in to the tangle of gear, ropes, and carabiners that hung all around us. Despair is the only word I know to describe my feeling as all of our food bounced down the wall and into the forest 2,000 feet below.

"What was that, did something just fall off the ledge?" Dean asked groggily.

How was I going to tell a hungry man that the last cans of fruit cocktail and bagels he had been dreaming about were now hurtling toward the scavenging squirrels and blue jays that roam the base of El Cap?

"Oops," was all I could say.

"What now?"

"Well, I'm sorry, but I just dropped the food."

"Perfect," said Dean as he lit his morning cigarette. "I couldn't have fucked up better myself."

At this, we started laughing. It was true. So many things had gone wrong on this climb that this was, as the French say, the coup de grâce—the final blow. There was nothing to do but pack up, share out the handful of lemon drops that Dean had stored in his pocket, then guzzle some water and put behind us the ten pitches that remained between us and the top.

Hungry but buzzing with an urgency to reach the summit, we swarmed up the steepest thousand feet of the Nose. By late afternoon on this third day we were moving up the last pitch. Ironically, on the first ascent Harding had led this pitch in the dead of night. As I climbed up this overhanging sea of rock, I marveled at the tenacity of this gritty fellow who was something of a shadow around the climber's hangouts in Yosemite. Like us, Harding had felt the pressure to escape the wall, but he had been on it far longer than we had—twelve days on his final foray. In his book, he describes his final fourteen hours by headlamp, painfully hand drilling the twenty-eight bolts that ascend the final over-hanging headwall, and from which I now hung: "By this time The Nose had really gotten to me. This thing had completely dominated my life for over a year . . . I was rather frazzled," were his words.

"Frazzled" certainly described our condition as we each popped over the rim of El Cap. We were hungry, thirsty, and bone-tired. As I peered over the rim one last time before stepping onto the flat granite slabs on top, I took note of the lay of the valley from this grand perspective. The cliffs and the roads and the meadows sprawled below me, with Half Dome and the bare granite backbone of the High Sierra curling around the horizon. It was if I were seeing Yosemite through a fisheye lens. It was a view I felt comfortable with, and it was a view I would see again, many times. Though I did not know it that day in 1979, by the end of the millennium I would make seven more ascents of this route.

Chapter 7

Big-Wall Thrills

The key to climbing well is to climb as much as you can. In Yosemite in the early 1980s, we indulged ourselves in climbing as if it were more than a full-time job. We worked at it five days a week, eight hours a day, and we put in a lot of overtime. The only problem was that the job of climbing was a job without pay. So the climbers there lived on the cheap, stretching the meager funds they accumulated during stints of seasonal employment as waitpersons, carpenters, smoke jumpers, maids, pizza deliverers, bicycle messengers, fishermen, gardeners, landscapers, concrete workers, roofers, shop assistants, ski patrollers, and every other short-term job there is. I managed to live in Camp Four for an entire summer on $75. Others lived there much longer on nearly nothing at all. To survive a climbing season in Yosemite—through the rains of spring, the heat of summer, the bliss of fall—you had to live by your wits.

The cash crop of Yosemite was the aluminum soda pop and beer cans that could be redeemed for a nickel each at the Yosemite recycling site. Tourists too impatient to harvest the five-cent value of the cans tossed an astonishing mass of beverage containers into the trash system of Yosemite. The orchards for this crop were the bearproof garbage cans and dumpsters dotted around the valley. Climbers were the fruit pickers. A meager living could be had from this.

I first learned about canning for profit when I encountered a scruffy Australian and his even scruffier British accomplice in a picnic area, pushing up the heavy lid of a dumpster and wedging a log under the lid to keep it open. As I watched, the Australian crawled into the huge steel trash bin and began noisily rummaging around, tossing cans out to the Brit, who gathered them into a shopping bag.

"What are you guys doing?" I asked.

"Existing," the Englishman said. He introduced himself as Tom, then he added that they were saving the cans from the landfills of Fresno, and saving America's environment while they were at it.

When the Aussie exited the dumpster, accompanied by a swarm of flies and yellow jackets, a family picnicking nearby and looking on with nothing resembling approval gathered up their lunch and left. The dumpster-diver introduced himself as Greg and explained that he and Tom were heading up El Cap as soon as they raised enough money to buy a new rope. They counted out the sticky cans they had foraged and told me that they had, this past week, gathered about eight hundred cans, the bulk of which were stashed in a cave behind Camp Four.

"A rope costs fifty bucks, so that means we need about two hundred more cans. Looks like another day of canning," the Aussie told his partner. Then the pair dived into the nearby Merced River, washed off the filth of their labors, and headed off.

Scarfing was another climber subsidy. It took place in the cafeteria and, like canning, was based on the fact that Yosemite tourists toss away most of what they buy. In a typical scarfing session a table of climbers would sit around drinking 25-cent cups of coffee and cramming themselves full of chemical-laden soup crackers and relish packets from the condiments counter, awaiting the next busload of tourists.

With trays weighed down by more food than they could eat, the tourists would pick at their macaroni salads, their scrambled eggs, or their french fries or whatever, until the bus driver honked the horn and the tourists fled, abandoning a bounty of half-eaten dishes. Swooping in like vultures, the climbers would grab the leftovers. The best tourists back then were the Japanese, whose robust national economy in the 1980s seemed to dictate that they should buy twice as much food as they could eat. Occasionally, scarfing led to errors in judgment. I watched Dale Bard, one of the fittest of the Yosemite climbers—he had climbed El Cap by scores of routes—intercept a tourist's half-eaten plate of bacon and eggs the moment the man left his seat at the cafeteria. Alas, the tourist had not abandoned his breakfast, he had only gone to the bathroom for a minute, and when he returned he was shocked to see Dale downing the last bite of his meal.

Avoiding campsite fees was another trick among valley regulars, and this was best accomplished by getting a berth on the Rescue Site in Camp Four. The Yosemite Search and Rescue Team was (and remains today) a loose-knit crew of climbers recruited by the National Park Service to perform high-angle cliff rescues. Free camping and minimum wages were the reward for risking your neck to save tourists lost on hiking trails or to remove injured climbers from cliffs. It was also just plain cool to be on the Rescue Team. Jim Bridwell, whether officially or simply by virtue of being the alpha male of the valley, seemed to be the chief of the Rescue Site, where he lived in a Bedouin-style tent that was party central. Under his watch the Rescue Site had also become a training zone. There was a pull-up bar tied to the fork of a tree, a rope ladder made with sections of PVC pipe, free weights lying about on a remnant of carpet, and a chain strung between two trees on which one could practice tightrope-walking—all useful tools for developing the strength and balance needed for Yosemite's climbs.

When I arrived in Camp Four, I claimed a piece of dirt covered in soft pine needles on which I could lay out my sleeping bag at night, as I had no tent, and I stored my few belongings in one of the bearproof, padlocked steel lockers in the camp. We called these heavy containers "coffins," due to their shape, and they were there to protect campers' food and gear from marauding bears. These hulking animals would steal anything resembling food and drag it into the woods, where they'd tear it apart and eat it. Littering the forest around Camp Four were shredded rucksacks that had once contained groceries, as well as toothmark-pocked cans and boxes. The bears ate anything that humans tried to hide from them, including containers of washing detergent, bars of soap, even whole tins of ground pepper.

This gypsylike lifestyle was all for a purpose: to climb for as long as possible on as little money as possible. By 1980 I felt an urge to climb that was insistent and compelling. If I could remain in Yosemite a little longer and accomplish a few more climbs by living cheap and dirty, then the means justified the end. Money and work were of little importance to us then, but money was, ironically, also the key to the climbing life. Years later, one climbing writer, Pat Ament, described me in those days as "a Chaplinesque, dirty-faced hobo of the Yosemite climbers' camp." For a few months of the year, this was true. These dirt-poor days were

Leading the famous Serenity Crack in Yosemite at age six-teen. (CHARLIE ROW)

among the best and the most carefree of my life, and though my friends were often scoundrels, I felt their friendship convincingly. Shoplifting, dining and dashing, siphoning gas, and other infractions in the name of furthering one's climbing dollars were common follies among some of the people to whom I trusted my life when I tied myself into a rope. Some of them, two decades later, are lawyers, doctors, and contractors, yet back then they were barely distinguishable from petty crooks.

Though I drew the line at stealing, I have often wondered what I would have done had I been faced with Yosemite's greatest free-money scam: the plane crash of 1977 when climbers salvaged a fortune in marijuana from a smuggler's plane that went down in the high country above Yosemite Valley. I envied the new racks of gear, the shiny new VW vans, the long and well-fed climbing road trips that a few climbers enjoyed from the fruits of that illegal salvage operation. But I also saw its dark side.

The strong odor of the "Lockheed Lodestar" weed, as Yosemite-ites called the marijuana that came from that plane, could be smelled even two years after the crash, as locals and visitors were still lighting up stashes of the mind-altering herb. According to a mix of fact and legend, the plane had, that February of '77, been sitting on a tarmac somewhere in Mexico, fueled to go, stuffed with 240 forty-pound bales of high-grade, red-haired marijuana. Its destination was some secret landing zone in the desert of California or Nevada. A shoot-out, some say, put the plane in the hands of rival drug traffickers, and the hijacked Lockheed Lodestar took off on its ill-fated flight.

Maybe the hijackers weren't savvy to the game of flying low over the contours of the land to elude U.S. radar, or maybe the owners of the cargo were so torched by the hijacking that they ratted on their own plane to the Drug Enforcement Agency. Either way, a high-speed pursuit plane intercepted the intruder and trailed it through southern California, ordering to it to change course, land, and be arrested. The pilots of the Lodestar freaked out. They flew deep into the High Sierra, far from roads or towns, running their fuel tanks low. Below them a deep winter snowpack clung to the mountains. As the plane's engines sputtered on vapors, they spotted a flat, white circle below them: Upper Merced Lake, sixteen miles as the crow flies from Yosemite Valley. The lake was frozen over with a two-foot-thick skin of ice.

In desperate straits now, the pilots lowered the undercarriage, eased the plane onto the lake, bounced once, then the ice cracked. The Lodestar augured in, the fuselage snapped in half, bales of weed spilled across the lake. The tail section containing most of the cargo sank, while the cockpit settled half-submerged into a crater of smashed ice, nose-pointing skyward. The pilots lay dead, still strapped to their seats. Soon after, during a window between snowstorms, a helicopter flight by the authorities spotted the wreck but deemed it inaccessible and conditions too cold and dangerous to venture into it, so a recovery mission was postponed until the spring thaw.

Story has it that word reached climbers' ears one rainy day when a few Camp Four regulars made a social call to a Park Service ranger's office. While they were indulging in a bit of small talk, the radio blurted out a report about the unidentified plane plowing into Upper Merced Lake. The climbers asked a few questions and learned that no cops or rangers would be heading up there until spring. Only one of the climbers who'd heard this news had the gumption to suit up in his winter clothes, clip on his beat-up cross-country skis, and head into the backcountry for a look. The others feared they'd get into trouble. But when their friend returned a few days later with a heavy backpack full of weed, the lure of easy money drew the rest of them up to the lake.

What happened next is tainted by the retelling of a hundred people who were not there and by the secrecy of the handful who were, but by the end of a few more days several Yosemite climbers were rich. Climbers zeroed in on the plane crash while authorities put off the recuperation efforts, mainly because the climbers thought nothing of trudging all day through thigh-deep snow to reach their destination. The survival instincts required by winter camping and the toughness to put up with being wet and cold for days on end is second nature to a lot of climbers, but, evidently, it was unthinkable to the DEA, FBI, and Park Service folk.

The first climbers to reach the wreck found easy pickings, and harvested the bales off the top of the frozen lake. Stunned by their luck, they instantly realized that the value of one bale of weed far surpassed the cost of their winter camping gear, so they dumped everything out of their packs and crammed them full of weed. Conveniently, the bales fitted neatly into a rucksack. As more climbers visited the lake, the

Discovering big wall climbing at age seventeen on the northwest face of Half Dome, 1977. (CHARLIE ROW)

Relaxing on the summit of Half Dome with Charlie Row. (CHARLIE ROW)

On the summit of the Nose in 1979 with Mari Gingery and Dean Fidelman. (JESSICA PERRIN-LARRABEE)

Twilight Zone (5.13b) at the Gunks. (SANDY STEWART)

Free soloing High Exposure
at the Gunks, 1984 (5.6).
(NED GILLETTE)

The Pirate (5.12d)
at Suicide Rock,
California, 1988.
(GREG EPPERSON)

The Green Ripper (5.12b),
Mount Lemmon, Arizona.
(GREG EPPERSON)

When
Legends
Die (5.13b)
at Hueco
Tanks,
Texas.
(GREG
EPPERSON)

Terror Vision in
the Needles,
California, with
Scott Franklin,
1989 (5.12a).
(GREG EPPERSON)

Chouca in Buoux, France
(5.13c). (OLIVIER GRÜNEWALD)

On the victory podium at Bercy with
Catherine Destivelle in 1988.
(OLIVIER GRÜNEWALD)

Verdon Gorge, France, 1990. (PHILIPPE FRAGNOL)

Breaking the 5.14 barrier on Masse Critique, in Cimaï, France, 1990.

(PHILIPPE FRAGNOL)

Laybacking
underneath
the Great Roof
on the Nose, 1993.
(JOHN McDONALD)

The classic Pancake Flake
pitch (5.11c) on the Nose.
(HEINZ ZAK)

My partner Brooke
Sandahl at the
Camp Five bivy.
(LYNN HILL)

The Glowering
Spot (5.12d) pitch
on the Nose.
(HEINZ ZAK)

A crucial moment of balance and precision entering the Changing Corners dihedral on the Nose (5.13c–5.14), 1994.

(HEINZ ZAK)

After completing my Houdini move
on the Changing Corners pitch,
one of the most difficult pitches
on the Nose (5.13c–5.14), 1993.
(JOHN McDONALD)

Alex Lowe on the summit
of 4810 in Kyrgyzstan, 1995.
(LYNN HILL)

Team North Face hanging out at base camp in Kyrgyzstan.
From left to right: Greg Child, Conrad Anker, Alex Lowe,
Lynn Hill, Jay Smith, Dan Osman, Kitty Calhoun. (CHRIS NOBLE)

With Nancy Feagin on the crux pitch of Serpentine (5.13b) on Taipan Wall in the Grampians, Australia. (SIMON CARTER)

Climbing Archimedes' Principle on the
Eureka Wall, Australia (5.12c). (SIMON CARTER)

Completing a new route in Ha Long Bay, Vietnam. (BETH WALD)

The Free Route on
the Totem Pole at
Cape Hauy,
Tasmania,
Australia (5.12b).
(SIMON CARTER)

An airy
perspective on
the second
pitch of the
Free Route.
(SIMON CARTER)

Negotiating the crux on
Calippo in the Dolomites,
Italy (5.13b). (BETH WALD)

Taking a break with Pietro Dal Pra in Erto, Italy. (LYNN HILL)

Making friends in Morocco. (BETH WALD)

Evening light on the Tsaranoro Massif, Madagascar. (GREG EPPERSON)

The crux pitch of Bravo Les Filles on the Tsaranoro Massif, Madagascar (5.13d/AO).

(GREG EPPERSON)

On the summit of Tsaranoro
with Nancy Feagin, left, and
Kath Pike, right, in 1999.
(GREG EPPERSON)

shore began to resemble a yard sale, littered with abandoned sleeping bags, tents, and other gear. Those things could all be bought again later.

A second wave of climbers ventured into the wreck itself. Poking around with ice axes, they retrieved bales floating near the torn fuselage. I heard talk that one climber saw a western-style down vest floating in a pool near the wreckage. He waded into the ice water to fetch it, but it was stuck on something.

"Jesus, maybe it's attached to a body," he exclaimed, retreating to the shore.

"So what if it's a body? Lemme go see," replied his less squeamish partner.

The vest was merely snagged on a chunk of ice, and when he slipped his hand into the pocket, out came $1,800 in crisp new C-notes and a little black book containing names and phone numbers of people whom the law, no doubt, would like to meet. Depending on which version of events you heard, the book was either burned on the spot or spirited away by its finder. Either way, legend has it that Mafia types as well as FBI types roamed the valley those next few months, making inquiries about that book and who took it.

Stories, maybe true, maybe not, grew out of this scene. Some said a billfold containing $10,000 was plucked from the body of the frozen pilot, while others talked of a briefcase stuffed with ten times that amount. There was also talk of metal cylinders stuffed with cocaine— worth ten times what the briefcase held. The cocaine existed, but no one (besides the authorities who did fish out a load of the stuff in the spring) has ever admitted finding it. One enterprising team did try to get their hands on the cocaine, though. They carried a chain saw to cut through the ice and then enlisted two deep-sea divers with dry suits and scuba gear to do the diving. The deal was to be that the climbers and the divers would split the drugs fifty-fifty. But the lake was too murky and nothing but marijuana was found. The chain saw got dumped beside the lake. Others used it to fetch more weed.

Days passed and the easiest-to-fish-out bales got snapped up. Finally, after some climbers had made as many as three trips to the wreck and at least twenty people had harvested a share of the wealth, the Park Service noticed tracks heading up the trail to Upper Merced Lake, so they posted a couple of rangers at the trailhead. Two climbers heading down with eighty-pound rucksacks dripping with strong-smelling resin saw the rangers just as the rangers saw them. Thinking quickly, the climbers turned around and pretended they were heading up to the lake instead of down to the valley. When the rangers ran up to them and asked what they were up to, they feigned innocence.

"Just heading to the lake for a couple days of winter camping," one explained.

"Sorry, guys, its off limits up there right now," countered a ranger.

"Oh, really? Too bad, we'll just head down and go somewhere else."

"Have a nice day, guys," concluded the smiling ranger.

Anyway, so the story goes.

Back in the valley, dozens of bales of weed sat in tents or behind Camp Four in caves, oozing a stinking mix of resinous water and aviation fuel. Though the plane may have run out of enough fuel to stay aloft, its tanks contained a smidgen of aviation gas that soaked the cargo when they split apart on impact. As climbers dried and sampled their harvest, the valley was racked with the sound of coughing. The leaves burned and sparked and filled the lungs with a noxious but mind-altering smoke. The local infirmary noticed a rash of cases of chemical pneumonia.

While recreational drug use was not unusual in Yosemite, owning a hundred pounds of wet weed was a new experience to the Camp Four crowd. What to do with it? One crew stuffed the trunk of a beat-up Cadillac with the stuff, headed to the Mojave Desert, found a remote patch of dirt, and spread the crop out in the sun till it was crisp. Like others, they then entered the seedy world of the middlemen who facilitate the sale of drugs. For the most part, it was a rags-to-riches sort of journey for those who scored from the plane crash. Scarfers and canners were suddenly eating New York steaks in Yosemite's swankest restaurant, the Broiler Room Grill, and treating their friends to the same every night. Partying like rock stars, they acquired the gear, cars, toys, drug habits, and even, for some, the houses they had always wanted.

Then the luck began to change.

I never went to the lake, but I stood in the circles of people in the Arcing Plot, listening to the tales of those who had. In my desire to find enough money to climb forever, had I been in the know in Camp Four that winter, I too may have been tempted to trudge up there and bring down a bale. These were still my freewheeling teens and the weed was manna from heaven. There was no guilt, no sense of laws broken by the plane crash harvesters. Yet I'm glad I wasn't there, for I'm certain my life would look a lot different compared to what it is today, and I cannot be certain it would be positive change. I believe in karma, and I believe that the marijuana that had brought small fortunes to many climbers was tainted by something worse than aircraft fuel.

The first tragedy to hit the nouveau riche of Yosemite came early in the spring after the plane crash, when late one night the rescue team was called out to help two climbers who were stuck up on a climb near Yosemite Falls. One of the rescuers, a hard-partying climber and plane crash veteran named Jack, headed into the night on his mission, but came back in a body bag. In the dark he had slipped to his death from a cliffside trail. Rumors—part of the paranoia that began to grow around the plane crash—suggested that he had been the one who found the address book, and that the criminals who wanted it had caught up with him. More likely—he had poor vision and wore glasses as thick as Coke bottles—it was truly an accident. But around the same time an ill wind blew into other lives, as well. There was the pair who had sold their weed and were trading up to an equivalent wholesale value of cocaine, in hopes of turning an even bigger profit. The exchange went sour when the so-called dealers pulled guns and took the climbers' $50,000. Rip-offs, busts, and bad deals abounded. Another fellow, on a cross-country trip, got out of his car, which was loaded with his newly bought kayak, bike, and big-wall rack, walked into the woods to take a leak, then came back to find a raging fire consuming car and all. Yet another plane crash beneficiary ran his van off the road when looking up at a cliff while driving; the crash killed his girlfriend. A couple who were go-betweens in the selling process were, two years later, reported in newspapers as having been found beaten to death somewhere in the south Bay Area, victims of a drug deal gone wrong. Agenting the plane crash crop had started their career.

To some, the plane crash episode represented high drama and adventure, and certainly for each tragedy there was a tale of a life made better by the sudden injection of cash. Yet the drugs and the money diverted the focus of some talented climbers from the sport they were brilliant at, aiming it instead at illegal, tax-free, easy-money endeavors. In the early 1980s the air was full of helicopters searching for pot plantations growing inside Yosemite itself. Many of the farmers were climbers. Those who were busted served time. Those who eluded arrest largely dropped out of climbing, having fallen into a world in which they were always looking over their shoulders, always nervous. Either way, Yosemite's cliffs were poorer for their choices.

The Nose introduced Mari and me to the cult of El Capitan. Back then, on the cusp of the seventies and eighties, climbers viewed the experience of living for days on end on a gigantic cliff as a mystical pilgrimage. These were heady times. We indulged in these "vertical retreats" as a means of reaffirming our belief in the virtue of abandoning material comforts in favor of the kind of character-building experiences that inevitably occur on these big-wall journeys. Through such intense experiences you get to know your partner's true nature without pretense. Mari and I were good friends and we worked well together.

The Nose had provided a good challenge for Mari and me and we wanted more, so we planned another El Cap route. This time we'd do one that was steeper, more difficult, and that would require us to learn more advanced aid-climbing techniques. This time we'd spend more time living in the vertical world. If Yosemite Valley is to the world of rock climbing what the Himalayan Range is to mountaineering, then for us, doing El Capitan by a route like the Shield would be the equivalent of tackling Everest.

The Shield is a big-wall experience altogether different from the Nose. While the Nose is steep, especially in the upper third of the route in the huge corners, the Shield is so overhanging that a drop of water falling from the top of the route would land in the forest 200 feet out from the base. The last chunk of the climb—a thousand-foot feature known as the Headwall—juts over the floor of the valley so dramatically that the first time I watched a party climbing up it, I was reminded of two flies crawling around the underside of a giant hot-air balloon. The only way to climb this overhanging wall is by slow and methodical aid-climbing tactics. Up on the Nose, Mari and I had often been able to stuff our hands into cracks and quickly free climb long tracts of the route. But the cracks of the Shield are not much wider than a piece of string. Into these we'd have to hammer tiny pitons, one after another for hundreds of feet. Hanging from our pitons in ladderlike slings called "aiders" and inching our way upward, it could take hours to climb 100 feet. Though I was more enthusiastic about the natural movement of free climbing, the dramatic, wildly exposed position that we'd get ourselves into on the Shield made the labor of aid climbing—which I have no interest in if taken as a style on its own—seemed worth the effort. Aid climbing would take us to a place on El Cap that no other method would allow us to reach.

The other aspect of climbing the Shield that would be a new experience for us was the way we would have to live on the wall. On the Nose we found spacious ledges to sleep on each night. The Shield offered no ledges until the top. Instead we'd have to take our own portable ledges for sleeping on, which we'd suspend from the belays on the overhanging wall. Sleeping, eating, climbing, even answering calls of nature, would all be done in an overhanging environment. We were entering the arena of hard-core big-wall climbing.

To say we were apprehensive about doing a climb as wild as the Shield was an understatement. But once the work began, there was no more time to be nervous. At that stage in our climbing every experience was new, so we were used to finding new ways to adapt to whatever situation we were in. We always seemed to find a way to make it work. On the Shield, however, we would *have* to find a way. Once we climbed onto the Headwall, we would have no choice about backing off; rappelling back down such an overhang becomes nearly impossible because the rope swings free from the rock. So once we passed this landmark, we knew we were committed. More common to mountaineering, this aspect of the sport is all about the mental space you occupy when you know there's no turning back.

Prior to setting off on the Shield we learned that two other teams wanted to jump on the route too—Randy Leavitt and Gary Zachar, both Californians, and one team from Arizona. Both teams had a wealth of big-wall experience under their belts. We agreed to let these all-male parties step in line ahead of us and we stalled our departure for a couple of days. We figured that letting the faster, wall-hardened climbers go first was the "gentlemanly" thing to do. We were surprised to see, on our first day on the wall, both teams rappel past us on their way down. First Randy and Gary came down because Randy had gotten a splinter of metal in his eye, then the team from Arizona followed.

"What's wrong? Why are you retreating?" I shouted up to one of the Arizona climbers above me. I wondered if the storm of the century was bearing down on Yosemite. Yet the sky was blue.

"We heard someone take one hell of a fall early this morning. There was a terrible scream. He must be way fucked up, or dead. It kinda freaked us out, so we decided to bail," came the reply.

Mari and I eyed each other, then explained the story behind this bloodcurdling scream. Mari's boyfriend, Mike Lechlinski, and Yabo had set off at midnight to climb the 3,000-foot-long Triple Direct route on El Cap in a day. When Mari and I arrived at the parking area below El Cap early that morning and saw the two of them standing by their car, we knew something had gone wrong. Mike was arranging their gear while Yabo leaned against the fender, smoking a cigarette, staring into the forest.

"What happened?" Mari asked.

"Yabo took an eighty-footer!" Mike shot back.

At this Yabo uttered one of the staccato sniggers he was known to emit whenever nervous or unsure of himself.

"Yabo, are you okay?" I asked, looking him up and down from head to toe, searching for blood or bruises. He appeared unscathed.

"Yeah, I'm fine. I was climbing in my tennis shoes since it was easy up there. I was climbing with a pack and a full rack of gear, but I didn't bother to put in any protection. It was four-thirty in the morning, so it was a bit hard to see. I was cruising fast until I was nearly at the top of the pitch, and suddenly I realized that I messed up my hand sequence. Just then my foot popped off the face and I took a huge whipper," came his sheepish admission.

"He was a hundred feet up, on the tenth pitch!" exclaimed Mike. "When I saw him flying through the air, I reeled in slack through the belay device, but I could see he had no pro between me and him. I thought for sure we're dead, he's gonna rip us off the wall. Strawberry jam, here we come. But then his rope hooked around a mysterious knob or feature just in the right spot to catch Yabo's fall. If he had fallen ten

**John Yablonsky cranking
on Planet X.** (DEAN FIDELMAN)

feet farther, he would have come crashing down onto Mammoth
Terraces. As soon as Yabo scrambled back down the last few feet onto
the ledge, I flipped the rope and it came tumbling back down! I don't
know how the rope snagged on that chunk of rock, but if it hadn't,
Yabo would have gone another 80 feet! I knew Yabo was not badly hurt
when he said, 'Let's go for it. We can do it.'"

Yabo laughed again in a quavering, shell-shocked way, then he lit
another cigarette. I looked him in the eye and shook my head, half in
disgust at his recklessness, half out of concern. This brush with death
was just the latest in a slew of near misses for Yabo. In a world where
people slip on the ice on their front doorstep and die, Yabo lived like a
cat with nine lives, defying the consequences of gravity, doing everything the dangerous way, falling with impunity. A few weeks earlier he
had been solo climbing a short, difficult crack of about 40 feet called
Short Circuit when his fingers had slipped out of the crevice. He had
pitched backward through the air toward a jagged jumble of boulders
that would have crippled him had he survived the impact, but miracu-

lously his armpit had hooked around the branch of a sapling. Bending and lowering him as gently as a bungee cord, the branch delivered him into the arms of his friend Steve Sutton, who happened to be standing there at the base. Another time, while Yabo was free soloing a 5.10d called Right Side of the Folly, he slipped off a wet hold on the second pitch. Somehow he managed to catch himself on another hold in midair before falling to the ground. There were getting to be too many tales of Yabo nearly killing himself. He was getting too comfortable with the idea of dancing on the perimeter of death.

The Shield still was there, though, awaiting Mari and me, so after hugging the boys and saying good-bye, we started jumaring up our ropes to Heart Ledge, where we had fixed them a few days earlier. As Mari started jumaring the ropes, she said as if to herself, "Someday Yabo's not gonna walk away from his crazy ways." It would take a few years, but she would prove to be right.

Now that the last of the men had retreated due to the horror of Yabo's primal scream, we had the wall to ourselves. It humored us to know that despite the more impressive range of experience that these teams had over us, we remained the determined ones, going to the top.

"A wall without balls," I jokingly said to Mari, referring to the term Bev Johnson and Sybille Hechtel had coined when they did the first all-female ascent of the Triple Direct on El Cap in 1973. The Shield, which loomed frighteningly steep over our heads, was now the sole domain of two women.

For the first two days of the climb we inched up El Cap's glacier-cut face, slowly gaining height by the unfamiliar mode of aid climbing, and even more slowly dragging up our haulbag. For good reason, climbers refer to the haulbag as the "pig." Haulbags are heavy, unruly, obnoxious, and they do not obey. They often get stuck behind a flake or small roof and stubbornly refuse to budge. Whenever our haulbag got stuck, one of us would have to rappel down to the bag and maneuver it around the obstacle, then herd it upward. Ours was loaded with so much equipment, water, and food that it outweighed both of us combined. So on the first few hundred feet of the wall Mari and I rigged a two-person hauling system. We each pulled out backward with all our might on the haul line, winching the bag's weight through a small pulley. Our pig crawled up the wall in small surges. Our skin was rubbed raw from pulling on the rope. Sweat poured out of us.

After two days on the wall, we became accustomed to living in a reality where survival required us to concentrate on each move and to evaluate the consequences of every action, whether it was hammering in a piton or clipping ourselves into our batlike hanging bivouacs. During those intense moments of total engagement, I would become acutely aware of that little voice of intuition that on the ground is so often obscured by the clutter and command of our day-to-day thinking. On the sixteenth pitch off the ground, while bashing a piton into an expanding crack (a crack that opens as the piton is driven deeper into it, making for a very unstable piton placement), the thought occurred to me that perhaps I should have hammered this piton a little harder. In the next instant, after I had clipped my little four-foot-long ladder of nylon webbing onto the piton and stood up in it, the piton ripped out with a loud ping. I flew 30 feet backward before a well-placed piece of gear caught me on the rope. The fall was over in less than a breath, but the memory of the need to listen to the quiet internal voice of warning was never forgotten.

Night was a precious time when we could relax, eat, drink, and gaze up at the stars—but only after we had fiddled for an hour rigging and suspending our sleeping bunks. Mari had it good—she owned one of the first portaledges ever made. This newfangled gadget was a six-pound collapsible cot consisting of an aluminum frame strung with a nylon sheet. It hung from six webbing straps all sewn together into a single loop, into which she clipped the anchor. It made a comfortable sailor-style bunk. My bed wasn't so deluxe. It was a banana-shaped hammock in which I slumped like a caterpillar in a cocoon. My first night in this was dire. In the corner of a dihedral, I hung in a bent position all night long, shifting from side to side in discomfort.

On the fourth day Mari led us up to the Headwall. The pitch she followed to get us there was dubbed the Shield Roof, and it was indeed a giant of a roof. Hanging upside down under the roof to place each piece of gear, she dangled in her aid ladders, whacking in pitons and placing nuts whenever possible. Among the more dubious devices she hung her body from were "copperheads." These are blobs of copper clamped onto the end of a thin wire cable, and they are used whenever the crack is too shallow to accept the blade of a piton. The copper blob is pounded with the pick of the hammer until it softens and molds around the irregularities of the crack. It then has the adhesive quality of a piece of duct tape, and you can hang a while on it before it gives up its grip and pops out. If you find yourself placing a lot of copperheads in a row, you know you are headed into territory with high potential for a big fall.

Hours passed while Mari led to the end of the Shield Roof. Finally, shouting down through the afternoon wind that blew our hanging loops of rope in a swirling dance, she let me know that she was off belay. I jumared up while removing a few precarious-looking copperhead placements she had hammered in. When I pulled around from the underside of the ceiling and joined Mari at the lip of the roof and at the start of the Headwall, I found that we were poised in an outrageous position. Under our feet, there was nothing but air. Above us rose 1,000 feet of smooth, overhanging orange granite. To either side of us the walls curved around out of sight. We seemed to be suspended on the edge of the world, and the two of us and our pig hung from three steel bolts the length, yet not quite the thickness, of a half-smoked cigarette. Feeling vulnerable, I instinctively checked the knot at my waist, the only thing securing me to the anchor. I could see now why this climb had been named the Shield: the feature we were on resembled the curving battle shield of a warrior.

We had reached the point of no return. It would be impossible to rappel down from here. It was now summit or bust. But we grew accustomed to the exposure of our perch, and once we set up our portaledge and hammock for another bivouac, the calm of twilight descended and Mari and I were finally able to rest. A distant strip of clouds in the west, over the plains of the San Joaquin Valley, glowed with brilliant colors. Hanging side by side in our bivouac cocoons, we munched bagels and crunched M&Ms. We had no fear of the height, only an enhanced sense of intimacy between us. Up here in this giddy place I felt as if we were the last people left on earth and secrets were of no further use. Perhaps because this was one of the rare times when we could speak woman-to-woman without a bunch of guys hanging around, the topic of our conversation revolved around our relationships with men. I gazed down to the snakelike curve of the Merced River and the green crescent of El Cap meadow.

"So how did you meet Mike anyway?" I asked Mari.

"I met him in high school on a blind date. I wanted to go to the high school prom with a friend of mine, but he was interested in some other girl, so he set me up with his friend Mike. After that night we were inseparable. I still have a picture of us together at the prom. But he'd be embarrassed to show this photo to anyone, since this was the only time he ever dressed up in a formal suit."

As I write this, twenty years later, Mike and Mari remain a couple.

"Was Largo your first boyfriend?" Mari asked.

"No, my first boyfriend was a guy named Charlie Row. In fact, I met him right down there," I said, pointing to the valley below.

"I met him on my first climbing trip to Yosemite when I was sixteen. Kathy and I had driven up from LA to meet with Chuck and

Thank God Ledge, the northwest face of Half Dome in 1977. (CHARLIE ROW)

Bob, who were staying in Camp Four. We were all sitting around a campfire the first night when Charlie came along and joined our group. He was seventeen and he'd just arrived back in camp after having climbed the Regular route on Half Dome. We sat talking, making eyes at each other, then he asked me if I wanted to check out one of the famous boulder problems in Camp Four, called Blue Suede Shoes, by moonlight. That was the night our romance began and we ended up spending our entire summer vacation in Yosemite climbing together. We did some great things together. Outer Limits. Serenity Crack. That was my first 5.11 and I had no idea how difficult this climb would be. I thought having thin fingers would be an advantage on this thin crack, but when I arrived at the crux, I realized that the crack was too thin to jam my feet in. I got totally pumped trying to hang on with one arm to place a piece of protection and I ended up taking a thirty-foot screamer. I also did my first big wall with Charlie. We spent three days climbing the northwest face of Half Dome. It was a great summer."

"So what's the story with Yabo?" Mari asked me. Her tone was more serious now. She was alluding to the fact that Yabo had a crush on me that I didn't reciprocate.

"Oh, I don't know what to do about that situation. Yabo is becoming obsessed with me. He has been, ever since we did the Direct Route on Half Dome. I was a bit wary of his intentions the moment he asked to come along with Dean and me. When Dean backed out at the last minute, I was left with the choice of either not going or doing the climb with Yabo. I was so psyched to climb the route that I decided to go anyway. Sure enough, the first night, when we were sleeping at the base, Yabo tried to kiss me. I wasn't prepared for this and I didn't know what to do."

"So what did you do?"

"I told him that the answer was no. He backed off a bit. But all the way up the climb I was aware of his needy presence. Now it seems that every time I turn around, Yabo is there. I love him as a friend. When we climb together there is incredible energy. But romantically—no way."

The conversation trailed off on that note. Lying in my hammock, I thought of Yabo. He was the adopted, troubled orphan in our tribe. Over the next few years this bizarre character on the climbing scene would be my greatest personal challenge. We would climb some of our best routes together, yet we would cause each other great anguish.

The next morning as we began climbing the 1,000-foot-long, over-hanging Headwall, we entered the realm of cutting-edge aid climbing. When Charlie Porter first climbed into this intimidating part of El Cap with his partner Gary Bocarde in 1972, they came away with a route that pushed aid climbing into a new dimension, because never before had a climb been created that was comprised of such tenuous features. They gave the Shield the most difficult big-wall rating of A5, though subsequent ascents have now hammered out and eroded the crack so that today it accepts larger pitons, and the rating is easier, more like A3+. Porter, however, faced a seam in the wall that was the thickness of a strand of hair and that was just millimeters deep. No piton fitted this crack other than the tiniest type, called a RURP. This hatchet-shaped piton is the size and thickness of a nickel, and its blade pokes into a crack no more than a quarter inch. The inventors of the RURP, Tom Frost and Yvon Chouinard (another blacksmith climber like John Salathè, and who went on to found the immensely successful clothing company Patagonia), dubbed their new design the Realized Ultimate Reality Piton—RURP for short. They figured that no piton could be smaller and still hold a climber's weight. Porter climbed the Headwall on the Shield using scores of RURPs—thirty-five of them in a row on one pitch. Porter was apparently quite cava-lier about launching off into the unknown on these micro-pitons, but when Bocarde jumared up the rope and pulled most of the RURPs out with his fingers, the pair were sobered, realizing that a leader fall would probably rip out every piece on the pitch and create a cata-strophic force that would tear the entire anchor and everything attached to it right out of the wall. According to Bocarde, he yelled up at Porter in a fit of black humor, "Charlie, I am cutting the rope if you fall." After the climb was over, it created quite a stir as being the hardest route on El Cap, though soon Bridwell superseded it with even more risky, technical routes like Pacific Ocean Wall and Sea of Dreams. But in its heyday the Shield was the ultimate wall. "Porter has gotten inside the RURP and is looking out," quipped the famous climber Royal Robbins, bestowing on this reclusive guru of big-wall culture the Realized Ultimate Reality Compliment.

Our progress slowed to a snail's pace as we coped with the difficulties of the Headwall. Poking out of the crack ahead of me were occasional RURPs that had been hammered in so tightly by other ascents that they could not be removed. Old and tattered bits of skinny webbing tied to these "fixed" RURPs flapped in the breeze. These little slings creaked like ripping fabric when I hung from them. They felt ready to break, so I hurried on to the next placement. The only thing in my favor was that my weight—around a hundred pounds—exerted less force on the RURPs than other climbers. The more solidly built Charlie Porter, or any other guy who had climbed the route since him, likely weighed nearly twice as much as I.

On the fifth day we exited the Headwall, hauling onto a large, sloping rock platform called Chickenhead Ledge, so named for the black knobs of intrusive diorite that poke through the bed of white granite. Sometimes these bumps resemble a head with a narrow neck, and some wit in the climbing world had likened the grabbing of them to strangling a chicken. With only one day left before we "topped out," we slept well here, knowing we'd be on flat earth by the next afternoon. Some of our pitches had taken us five hours to lead. I wondered if I would bother doing another big "nailing," or piton-bashing route, ever again. It was so slow and tedious at times! We'd later learn that in the time it took us to lead three pitches on our day on the Headwall, Mari's boyfriend Mike, with John Bachar, had climbed all thirty-three pitches of the Nose route!

The next day—our sixth since leaving the valley floor—we pulled over the edge of El Cap. Twenty-nine pitches lay behind us. The relief of the climb being over and the elation of finally standing on top was enhanced by the presence of John and Mike, who had hiked to meet us on top, just as Mari and I had done when Mike and John reached the top of the Shield. In fact, that was when John had suggested that Mari and I climb this route together. After hearing about what a sensational climb it was, Mari and I had looked at each other and said, "Yeah, why not? Let's go for it." Though it was a lot of work, living in such a spectacular vertical world had been well worth the effort. Weighed down by our haulbag and by coils of ropes and racks of pitons, we wobbled on our legs, but we were grateful to be able to walk again and return to the comforts of a hot shower and some fresh food.

Ours had been the first female ascent of the Shield. It was something to be proud of, yet rather than feeling that we had done something "apart" from men, we felt we had done something "equal" to men. Before starting the Shield, I had read with some chagrin in Galen Rowell's book *The Vertical World of Yosemite*, "Women are conspicuously absent from the climbs in this book. I have no apology to make here because it is not my place to change history. There simply were no major first ascents in Yosemite done by women during the formative years of the sport."

Our sport back then was directed by a fraternity of men, and there was little encouragement or, frankly, inclination for women to participate. Yet women climbers were out there. True, there were precious few

Bev Johnson on her ten-day solo ascent of the Dihedral Wall on El Capitan in 1978. (MIKE HOOVER)

of us, but it reassured me to know that we had a presence. Though some people may have taken note of our ascent of the Shield, women had climbed big walls before us. The first all-female ascent of El Capitan had been Beverly Johnson's and Sybille Hechtel's ascent of the Triple Direct route in 1973. Then, in 1977, Barb Eastman and Molly Higgins made the first all-female ascent of the Nose. Self-taught and determined, Barb and Molly made a respectably fast three-and-a-half-day ascent of their climb—the same speed as Mari, Dean, and me.

But if I had a role model or heroine during my formative years of climbing, it was Bev. She had been up El Cap many times before me, on first ascents with her boyfriend of the time, Charlie Porter; with other women; and alone. While books about climbing touted El Cap climbs like the North America Wall, put up by Robbins, Chouinard, and others as being landmarks in climbing history, I personally found it significant to know that Bev had made a ten-day solo ascent of the Dihedral Wall route on El Capitan in 1978. Her effort is barely mentioned in the climbing books, but after our climb of the Shield I appreciated Bev's tenacity all the more. All the gut-busting work that Mari and I had shared—leading, hauling, everything—had been done by Bev, as a team of one, on the Dihedral Wall. I was awed, but not just by the know-how and hard work she'd put into her ascent. It was the courage and confidence that it took to put herself on the line, to do something on the cutting edge—to climb one of the world's greatest big walls in one of the most challenging ways possible: solo. She had succeeded and she'd given women climbers like me enormous confidence to be ourselves and not feel limited by being a minority in a male-dominated sport. Ever since I heard Jim Bridwell talk about Bev and her exploits, I felt we had much in common.

Chapter 8

Adventures with Largo

If I had to pick a place and a time when my romance with John Long began, I would choose the Arcing Plot in Yosemite Valley, in the summer of 1978. One afternoon John, a self-styled bard, had dashed off a humorous ballad and was reciting it to the gathered crowd of climbers. As I listened, it became evident that he had carefully rehearsed his poem, because his delivery—with barrel chest thrust forward to better project his deep voice and with hands mincing like an orchestral conductor—was flawless. I was taken less by his poem or his theatrical presence than by the childlike sweetness of his act: a desire to share something of his own creation with the climbers he spent his life with, and to make them laugh. He titled his poem, "Must Be No One's Fool."

Sitting in bliss in my nylon seat
Paying out the rope
Caught three whistlers—one, two, three
Almost gave up hope.

Looking left, then staring right
To my mind's dismay
A naked maiden soloing
But ten yards away.

I tied the bonehead off but quick
And laced my boots up tight
Then untied and prayed to God
And soloed ten yards right.

She glanced down claiming hold-a-plenty
Though I saw not one;
But after all, my eyes were glued on
Loins which shone in the sun.

I cranked, I edged, my fingers bled
But no advance was gained.
The maiden chalked and high-stepped on
And woe, my heart was pained.

She topped out soon thereafter
Voicing down to "play it cool."
I answered back that "Climbing wise,
I was no one's fool!"

Ten feet from the summit
She observed my face's frown
And bless her soul, she quickly tossed
The sacred perlon down.

I grabbed the cord, and thanked the Lord
Then tied my carcass in.
I cranked like hell; I almost fell
The holds were terribly thin!

A mantel quick, then pan the scene
No maiden to be found.
Bereaved I paced, then stumbled 'cross
A note upon the ground.

"Dear handsome one, a nice display
And though you make me drool
The man I need, climbing wise,
Must be no one's fool."

After John finished, he cast a searching glance toward me. His clear blue eyes seemed to ask, *Am I your fool?*

A few days later John and I found ourselves bouldering together among the granite rocks behind Camp Four. Walking from one rock to another and doing one boulder problem after another, we displayed our very different styles of climbing. To overcome the same set of moves, John would use his large, powerful frame to leap dynamically, or "dyno," past difficult sections of rock, whereas I would pad carefully over the same terrain, clinging to minute holds that John's thick fingers could not grip.

"Let me see those little mitts of yours," John demanded of me after I hopped down from the top of one boulder problem.

Snatching my child-sized hand, he laid it over his bearlike paw. "Hah," he boomed with a laugh. "It's cheating to have such small hands!" His fingers were like giant sausages in comparison with my pencil-thin digits. The difference in size, and in our respective body weights, meant I could crimp my fingers onto smaller holds and slip my hands into very thin cracks. Yet John was far from ham-fisted in the way he moved. On rock he climbed gracefully, and when he took my hand there was gentleness in the way he brushed his fingers against mine. For the rest of the afternoon we wandered the alley of boulders, moving closer and closer together, like a pair of magnets gradually realizing their attraction to one another.

While "spotting" each other on difficult boulder problems, we exchanged soft touches and words of encouragement. The role of the spotter is to protect the climber from landing in a harmful way in the event of a slip, just as a gymnast has a spotter standing by to break her fall if she botches a somersault. The spotter stands at the base of the boulder ready to catch an airborne climber by grabbing her around the hips and directing her onto the ground, feet first. This aspect of bouldering is reminiscent of a dance duo, and it has a certain grace to it. The harmony between John and me was palpable that day, and from then on we could be seen together on crags from California to Colorado.

In those days John was living with his folks while finishing his master's degree in theology at Claremont College in the Los Angeles area. At twenty-six years old he was eight years my senior, and he was at the top of his game in climbing, having made ascents like the legendary one-day blitz of the Nose. Even though he was intensely physical by nature, being a devotee of weight training and sports like baseball and basketball, he also believed in a life of the mind. Theology appealed to him because the subject grappled with the universal truths of life.

**Under John's wing in
Yosemite Valley.**
(TILMANN HEPP)

There was also, I suspected, a reason behind John's regimen of weight training and his cultivation of potentially frightening physical strength: as a child he had been treated roughly by his adoptive father. John was nonviolent by nature, and as he grew up, and grew stronger, his father became less inclined to lay his hands on him.

As for me, I was attending classes at Fullerton College, also in the Los Angeles area. Uncertain of what I wished to pursue as a career, I took a smattering of courses like Western Civilization, Calculus, Philosophy, and Zoology. I was young and I figured I would find my path as time went on. Between classes and part-time jobs, I trained with John two nights a week at a gym in Redlands, where he traded janitorial services for a membership. John threw weights around like a pro, and was as familiar with the machines and the racks of iron as he was with the muscle groups in his body.

John believed that weight training could benefit our climbing, so he suggested certain exercises to develop power and endurance. Initially, I wasn't so sure if I agreed that this form of exercise could help my climbing. Weight routines focus primarily on pushing weight away rather than pulling it toward the body, the opposite of the motions in climbing. Yet I understood enough about physiology to know that training the opposite muscle groups would keep our bodies balanced. Lifting weights could work those underdeveloped muscles, help prevent injuries, and develop greater overall strength.

One night in the Redlands gym, one of John's buddies, a power lifter named Jack, watched me on the bench press. After warming up by doing several repetitions with light weights, I had added plate after plate of iron in small increments until I was lifting 125 pounds—20 percent more than I weighed.

"You could probably break the world record for women in your weight class if you trained seriously for a while," Jack suggested casually.

"Really?" I asked, instantly curious about the idea.

"Yeah, the record for the bench press is about a hundred fifty pounds for a woman your size. You could probably get there with six months of training if you really wanted to."

I looked at John, to see what he thought of the idea.

"Go for it, Lynnie," he said without hesitation.

John's unflinching encouragement that I should take up this challenge typified one of the positive elements of the relationship we were building then. While climbing with me, he had identified a side of my psyche that I was only partially aware of—the side of me that had to do with determination and the ability to focus on a goal.

After a few months of regular training, I achieved my goal of bench-pressing 150 pounds. The week after tipping that scale, I signed up to compete at a local weight lifting meet in a seedy neighborhood gym. Inside, the sweat-filled atmosphere was claustrophobic. Lost in a crowd of huge weight lifters wearing knee and back braces, I felt completely out of place. When it was my turn to try bench-pressing 150 pounds, I was unable to budge the bar. The mental calm I had used to direct my energy to lifting almost an additional third of my body weight a week earlier was nowhere to be found in this dingy gym full of strangers. At that point I realized that my ability to focus my strength and willpower also had to be accompanied by the right atmosphere and directed to something I cared about. Open space, a cliff surrounded by fresh air, trees, and fun-loving friends—those were places where I could summon my passion and determination. Though I continued to practice weight lifting for brief periods during the winter season over the years, I never entered a competition again. Subsequently, I learned that the world record in my weight class had far surpassed 150 pounds by women who used steroids. The idea of achieving better performance through artificial substances repelled me. It seemed both destructive to the body and as dishonest as claiming the first free ascent of a climb that had been made easier by chiseling holds into the rock.

One afternoon in the spring of 1980 after riding my bicycle from Fullerton College back to my mother's home where I was living, I received a phone call from Beverly Johnson, of El Cap climbing fame. She explained that she and her husband, the cameraman Mike Hoover, were helping to produce a made-for-television outdoor athletic competition called Survival of the Fittest. The competition would take place in and around Yosemite Valley and it would involve events like the Climb and Rappel, the Aerial Obstacle Course, Swimming and Kayaking, and the Survival Run. Other women who had signed up included Julie Brugger and Anne Tarver, both good rock climbers, a Swiss cross-country ski racer with Olympic experience named Gabriella Anderson, as well as a parachutist and a professional jockey. Win or lose, there was money in it.

"We'd like to invite you to compete. What do you say?" Bev asked.

The free-form style of these events related to my own form of athleticism. The idea of competing in an outdoor arena with and against other women who shared my passion had instant appeal. Plus, I could use the money to help pay for my college education and finance my next season of climbing.

"I'll do it," I answered.

Had the offer to compete in Survival of the Fittest come from someone other than Beverly Johnson, I may not have been so quick to accept. My admiration for Bev as a climber, as a woman, and as a person of integrity with an authentic love of adventure gave the event a seal of approval. Though I had never met her in person, after our brief conversation I had come away feeling as if we had known each other for years.

Bev had impressive climbing credentials and now she traveled from hemisphere to hemisphere making adventure films. She had sparkling eyes, long dark-blond hair, and a sweet-looking face. But what set her apart was her open nature and her way of making people feel instantly comfortable. From the first moment I saw Bev, I felt at ease in her presence. Though Bev was a lighthearted and natural person, she could also be controversial and disarming in conversation. Legendary was her much-quoted quip to Ken Wilson, the editor of the British climbing magazine *Mountain*. During an interview Wilson asked her how many 5.10 climbs she had led. "But Ken, it's not about how many 5.10s you have led, it's about how many 5.10 leaders you have laid," Bev replied facetiously to the taken-aback interviewer.

After a few weeks of preparation and training, the competitors and TV crew gathered in Yosemite at Nevada Falls, a foaming geyser of water that spills loudly over a cliff beside the trail that leads to Half Dome. Here, on a cliff face beside the waterfall, the first event—the Climb and Rappel—would be launched.

Prior to the event, Bev greeted me warmly. Standing beside her was Mike, her husband and the mastermind of the show. Mike was a climber himself, but he had shifted his focus to become a hard-driving TV cameraman and producer. A commanding figure with an intense gaze and a six-foot-five-inch frame, he exercised absolute control over the show, and he was not above shouting and screaming at his under-lings if he thought it would push them to do a better job. His adventure documentaries, many of them shot with Bev, took him to every conti-nent including Antarctica. In 1982 the pair would head to Afghanistan to document the story between the Soviet invasion and the mujahideen resistance for NBC News. Amid tanks, bullets, and helicopter gun-ships, Mike found the ultimate journalistic high: working as a war cor-respondent.

Despite Mike's intimidating presence, I could tell he liked me and accepted me as a kindred spirit in the climbing family. When the com-petitors arrived at the trailhead in front of Nevada Falls, Mike explained our course. It started at the base of a low-angle rock face 50 feet high. Dangling down the face lay several thick gym ropes that we would have to grip and haul ourselves up on. Once at the top, we'd run up a steep hillside to a trail that led to the top of a cliff on the other side of Nevada Falls. Thinner ropes hung over that cliff and we'd use these to rappel down for 400 feet. Whoever touched the ground first, won. It was simple stuff for a climber, but the more aerobically fit ath-letes had an edge in the uphill running section.

Standing with my toe behind the starting line, I felt butterflies in my stomach. I felt confident that I could haul my body up the rope quickly, but I was less certain how well I would fare in the running part of the event. I looked at the faces of my competitors, trying to read their feel-ings. John had warned me not to underestimate the women I was up against. Each had specific skills and advantages in the different events, even though it seemed that the all-body and rugged nature of this out-door contest favored the climbers. "Watch out for Julie Brugger," John had said. "She's a runner, a mountaineer, and she was the first woman to lead Lunatic Fringe." This classic Yosemite crack had a reputation for being a strenuous route. Julie was doing climbs that few women had done before, and I respected that.

The starting gun cracked off its signal and everyone sprinted for-ward. At the cliff I clenched the rope and climbed it quickly, then scrambled over loose rocks and through sharp manzanita brush to the top of the hillside. Only minutes had passed, yet by the time I reached the trail I could taste the bitterness of my burning lungs as I heaved in and spat out large amounts of air. By the time I reached the top of Nevada Falls, my legs felt wobbly. I was the first one to arrive at the rappel. A course marshal waved me toward the rope closest to the waterfall.

When I grabbed the rope and lifted it up a few inches to poke a loop of it into the rappel device that hung from my harness, I was surprised at its dead weight. Spray fanning out from Nevada Falls had soaked it, making it swollen and heavy. I realized vaguely that arriving first at this point in the race was in fact a disadvantage. For the sake of getting a good shot of me framed against the waterfall, the marshal had directed me to the rope right beside the cascade. It was wetter and heavier than the others and my time suffered for it, as the damp nylon kept jamming in my rappel device. I couldn't get any speed until I was 200 feet down the wall. At that point Anne Tarver, a climber from Seattle who frequented Camp Four, came running vertically past me. Though I managed to catch up and pass her for a split second, my rope hung up again moments before the end. Anne slid by me and seized first place.

I was disappointed to have come in second place due to a glitch in the rappel system, but my disappointment didn't last long. The next day, just before the Aerial Obstacle Course, Mike and Bev told me that they were confident I would win. I felt flattered. This comment motivated me to prove them right.

The Aerial Obstacle Course was perfectly suited to my skills, held on a ropes course strung from a series of platforms perched 20 feet off the ground. Competitors started the event with a rope-to-rope Tarzan swing that led to a strenuous rope climb, then a swaying tightrope across a river. At the end came a breakneck-speed ride on a zip line into the river. First to splash into the water won. Though I stayed in front in this event, I was conscious of Julie always inches from my heels. Every time I saw her out of the corner of my eye, I found a burst of energy to keep me ahead. In the back of my mind a mantra kept chanting, *Concentrate. Keep your eyes on the ropes. All the way to the end.*

Years later I would hear that during this leg of the race Julie had connected eyes with me and had seen something icy and determined in my gaze. "Lynn looked right through me. When I saw her eyes, I knew I couldn't beat her," she had told a friend.

I crossed the finish line first. As I rested and let my breathing return to normal, I began to comprehend that something like an inner being was guiding me, finding me energy when none was left, pushing my feet forward to keep me ahead of the pack. This inner being could not let go. Recognizing this tremendous force of determination I possessed was nothing less than a revelation for me. I realized I was different from most of my competitors. Sure, we were all fit and strong, but I was willing to give whatever was necessary to achieve my objective. This is what Julie detected in my eyes.

Nevertheless, next day I came in fourth place in the Swimming and Kayaking event. Even a mental edge could not overcome such unfamiliar skills. Julie crossed the line ahead of me, but even so, I carried the lead in points. If I came first or even second in the final event, the Survival Run, then the contest would be mine. But as I was chatting to one of the male competitors, whose contest was running concurrently with the women's, I learned that first prize for the men was $15,000, while a first for the women awarded only $5,000.

This seemed grossly unfair, and it offended me deeply. I raised the issue with the other women and suggested to them that we should boycott the show. At first, my idea was met with reluctance. It was argued that the men competed in six events and the women only four; what's more, the two events that the women were exempt from were of a violent, medieval nature. One was a one-on-one jousting match with batons in which the men had to batter each other and to try to topple their opponent off a log spanning a river. The other was a downhill footrace on a course that was huge, steep, and rocky. It looked like a sure way to break an ankle.

That aside, my objection revolved around simple math: the women were doing two-thirds of the work for one-third of the money. I felt it was demeaning to us all. By the end of the discussion the women competitors agreed to stand up for what was fair. But word of unrest in the women's camp spread like wildfire. Before I had a chance to confront him, the production manager, Bob Bagley, marched up to me.

"I hear you have proposed a boycott," he said, cutting right to the chase.

"Yes, I don't understand why the top prize for the women is five thousand dollars and the top prize for the men is fifteen thousand. I understand that the women are competing in four events and the men in six, so if you want to be fair the women should be paid ten and the men fifteen."

"Okay, you have a point," Bob conceded, "but I wasn't responsible for that decision and it's too late to change it now. The budget for this show has already been allocated for this year. I promise you we will raise the prize money for the women's comp next year. If you boycott this last event, we'll cancel the women's show right now and no one will make any money. But if you win, you'll be invited back to compete again next year."

I guessed that he was bluffing about canceling the women's show over our threatened protest, but if he wasn't bluffing, everyone would lose. We decided to trust his promise and keep going. I wanted to finish the competition as much as anyone, and I felt satisfied that I had spoken up.

The last event of the show was the Survival Run. For me it was a humbling learning experience. The course was a four-mile cross-country run through the hills near the Stanislaus River. This race favored Gabriella Anderson with her marathon endurance and aerobic capacity. At the starting line I looked over and tried to read something in her eyes. She looked dead ahead, ignoring me. A veteran of countless races, she had learned to avoid the prying eyes of competitors; she knew the power of "the look" and its ability to "psyche out" an athlete. I was about to compete against an Olympic-hardened cross-country ski racer with plenty of aerobic endurance and mental toughness. In fact, four years later at the 1984 Summer Olympics in LA, Gabriella would stagger over the finish line of the marathon in yet another Olympic event. Nevertheless, her training had always been on level tracks, whereas I had the reflexes for running on rough terrain. I knew the feel of granite and loose rubble under my feet, so I'd learned to quickly correct for the slippage and roll that comes with a run through the wilderness.

When the starting gun echoed across the valley, I bounded down the rocky slope. I knew I couldn't beat Gabriella on the flats, so my strategy was to go like blazes on the steep terrain and try to maintain my lead from there. I hit the bottom of the hill first, leaving Gabriella to pick her way down the scree. But she was like the wind when she hit the flats. She soon took the lead, and I watched her figure disappear into the distance.

Her commitment to cardiovascular training was evident, as was my lack of it. When we splashed into the river to swim across, I closed the gap slightly, but it was to no avail: she crossed the line twenty seconds ahead of me. Racing against Gabriella inspired me to run on a regular basis from that day on. My daily jogs soon became my most peaceful time of the day, when I could let my thoughts go uninterrupted and let the rhythm between my mind and body settle into a natural harmony.

Though Gabriella won the Survival Run, I had scored enough points overall to win the contest, and the cash. The following three years brought me more invitations to compete in Survival of the Fittest, in events as far away as New Zealand. Each year I won. True to their word, the producers raised first prize for the women to ten thousand dollars. When NBC canceled the women's segment of the show, it was, I heard, because the producers couldn't find anyone to beat me. Whether or not this was true, I became increasingly aware of how few women were pushing the limits of climbing and endurance like I was, and of how my passion had led me very much into a man's world.

Bev Johnson was one of my first role models because she too was a strong woman who boldly followed her passions. Several years later, in 1994, just as I was writing a profile about Beverly Johnson and her impact on me as a young climber, an uncanny, devastating thing happened. I received a phone call from Jim Bridwell, who informed me that Bev had been killed in a helicopter crash in the Ruby Mountains of Nevada. Also killed were the pilot, a ski guide, and Frank Wells, president of Disney Productions. Only Mike had survived, with serious injuries from which he would eventually recover. Though our encounters over the years had been brief, I regarded Bev as my "adventure sister." I thought about the last time I had seen Bev, when we had breakfasted together before an outdoor industry trade show in Salt Lake City. Over coffee we had exchanged stories about our travels and talked about future plans. As always, she impressed me with her abundance of positive energy, yet that meeting also left me feeling unsettled. In every tale she told, in every place she described, someone had died, right in front of her. In the mountains of the Karakoram it had been a filmmaking colleague who'd died of hepatitis; in Antarctica her friend the aviator Giles Kershaw had been killed when his gyrocopter crashed onto the ice. And there were others. Though no doubt affected by these losses, Bev spoke about death with ease, as if it were an occupational hazard. She was not cavalier or callous, but she accepted death as part and parcel of being a war correspondent, an adventure filmmaker, a pilot and a climber, and an explorer of third world jungles, mountains, and ice caps. Perhaps she had seen enough death to overcome the fear of it that weighs on most of us; or perhaps by accepting the impermanence of life she was more able to accept the world as a playground full of possibilities, with no challenge too grim to face. Whatever the truth of Bev's philosophies, the news of her death hit me hard. I had lost a soul sister.

When the school year ended in June 1980, I spent $3,000 of my $5,000 prize money from Survival of the Fittest on a Volkswagen van. John and I loaded it with camping and climbing gear and groceries, and we hit the road. The road trip lies at the heart of American rock climbing. It's a summer ritual of cruising down highways and back roads, passing through small towns, and camping and climbing at crags that dot the countryside. For rock climbers, it is the embodiment of freedom.

Our plan was to drive throughout the western states for several months, hitting Yosemite; Granite Mountain, Arizona; and Eldorado Canyon and other meccas in Colorado. John was an enthusiastic leader, primarily motivated to pioneer first ascents wherever we went. I was an accomplice on these exploits, grateful to be learning. As we cruised along in the van, the tape deck blared out John's favorite music—Al Di Meola, John McLaughlin, and Paco de Lucia—while John, a drummer who played in a couple of bands, pounded on the dashboard with his thick fingers.

Our first stop was at a large massif of brown stone a few miles outside Prescott, Arizona. Granite Mountain, as it is called, rises from a landscape of weathered boulders and saguaro cacti stretching their spiky arms toward the sky. Climbers had been coming to this Sonora Desert crag for years, and they had charted a lot of routes here. But John knew that the steepest climbs had not been done in the most perfect style: they still had sections of aid in them. This meant that although the climbers on the first ascents had gotten to the top of these routes, they had hung on their gear when the going got extremely hard or strenuous. John's plan was to eliminate the aid moves and make first free ascents of these routes. In the 1980s, there were hundreds of climbs across America awaiting an FFA, as we called the first free ascent. They were like prizes waiting to be snatched by climbers with the right combination of strength, talent, and technical ability.

On Granite Mountain we zeroed in on a crack climb called Coatamundi Whiteout, named after a song by Frank Zappa. For this route a friend of John's from LA, Keith Cunning, joined us. Locals had been trying to climb it free for some time and I could see that even with aid it was difficult. If we were going to "free it," then it would be a war of attrition that would take effort from all three of us.

I went up first, sinking my fingers into a rough, thin crack for ten feet. I slotted a small stopper in the crack, then realized that I faced a difficult move to traverse left to join the horizontal crack under the giant overhang above my head. I managed to crimp my fingers onto a few tiny flakes, stood on some crystals of granite on the face below, then reached over to jam my fingers into the horizontal crack. I was able to hang on just long enough to fiddle another piece of protection in the crack under the roof. I tried making another move out left, then fell off onto the nut.

Keith went up next. He climbed a little farther, added another nut to the crack, and also fell off. Placing protection while balancing on such thin holds was immensely strenuous, so each time we fell, we left the rope in place at our high point so that each "fresh" climber had the benefit of a top rope up to the highest nut. This was called "yo-yo" style. John went up last and made it past the highest point we had climbed to, then he continued along the horizontal crack until he arrived at another roof that was split by a wide crack. After making a few fist jams and wedging his feet in the crack above his head, he pulled around the roof and onto the ledge that marked its end. He had "bagged" the first free ascent of Coatamundi Whiteout, a fierce 5.11, though with effort from his partners. Belayed from above by John, Keith and I free climbed the route to the top.

Minutes after we hiked back to the bottom of the cliff, two local climbers arrived at the base of Coatamundi Whiteout and explained that they had planned to attempt to free climb this route that very day. They had trained for months in preparation, they told us, and they were disappointed to discover that John Long and his girlfriend had scooped them!

"You snooze, you lose," said John as we hiked back down to the van.

I have to say that I felt sorry for these guys, since we had bagged the prize route of their local area right in front of their noses. Many climbers consider new routes sacred possessions and "ownership" is determined by whoever becomes the first person to climb a new route. Much like the ethic in surfing regarding first priority on a wave, climbers have their own code of ethics regarding who gets priority in doing the first ascent of a climb. Those who spot a new line and are the first to try climbing it have the first shot at it. But in my mind, there is no such thing as ownership of a route. And this would not be the last time I scooped someone on the first free ascent.

The Volkswagen then took us east, into southern Colorado to the old mining town and soon-to-be ski resort of the nouveau riche, Telluride. Lush alpine forests, waterfalls, and jagged-edged mountain ridges surround this valley of the San Juan Mountains. We had traveled here to house-sit for the great American climber Royal Robbins, who had done the first ascent of Half Dome in 1957, the first big-wall route in Yosemite Valley, as well as many other historic first ascents in America and abroad, and who was now earning a comfortable living with his eponymous clothing company. Royal had, months earlier, hired John to promote his line of outdoor clothing by doing slide shows in climbing shops. Now he was letting us use his vacation home in Telluride while John launched a business in which he and I would be rock climbing guides. Generous to a fault, Royal had even invested in John by printing up a stack of brochures, with John's picture on the cover, advertising our services.

All along the winding mountain highway, John talked up the idea, but it wasn't until after we arrived in Telluride that I realized our business was nothing more than a brochure. Somehow—and John wasn't sure how—paying clients were supposed to find us. Telluride in 1980 was not the chic mountain town that it is today, but a small mountain village far from any city. It wasn't at all a mecca for climbers. During our entire two-month stay, we didn't guide a single client.

But we didn't care. Instead we climbed at the nearby Ophir Wall, a 500-foot granite cliff. There, I made a major breakthrough in my climbing, with the FFA of a route called Ophir Broke. Just as on the climb at Granite Mountain, John and I took turns yo-yoing our way up this overhanging face with a crack splitting the wall above. For John, the initial moves getting to the crack were not much of a problem because he could reach past a long blank section to a vital hold. However, when he arrived at the crack, he could not wedge his big hands into the thin fissure, and he repeatedly fell. For me, the trouble was on the initial overhanging face below, where no matter how high I reached, I was still inches short of that vital hold. After several tries, I realized that the only way for me to overcome this blank section of rock was to execute a move that would be, at that time, perhaps the hardest single move I had ever done. Using the kind of code talk that climbers employ to describe sequences of moves, I told John of my plan.

"I'll set both my feet up high onto those two small edges, then slap my hand up to that tiny edge, catch it for a moment, then I'll dyno again to the good hold," I said.

Tom Frost, Royal Robbins, and Yvon Chouinard bivving in the Black Cave on the first ascent of the North American Wall on El Capitan in 1964.
(CHUCK PRATT)

"Whoa, Lynnie, I can barely see that micro hold you're planning to use. But give it a shot. Go for it."

I proceeded to set both my feet up high onto two small edges, then I popped my hand up to the tiny crystalline edge for just long enough to still myself and find that perfect zero-gravity moment that exists somewhere between falling off and jumping higher. A moment later, I shot my hand up again and caught the vital hold. Once I latched on to this hold, I was able to reach the thin crack and continued jamming to the top. When I arrived at the belay, I was surprised that I'ad succeeded on such a hard climb before John. Today the route is rated at 5.12d, and in 1980 there were very few climbs of such a grade. Though I did the FFA of this route, the guidebook to the Ophir Wall credits John with the FFA, probably because in 1980 I was an unknown climber, just a protégé of Largo.

The big lesson for me here was to realize that despite what appeared to be a limitation due to my small stature, I could create my own method of getting past a difficult section of rock. John's size and power enabled him to make long reaches and explosive lunge moves that were completely out of my range. I, on the other hand, often found small intermediate holds that John couldn't even imagine gripping. But more importantly, I realized that no matter what our physical differences, with the right combination of vision, desire, and effort, just about any climb was possible. Short or tall, man or woman, the rock is an objective medium that is equally open for interpretation by all.

After two months of unemployment in Telluride, our skills were put to use when Royal invited several of his best clothing dealers to Telluride for a company event. These folks, who owned large outdoor stores across the United States, had little experience climbing, so Royal decided it would be fun for them to try their hand on the rocks. He hired John to take them up some easy routes in a granite cove named Cracked Canyon. I volunteered to help by setting up ropes and belaying people on beginning-to-moderate-level climbs throughout the day. After coaching people up climbs all day long, I was in the habit of explaining the moves and shouting out the "beta," as climbers call such directions. At the end of the afternoon, Royal suggested that we do a more challenging climb together on the other, steeper side of Cracked Canyon. He started up a route rated 5.10d that I had done so many times that summer I knew every move by heart. When Royal reached the crux moves below an overhang, he hesitated, puffing and shaking out the fatigue in his arms. It was then that I unwittingly began shouting out advice about how to do the crux moves. As I watched Royal become increasingly frustrated and fail to get past the crux, I felt embarrassed that I might have insulted the dignity of this climbing legend. Perhaps he was distracted by my comments or maybe he was concentrating on avoiding painful movements with his arthritic wrists. I thought, *Why should I be giving Royal advice about how to climb this route, especially since I don't like it when other people do the same while I'm climbing?* Royal's polite silence in the face of my ignorance spoke louder than words.

At the end of our summer in Telluride, I took stock of our finances. The $2,000 I had left from Survival of the Fittest was all but spent, and we had brought in virtually no further income. It was time to end our road trip and earn some more money. But where?

"Vegas!" John suggested when I told him we were broke.

"Vegas? Why Vegas?"

"It's a warm winter hang, there's plenty of work, there's a university you could enroll in, and my buddy Randy Grandstaff has a big house with cheap rent."

John always had a plan or a scheme, and I was a free spirit, so we gassed up the Volkswagen and headed west. On the outskirts of Vegas, adjacent to the airport, we found Randy Grandstaff's place. Today condos and shopping malls have overwhelmed this part of the city and Randy's old place has long been torn down and built over, but back then this location seemed practically rural. Randy, a loquacious climber always fond of company, offered us a room for $150 a month. This is where we lived, on a shoestring, for seven months. Sixties decor featuring electric-blue carpet, leaky bathroom faucets, and rust-streaked tubs, a sand dune that kept blowing under the back door like an unwanted stray dog, and the regular roar and rattle of jets gave our pad a white-trash flavor, but the spectacular climbing at Red Rocks was only minutes from our home.

We had arrived in Vegas in late September with barely any money, and it was too late for me to enroll in the University of Las Vegas for the semester. We needed work badly, but the jobs that were available were low-paying menial jobs. Since we were in the home of gambling joints, John figured the best way to earn some quick cash was to find work as a dealer in one of the casinos.

"I've got a great idea," John said one day.

"What is it?" I asked.

"Baccarat. I'll take a card dealer's course and learn the game. The course takes three months. Grandstaff's old man is a pit boss in the Sands Hotel. He's got the juice to get me a job on the tables."

I paid John's enrollment fee, then realized that we were nearly flat broke. Soon thereafter a strange opportunity arose. We ran into Dan Goodwin while bouldering in Calico Basin.

I'd first met Dan in Joshua Tree just after he had left the commune where he had been living for the past several years. Dan, a strikingly handsome man with bright green eyes and dark blond hair, described the commune to me while we were hiking out to the Wonderland Area of Rocks deep in Joshua Tree. It was a hot day and we were the only people for miles in this vast desert, except for a small group of friends who were lagging behind us. As Dan extolled the utopian commune life, he began to strip off all his clothes. Strutting naked, feeding his already perfect tan, he talked about abandoning hang-ups regarding nudity. His free-spirited lecture made me feel uninhibited about taking off my own top. But when our friends caught up with us, they took one look at the nudity before them and stared at us as if we had lost our minds. When I glanced down at my bare white chest, I felt awkward and embarrassed. At the same time, I wondered why a woman's bare chest should be a source of shame among friends. I recognized that most people's beliefs about what is appropriate to wear is based on cultural traditions rather than personal choice. Women in Afghanistan can be stoned to death for showing too much skin. Many Muslim women wear veils to cover their faces and long robes to cover their arms and legs. European women sunbathe topless on public beaches. In some African cultures people walk around half naked all their lives. To me it seemed natural to be topless among friends. Even so, I threw my top back on.

While bouldering at Calico Basin that day with John and Dan, we talked about our trouble finding employment in Vegas.

"What are you doing for work, Dan?" asked John.

"I'm a live performer in a bar on the Las Vegas strip."

"You mean you're a male stripper?"

"Not exactly, but sort of." Dan then described his Vaudevillian line of work. His performance began when he strolled onto the stage carrying a backpack and a climbing rope slung over his shoulder. To musical accompaniment and some kind of dance, Dan would shed his clothes until he was wearing nothing but a G-string. Dan then suggested that I could earn some quick money in the same nightclub.

"No, thanks," I said with a laugh, remembering my last experience with Dan and his nudity.

"I'm serious. There's a female boxing match there every Thursday night. You'd be perfect."

Not nudity but a boxing match? Before I had a chance to respond, John blurted out, "Go for it, Lynnie, it'll be hilarious!"

I signed up, and in the spirit of the event I picked out a pair of shiny blue running shorts with white stripes down the side and a red, yellow, and blue Lycra top I had purchased in a closeout sale. On Thursday night we fronted up to a seedy bar located at the entrance to the city, just past the sign that says WELCOME TO LAS VEGAS. A flashing neon sign on top of the bar announced, LIVE ENTERTAINMENT DAILY. In the bar a boxing ring sat center stage. Spotlights shone onto the white mat and red ropes surrounded the ring. The clientele were urban cowboys, beer-bellied truck drivers with armloads of tattoos, and older men who looked like they hadn't left the bar in a decade. The manager handed me a pair of oversized boxing gloves that looked more like pillows. Then he brought me into the ring and introduced me to my opponent, who was several inches taller than me with straight blond hair and pencil-thin arms.

"You fight three one-minute rounds with thirty seconds' rest in between. Good luck, girls. Now go to it," he said tersely.

The bell rang, the punches flew. Though my opponent was trying her best, I had more force behind my punches. After our brief bout, I was declared the winner. The referee raised my arm above my head in victory. The drinkers raised their glasses.

"Way to go, baby," they slurred as one.

I was laughing with them at the absurdity of it all until I caught the eye of a friend whom John had encouraged to come along. She wore a look of embarrassment that matched my own, confirming to me that I had just done something utterly silly. When the manager handed me a measly $20, I felt even more ridiculous.

Although that was my first and last live performance in Las Vegas, Dan's stage career continued to evolve. His next performance was at the Tropicana Hotel and it was loosely based on Oscar Wilde's *The Picture of Dorian Gray*, about a man who sells his soul to the devil in return for eternal youth. Dan invited John and me to his show, which played to a large crowd. When the curtain lifted, a carriage rolled onto the stage from a cloud of smoke created by dry ice. Out of the carriage emerged Dan, wearing a top hat and tuxedo. Accompanied by soft striptease music, he tipped off his top hat with a flourish of his cane, then slipped off his white gloves, which magically burst into flames. Then off went the rest of his clothes until he was down to a G-string. At this point he grabbed a pull-up bar hanging from the ceiling of the carriage and started flexing his body into a variety of gymnastic poses, giving the audience a good look at his rippling back and buttocks.

But Dan's magnum opus came later that winter when he soloed up the outside of the enormous Sears tower in Chicago, wearing a Spiderman suit. The stunt earned him the nickname Spider Dan. This audacious ascent—for which he was arrested—was accomplished by using sky hooks and industrial suction cups that he occasionally clamped onto the smooth surface of the glass and marble exterior of the skyscraper. The whole event was a gimmick to promote a pyramid scheme that sold health food made of plankton; halfway up the building, he stopped in full view of journalists to eat some of this special product. Dan offered me a sales position in his plankton-selling enterprise, but I declined. I thought it would be better to finish college.

By early 1981 I was taking classes at UNLV and holding down an array of menial jobs. I polished brass at a furniture store; I slapped price labels on new products at an Alpha Beta supermarket; I worked at a pizza joint; and I was a hostess at JoJo's Restaurant on the Las Vegas Strip. In the space of seven months I had five different jobs. On my last day at JoJo's (I was fired allegedly because I left the front lobby unattended too often while using the rest room) I stood in the lobby watching black smoke billow from the MGM Grand Hotel as it burned to the ground. Eighty-four people burned to death, died of smoke inhalation, or jumped out of windows. Six hundred and seventy-nine people were injured. It was a terrible scene to witness and it made me realize how trapped I felt in my own life in this boomtown. The superficiality and tawdriness in Vegas depressed me.

When John returned from climbing at Red Rocks that evening, I had to tell him I had lost my job. While I was going from job to job, John hadn't found work as a card dealer like he had hoped. By the time John graduated as a baccarat dealer, he found that people wait for years for an opening at a card table. His connection's "juice" was a little dry, and so John never dealt a card in Las Vegas. We didn't have enough money to pay rent, buy food, and pay for my college tuition. Our cupboards were truly bare. We were learning the hard way that nothing is as easy as it appears in glittery Las Vegas.

"You really need to get a job," I said flatly as John was unpacking his rucksack. Within a few days John was sitting in a glass booth surrounded by gas pumps, working a cash register. For John, this was the perfect job. In between making change he read literature or wrote the stories that eventually became his bread and butter.

Bleak as Vegas could be, the canyons of Red Rocks kept me sane. In the spring of 1981, John, Randy Grandstaff, and I made several first ascents that were wonderful, if dangerous, vertical journeys. In Pine Creek Canyon there was Heart of Darkness, a climb that forced us to climb far beyond our protection on an uncertain sea of sandstone. At one point, as I led, a flake suddenly broke off and I went flying backward through the air for 35 feet before my fall was stopped by a small wired nut wedged in a tiny crack. The plummet left me dangling upside down under a small roof, dazed but unscathed. John and Randy, who had watched me fall, seemed more shaken up than me. I was so surprised to have fallen that I immediately lowered back to the ground, then quickly climbed my way back up and finished the pitch. We could have tamed this route with bolts, but in those days bolts were out and boldness was in. We climbed with daring and confidence and we felt great satisfaction from these efforts.

But the most beautiful free climb we did that year was a ten-pitch face route called Levitation 29. John and I made the first free ascent of this route, accompanied by the two climbers who had made the first ascent using aid, Jorge and Joanne Urioste. The mysterious-sounding name Levitation 29 had to do with the climb having been made on Joanne's twenty-ninth birthday, and the idea that levitation would be helpful to rise up this sheer 800-foot wall. One of my best memories of our Las Vegas days is walking across the desert to this sun-soaked towering cliff in Oak Creek Canyon. We crossed paths with a ring-tailed cat and a few bighorn sheep and as we cruised through the desert, my eyes kept resting on the countless rainbow-colored sedimentary boulders along the path. John and I climbed fluidly together that day on Levitation 29. Whatever challenges Vegas handed us on the domestic front, John was an ideal playmate on the rocks.

When the spring semester ended, the desert started heating up. As Vegas became a furnace, John and I were beginning to question our

On the first free ascent of Levitation 29 (5.11c).
(JORGE URIOSTE)

purpose for staying there. I was just biding my time at school, our jobs were unsatisfying, even the bad wallpaper of our rented room gave me a headache. The question was, where to next?

It was a phone call that gave us the impetus to make our move. The call was from Mike Hoover, who wanted to hire John to go to Venezuela to try to make the world's longest rappel down the cliff beside Angel Fall for *The Guinness Book of World Records* TV show. Both John and I had worked on a few TV projects already. John had recently been paid to write the script for a climbing film set in Colorado that featured my friend Beth Bennett and me doing a route called the Naked Edge. John had always believed that we had a career in adventure film, and now it seemed that the moment was right for us to move back to LA and closer to the land of Hollywood. In the time it took us to pack our van, we were headed back over the state line toward my family and the J-Tree crew we had missed so much during our time in Nevada.

Chapter 9

From Vegas to Hollywood

Back in Santa Monica John and I lived in a second-floor apartment on the corner of Lincoln and Montana, eight blocks from the beach. At sunrise the faint sounds of breaking waves and squabbling seagulls filtered through our window, but by rush hour the air was filled with the roar of cars and buses. John had returned from Venezuela after his televised Angel Fall rappel more convinced than ever that we could earn a living from Hollywood. With that in mind, he spent days at the kitchen table working on proposals to pitch to TV production companies suggesting outlandish stunts, and he wrote far-fetched but funny tales like "I Smoked Pipeloads With the Yeti" that occasionally appeared in magazines like *Climbing*.

These times started out as lean as our Vegas days. John spent most of his time writing, and I went to Santa Monica College, where I majored in biology. I also worked part-time at an outdoor store to help pay for my college education, but the majority of my income came from occasional television jobs. Besides my annual gig on Survival of the Fittest, I had performed on other TV shows such as the *The Guinness Game, That's Incredible!*, and *Ripley's Believe it or Not*. In the early eighties, television was just beginning to discover the world of adrenaline sports, and feeding this fad came a host of new shows. Each of these tried to outdo the other with spectacular never-been-done-before feats. These jobs represented both the easiest money I ever made and some of the most absurd undertakings of my life.

A feat for *That's Incredible!* was perhaps the most ridiculous stunt I ever did. On this show I was asked to climb over a hot-air balloon flying at an altitude of 6,000 feet. This was a world's first for obvious reasons: it was sensational and perilous, but more importantly, no one had ever been motivated to perform such a senseless stunt. I was, however, moved by the offer of $4,000.

Nothing like this had ever been done before, so I had to plan out each detail carefully. My first challenge was to figure out how to make a rope ladder and attach it to the hot-air balloon. With John's help, I made a long rope ladder using short sections of PVC pipe threaded onto parallel strands of an old climbing rope. The rope ladder would be draped over the balloon and attached to a large metal ring six inches in diameter that was fixed to the balloon's apex. The ring was the only solid connection to the balloon, since the top of the balloon was covered by a loose piece of parachute fabric. The pilot could regulate the height of the balloon by pulling strings attached to the parachute, thereby allowing variable amounts of hot air to escape through the opening. One potential problem was that the metal ring could heat up to nearly 250 degrees, since it lay above the propane-fueled burner that constantly gave off jets of flame. My concern was that the hot metal ring could melt the nylon rope tied to it, my only contact to the balloon. We brought along an asbestos mat to drape on top of the balloon to diffuse the heat, and just in case something went wrong, I decided to carry a small reserve parachute on my back.

"Lynnie, I've got a great idea," John said as we were preparing the ladder. "When you get around to the other side of the balloon, you should cut your feet loose and pretend you're having a hard time. Then just let go and parachute to the ground."

My parachute experience was limited to a one-day crash course involving two static-line jumps from an airplane. I considered the idea for a moment, then dismissed John's notion with a smile. The stunt I was about to perform was crazy enough and I figured it would be foolish to trust my life to a single reserve parachute.

On the day of the filming we rigged the ladder over the balloon and the pilot inflated it with frequent blasts of flames from the propane burner. The canopy rose like a mushroom, 45 feet tall. The pilot had never steered his ship with a person clambering over it, so he appeared a bit nervous as we prepared to set off. I was surprised to find out that he didn't even carry a reserve parachute. Like the captain of a fishing vessel, if a disaster occurred, he would go down with the ship.

The balloon drifted in a strong north wind across the arid flatlands north of LA. After we rose to an altitude of about 6,000 feet, we received a call from the cameraman inside the helicopter saying, "We're ready to roll."

The thundering sound of the helicopter circling around us added to my sense of excitement as I eased my weight onto the ladder and began my ascent up the side of this strange floating sphere. Because of the inverted pear shape of the balloon, the first part of the ladder was overhanging and unstable.

"Be careful on top of the balloon," the pilot said, as he pointed a small camera at me.

My weight pressed against the balloon walls, deforming this air-filled bubble as I disappeared into the folds of multicolored nylon. When I reached the top of the balloon, I could feel the rush of hot air from the burner directly below. I stopped briefly to wave at the helicopter circling around me. To stand upright on top was out of the question. The only thing suspending me 6,000 feet above the ground was the ladder draped over a soft billowing pillow of air and fabric. If I were to fall off the ladder, I would tumble through the opening, into the searing interior of the balloon toward the flames of the burner. I stayed on the summit only long enough to savor one beautiful sensation of total stillness. Even though we were being propelled by a stiff wind, I felt like a drifting feather.

As I descended the other side of the balloon, my weight not only pressed into the canopy, creating a deep crease, but it pulled the top of the balloon over so that it looked like an overhanging brow. Dangling over this deformity, the ladder swung in midair, so when it came time to climb back into the basket, I found myself hanging several feet below it. Maybe I'd be using my parachute after all, I thought, as I dangled in space. The only way for me to climb into the basket was to pull up and suspend myself with one arm, then reach up a full arm's-length away to a square step cut out in the middle of the basket. Fortunately, I was able to reach this secure hold, then I made one more strenuous move to reach the top of the basket before climbing in beside the pilot.

"Okay, I'm taking us down," he shouted, adding that the fast wind had taken us over the landing zone more quickly than he had planned.

The view of the ground skating by and the helicopter circling around us was dizzying. The pilot pulled on the strings to release a blast of hot air and we started a rapid descent. The ground came up with unnerving speed. The basket hit the earth with a jolt, tipped over, and dumped us onto the ground. Ahead of us the canopy sagged, deflated, and flapped. The TV crew and my sister Trish were there to meet us on the ground. With considerable relief we toasted our "world first" with champagne.

Perhaps even more unnerving than this stunt was my guest appearance a week later in the show's Hollywood studio. Jamie Lee Curtis, the anchor of the show, introduced me to the viewers as I rappelled onto the stage in front of a live audience.

"Were you scared up there?" she asked.

During rehearsals the director had picked up on my reticence about being in front of the camera, so he made it easy for me: "Not as scared as I am right now," I replied, reading my line from a card held up in front of the stage.

Soon after, John sold another stunt to *That's Incredible!* and we found ourselves back in the air. This time the objective was to make the world's longest rappel from a helicopter. John's Angel Fall expedition had set out to establish this record a few months earlier, but a violent thunderstorm had blasted into him and Jim Bridwell, his partner in the stunt, when they were halfway down the ropes. The torrential downpour had nearly drowned the pair, but they were taken on an even more harrowing helicopter ride afterward when they were lost in the rain and fog and nearly out of gas. Luckily they spotted the lights of a landing zone and made a crash-landing onto the runway. John now figured that rather than make the world's longest rappel down a cliff, we could establish the record by dangling an even longer rope out of a helicopter. As a second aerial feat, John concocted a plan for me to zip through the air on a rope strung between the helicopter and a hot-air balloon.

Our takeoff point was a dry lake bed near Edwards Air Force Base, a place where land speed records are often attempted. On the ground we carefully laid out two immense ropes 1,800 feet in length and we attached one end of each rope to the helicopter. One rope was for me to rappel down, the other was for John. We loaded ourselves into the chopper and when it rose to 2,000 feet, we made ready to attach ourselves to the rappel devices already attached to the ropes. But the ropes were so heavy that neither of us could lift them to slide ourselves past the skids of the helicopter. We had to land and preconnect ourselves to the rope below the skids, then lift off again. This time we had it right, and John and I set off rappelling side by side. Although there was enormous friction created by the rope sliding through the rappel gadgets clipped to our harnesses, the farther we descended, the harder it was to stop the rope from racing through the metal rappel device. About 1,000 feet down, the metal rappel device had become so scorching hot that the exterior fibers of the rope began to melt. I spat on it to see how hot it really was and watched the droplet of saliva sizzle like a frying egg, then evaporate. John didn't appear to be having an easy time of it either.

"My legs have gone numb, and that ain't all that's numb either," he shouted with a grimace. The leg loops of his harness had cut the circulation off in his thighs and he was suffering a maddening bout of pins and needles. Cameras zeroed in on each of us to catch the expressions of the "record breakers" as we dangled at the ends of our ropes and the helicopter lowered us back down to earth.

Strong winds forced us to cancel the rope traverse from helicopter to balloon, but to add an exciting twist to the show, a stuntman on the set whom we had befriended, Darr Robinson, proposed that he and I go back up in the chopper and complete the act. He and I headed back up in the air dangling side by side from the ends of the rope. This time, though, when we arrived about 3,000 feet up, Darr slid down the rope and slipped off the end. After a few seconds of free fall he opened his parachute. The helicopter then lowered me down to the ground. The producers loved our act.

John and I got to know Darr better over the next few months. An established stuntman known for his wild aerial free falls, Darr was treated with respect on a film set. Darr held the world record for the highest free fall from a helicopter into an air bag—from a height of 311 feet! His new idea was for a woman to set the highest free fall world record by dropping from a helicopter 175 feet up in the air. Darr asked if I might be interested in learning the art of free falling into an air bag.

"You'd be great at it, since you have such good body awareness from gymnastics," he told me. "All you have to do is rotate over and land flat on your back."

Darr offered to teach me how to make a stunt fall in his backyard practice area. If I did well, he'd hire me as the backup woman for the filming of the stunt the following week. I would be paid $5,000 if the designated jumper chickened out. The money was impossible to resist.

From a perch 50 feet up in a tree, I looked down onto a twenty-foot-thick air bag below that Darr kept inflated with an air compressor. He'd coached me through the jump in theory; now I had to take the plunge. Poised on the edge of the platform, I swallowed the knot of adrenaline stuck in my throat and pitched forward. Lawns and swimming pools in the surrounding yards turned a circle and I landed with a painless flop. Minutes later I jumped again, landing perfectly once more. But on my third jump, I rotated too far and landed at an angle, painfully crunching my chin into my chest. As I walked away from the air bag, I felt glad I was only the backup and not the woman in the spotlight this time.

On the film set the next week the woman who was vying for the record nearly killed herself. I was introduced to her on the day the stunt took place. When I saw her waiting for her turn, holding her newborn infant in her arms, I felt very sorry for her—and for me—for having to go to such drastic measures to earn a buck. No matter how much money this stunt might pay, it wasn't worth the risk of becoming a quadriplegic. I couldn't even watch when she finally stepped out of the helicopter. As it happened, she very nearly missed the air bag. She surprised everyone by walking from the landing without injuries. Figuring out how to do innovative stunts was interesting, performing them was exciting, and the money was good, but my flirtation with Hollywood was beginning to feel demeaning.

It was at a casting audition in Hollywood when I realized I had immersed myself in a world of utter nonsense. By then, my appearances on *That's Incredible!* had gained me a talent agent who sometimes found me TV work that utilized my athletic skills. She had sent me to an audition for a soft drink commercial, telling me only that the commercial was looking for a fit young woman. But at the casting I found myself in a room full of meticulously coiffed women who looked ready to enter a beauty contest. I felt totally out of place. I knew for certain that my career as a TV extra was unlikely to blossom when a video camera was aimed at me and I was asked to pretend that I was flying through the air, riding on top of a soft drink bottle.

"Give us a big smile, stick your arms out in front of you like you're riding through the air, and yell, 'Whoopee!' at the top of your lungs," the producer told me.

I raised my arms like a sleepwalking zombie and squeaked out a half-hearted yell.

"We'll get back to you," said the casting director. He never did, and I never auditioned for another commercial.

Instead, I felt more certain than ever that I needed to finish my studies at college and build a more meaningful career. Several years later I picked up a newspaper in LA and saw that Darr had died after puncturing his spleen in a motorcycle accident.

Money from occasional stunts and my part-time job was enough to pay the bills and my college tuition, but the real cash cow for me was the Survival of the Fittest competition. I trained for it with a daily running routine at the campus track at Santa Monica College, yet I had no real idea how athletes formally train for aerobic performance. My own method was simple: I ran at a pace that I could barely maintain for forty minutes. Then one day at the track I heard a woman shout to me while I was sprinting along.

"I'm the track coach and I want to talk to you," she called.

She introduced herself as Anna Biller, a coach and a good enough athlete herself to have come in fourth place at the 1980 Olympic trials in the 400-meter hurdle event. She was curious why someone who was not on the track team would train at such an intense pace. I explained that I was preparing for the Survival of the Fittest contest, and that as a climber I was accustomed to pushing myself.

"I can help you train for that competition if you join the track team. We train every afternoon. If you're interested, meet us here tomorrow at three."

There was a charisma to Anna that made her invitation impossible to resist. When I joined her team the next day, we began a close friendship that has continued for nearly twenty years.

As a coach, Anna analyzed every element of the run. She focused on subtle nuances like the way we planted our feet on the ground, or the art of driving our arms forward with a precise tempo to add force to our pace. By concentrating on these motions, I found that my mind was distracted from the fatigue of running. Monday afternoons—the toughest day of her workouts—consisted of ten intervals of a quarter mile done at maximum intensity. Anna stood on the side of the track with a stopwatch in hand, shouting out our times as we ran by. Week after week, I felt my aerobic capacity improve. Coincidentally, one of my classmates was Hans Messner, the younger brother of the world-famous mountaineer Reinhold Messner, who had climbed Everest without oxygen. Like Reinhold, Hans had the right genes for incredible lung capacity. Whenever my legs felt like rubber and my lungs burned, Hans was there right with me, urging me on, just as Anna urged us on.

Whether Anna was aware of it or not, her track team sometimes doubled as a halfway house for students whose direction in life was faltering. One day while I was sitting beside the track lacing up my training shoes, Anna introduced me to Karen, a new member of the team. Karen would prove to be a talented runner who also pushed hard in our workouts, but I soon learned she had a checkered background. Transferred to Santa Monica by another college where she was failing, Karen had been a teenage runaway and a victim of sexual abuse. She had fled her East Coast hometown and had roamed the streets of LA until a Catholic priest in Venice had discovered her sleeping in his church. He'd found her a foster family and had helped her get back into college, but a short temper and a history of flunking out had caused Karen to drift from school to school. Santa Monica College was the end of the road for her, and with her poor grades Anna had had to fight hard to get Karen on her track team. Running proved to be a way for Karen to find a focus for her energy, yet she could be volatile. Angered by something Anna once said during practice, Karen hurled of pair of spiked running shoes at her. Even so, the two of us became friends. I understood Karen's troubled side much the same way I understood my good friend Yabo.

Since my return to LA I had rekindled my friendship with Yabo. Almost a year had passed since we had climbed together, and in that time I missed the way we brought out the best of each other's skills and passion on the cliffs. Even two decades and thousands of climbs later, I still consider some of my climbs with Yabo to be the most inspired ascents of my early days in Yosemite. Yet I did not miss the obsessive nature of his attraction to me.

When I met Yabo, I was eighteen and he was twenty-two. I was just beginning to discover many things about life, and climbing was the most powerful experience I knew. Yabo and I developed a strong bond through our shared passion for free climbing. Our purist approach to climbing reflected our attitudes toward life: we cherished being simple, direct, and natural. We both believed that the current trends of popular culture such as wearing fashionable clothes, driving around in fancy cars, chasing money, and other material pursuits were spiritless diversions from our true path: the pursuit of the perfect free climb. Our holy grail was a climb on which we gave our personal best in the most "pure" style we could manage—if possible, on a route that had never been climbed before. In those days—the early eighties—"pure" style meant that we begin a route at the bottom of a cliff and climbed to the top without hanging on the rope or equipment to bypass hard moves. The idea was to figure out how to free climb every move without falling while placing "natural" protection in the rock along the way. Instead of placing protection bolts or pitons, which permanently scar the rock, we used removable stoppers, which slip in and out of cracks. (In those days we didn't have spring-loaded camming devices.) Yabo and I set out on these routes with just a meager collection of my gear, plus whatever Yabo had managed to either find or borrow from friends. Our objective was to push ourselves the farthest without falling or using the help of our equipment to ascend. The goal was to enter the unknown and embrace it, to free climb every move without altering the rock. If that meant you came to a blank section and had to climb 50 feet without protection, then that was the pact you made with the rock. These ideals were our golden rules. They gave our efforts meaning.

I understood the "noble savage" in Yabo's character that drove him to push to try his absolute best. In this regard, Yabo and I found kindred spirits in one another and we formed a strong team, doing many routes that pushed us to our limits. Although since then I've made huge leaps in ability using modern sport climbing techniques and equipment

Yabo demonstrating his tenacity in Joshua Tree while Mari Gingery, Chris Wagner, and Charles Cole look on. (DEAN FIDELMAN)

(such as bolts), this approach of doing "the most with the least" is still the virtue that I hold in highest regard.

Although I had faith in Yabo's ability, I began to seriously question his judgment after a harrowing experience on the first ascent of a route called the Scariest of Them All. This ten-pitch route on Fairview Dome located in the granite highlands above Yosemite will not be found in any guidebook. We never bothered to report this climb because after we completed it, we realized that it was unlikely that anyone would even think about repeating it. Should someone stumble across it and do it in the same "pure" style as we had, and survive it, then they could call it their own if they wished. We left no trace of our passage on that blank, unprotected face.

The climb began inauspiciously one summer in 1979. Yabo and I had been climbing together every day for over a month. Yabo had been following me around everywhere and he even slept right next to me in the rescue site in Camp Four. The weather was getting hot in the valley, so Yabo suggested we go climbing in Tuolumne Meadows, where the weather was substantially cooler. Since Fairview Dome is the tallest, most shapely of the smooth granite domes of Tuolumne Meadows, we headed directly there. We hiked across a wildflower-covered meadow toward this 1,000-foot slab to set up camp for the night. As we walked, Yabo began talking about doing a new route on a face that he had had his eye on for a long time. His excitement over the idea of this new route quickly transformed into another mood, though, as his talk turned to the issue of his affection for me. This is when I saw Yabo seriously lose control the first time.

"Goddamn it, Lynn," he shouted, hyperventilating with anger, "I can't stand this anymore. I love you and if I can't have you I'm gonna solo up this cliff and jump off."

"Don't be ridiculous!" I said, not wanting to believe in the seriousness of this threat. "Let's go climbing instead. Let's do this new route you have in mind."

This jarred him back to reality. Instead of a death-defying display of soloing—which I knew to be, in reality, a ploy of emotional blackmail—Yabo would have me tied directly to him on the other end of the rope. But was doing a new route on this blank, 1,000-foot cliff with a madman a sensible act? Adding to the sense of danger confronting us was our lack of a bolt kit. If we climbed ourselves into a dead end up on that sea of shining rock, we would have no way to drill an emergency anchor and make an escape route back down. But Tuolumne was Yabo's home turf and I trusted that underneath his impulsiveness he knew what he was doing. Yabo's commitment to free climbing was so convincing, he sometimes appeared to have a mystical quality. As he slung our minimalist rack of gear over his shoulder, I felt a sense of blind faith. In reality, though, I had no idea what I was getting into.

Yabo began leading the first pitch up a steep shield of rock so smoothly polished by an ancient glacier that it shone like a mirror. Standing on a small ledge 100 feet off the ground, he belayed me up. Then it was my turn to lead. Above me rose a shallow left-facing dihedral leading to a blank, burnished face above. No climber had ever set foot on it. I climbed over to the base of the small dihedral, placed a small hexagon-shaped metal wedge in the crack, clipped the rope into that, then continued up for 15 more feet until the crack ended at a smooth, nearly featureless face. I had no idea where this vague path up the rock would take me, but I knew that the next 20 feet would be very difficult.

"Yabo, watch me. This looks very hard and insecure. If I fall from here, I'll hit that ledge sixty feet below me."

"I'm watching you. Go for it, you won't fall," Yabo shouted convincingly.

I believed him. Balancing upward, I entered an irreversible sequence of delicate moves. The only holds were tiny crystals so insubstantial that I could barely feel them with my fingers or feet. Soon my last piece of protection lay 30 feet below me and there were no cracks in sight in which to place another nut. With each move higher, the consequences of falling became more serious. I remained focused on maintaining perfect body position, and controlling the exact angle of my foot placements and weight transfers. One false move here would most likely be painful, if not fatal. I had willingly climbed myself into this situation, now I had no choice but to climb myself out of it.

After 10 more feet of climbing, I arrived at a small ledge and let out a sigh of relief that the ordeal was over. I slotted a single small nut into a crack, secured the rope, then called out, "Off belay." I pulled in the rope as Yabo climbed up to me.

"Good lead, that was really hard," Yabo said simply when he reached me. I had no idea what level of difficulty I had just climbed, though I knew it was extremely hard, with death-fall potential. The concentration had been so intense that I had felt my whole being absorbed in the experience. Yabo looked at me with eyes that seemed to say, *See what you can do if you go for it?* Then he set off on the next pitch. As I held the rope for him, I gazed over rolling granite domes and distant thunderclouds rising into the High Sierra sky. The blues, the greens, the rock tones, all seemed to shine more brightly in that moment.

The rope ran out foot after foot as Yabo climbed into the blank territory above us. Sometimes he'd pause as if baffled at the lack of holds, but then he would make a few rapid puffs to oxygenate his blood and push on deeper into this risky game. He seemed to will the rock into submission. At times his legs shook, at other times he teetered on the brink of falling before slapping his hand up to catch a higher hold. By the time he was 50 feet out, I realized that if he fell, he would rip out the nut that anchored us to the cliff and we'd fall 200 feet. But never did I doubt that he would climb up and place another piece of protection or find a tiny ledge to stop at before coming to the end of the rope.

We passed the rest of the day like this, and when we reached the top of Fairview Dome, we were in a state of adrenaline overload. We had just done something dangerous and brilliant. We had not compromised the rock with bolts or pitons. It would not have been possible without total belief in our own, and in each other's, abilities.

We were on a high, and not long after that climb we found ourselves climbing the 1,500-foot-long Chouinard/Herbert route on Sentinel Rock, which sits high above Yosemite Valley. We were partway up the climb and about 2,000 feet from the grassy floor of the valley when I passed our shoulder sling full of gear to Yabo. In a cavalier moment, Yabo threw it up in the air with the intention of passing his arm through the sling when it was in midflight. But he missed, and the gear clattered hundreds of feet down the cliff to the ground.

"Good one, Yabo, now what?" I asked in utter disbelief.

Dropping one's rack is perhaps the most costly mistake a climber can make, but we were lucky. Above us were two more climbers. They gave us three carabiners, which we used to rappel several pitches back to the ground. At the base we retrieved our scratched and dented gear, then we sat on a rock in the sun.

I figured our day of climbing was over. It was three-thirty P.M., too late to do anything else.

Then Yabo suddenly said, "Let's go for the summit. We can do it. If we climb simultaneously, we'll make it to the top before dark. We'll have to be fast, but we can do it."

The idea of climbing up this entire wall in one fast motion was a temptation I couldn't resist.

"Okay, let's go."

Yabo took the lead and I followed. Instead of leading the route pitch by pitch while the other person belayed, we climbed continuously for hundreds of feet with the rope strung between us. Should one of us fall, the only thing that might stop us from hitting the ground were the meager pieces of protection Yabo placed along the way. Yabo was raging with the intensity of the moment, racing the lowering sun, and he placed very little protection. I didn't dare fall. After a few hours, we arrived at the top with just enough evening light to find the trail down to the valley. Again, as on Fairview Dome, we buzzed with the feeling of flaunting danger. But although climbing with Yabo was exhilarating, I was beginning to wonder how many adventures like this we could pull off before one of us got hurt. With Yabo's frequent, if theatrical, suicide threats, I began to wonder if the risky climbs we did together were a subconscious attempt on his part to lure me into a situation in which one of us would be killed. After that summer of '79, I decided to make a concerted effort to back away from Yabo.

The next time I saw Yabo was about a year later, at the house of Dean Fidelman, my friend from our ascent of the Nose. Yabo, of no fixed abode in those days, was boarding on Dean's couch when he wasn't climbing in J-Tree or Yosemite. As soon as I saw Yabo there that night, I knew I was in for some trouble. Sure enough, as soon as Dean went to bed, Yabo started backing me into an emotional corner.

"Lynn, do you know I can't stop thinking about you? I love you. We're soul mates. I know we could be perfect together," he said in an all-too-familiar tone. Nothing I said could penetrate his convictions.

"But Yabo, we've been through this before. You know I'm in love with John. You and I are just good friends. That's just the way it is."

His mood darkened the more I tried to reason with him.

"If we can't be together, I'm gonna commit suicide."

"Come on, Yabo. Don't do this again," I said, as Yabo began banging his head very hard and deliberately against the wall.

"Yabo, stop it!" I yelled, shocked and appalled.

"You don't think I can kill myself?" he sniggered. His eyes grew large. He looked suddenly possessed. Then he clenched his fist and punched himself in the eye. When he looked up, I saw he had surely given himself a black eye. I gaped in utter astonishment at what was happening. On one hand I felt a torrent of pity for my mixed-up friend, on the other I was afraid of what he might do.

"Dean, get in here, Yabo's going crazy," I yelled.

It was past midnight and Dean was in bed sleeping. He entered the room, rubbing his eyes. Dean knew of Yabo's obssession with me, but he also had an understanding and tolerance of Yabo that few could match. Perhaps they shared some elements of a difficult childhood, or perhaps Dean just had a kindness and insight into his friend's troubles. He sat Yabo on the floor. Cross-legged, they faced each other. Yabo was panting in rapid bursts, and his eyes welled with tears of frustration at knowing he could never have what he proclaimed to want most out of life: me.

"Calm down, Yabo, take a chill pill," Dean said sternly but compassionately. His voice had a soothing quality. Slowly, Yabo eased off a bit.

"I'm sleeping in Dean's room. You can sleep on the couch," I said.

Yabo nodded. We retired to our separate beds. Dean and I had shared enough nights on the sides of cliffs to be unperturbed by an emergency bivouac under such circumstances. But at three in the morning Yabo crept into Dean's room and curled up next to me.

"Oh, Jesus, Yabo," Dean said in exasperation, as he looked at Yabo snuggled like a puppy beside me, quietly sleeping. In Dean's bohemian outlook, this was just another day in the life of two crazy climbing buddies.

This was my first encounter with the self-abusive side of Yabo, yet it was not the last. A few weeks later we found ourselves together in Joshua Tree. I was leery of Yabo's intentions and uneasy about the effect my presence seemed to have on him. I felt comforted by a large group of friends, but this social atmosphere only seemed to drive Yabo further over the edge. By the end of the weekend he had transformed his frustrations over me into a binge of free soloing that to this day is talked about around campfires throughout the climbing community. He began the day with unroped ascents of several hard 5.10 routes like Right Ski Track and Bearded Cabbage, then he worked his way up to an overhanging 50-foot 5.12 called Leave It to Beaver. This route he climbed without a rope not just once, but twice in a row. The legend of that ascent describes a manic Yabo flinging himself at the rock, and nearly falling off 60 feet above the ground. Apparently he was so pumped that the fingers of one hand slipped off at the precise moment that the fingers of his other hand caught the tiny hold he had been hanging from. The entire spectacle was intended to impress or to horrify me, and it did, along with all his other friends, who begged him to stop his soloing frenzy before he smashed himself to pieces on the boulders below. As I headed back to the campground at the end of the day, Yabo walked by and announced that he was going to free solo another difficult climb called Hidden Valley Shakedown. Since he would be alone, I felt obliged to be there in case he fell. It was agonizing to watch his body tremor with fatigue as he climbed unroped, 40 feet above several jagged boulders.

By this stage Yabo was using soloing as a weapon. He flaunted it the way a potential suicide waves a gun around. It was a way for him to purge the angst inside himself, as well as to demand attention from his friends and me. Cultivating risk was a part of the Bushido-like code that Yabo lived by. Everyone who climbed with Yabo has a tale of how he could turn a peaceful day of climbing into a dangerous test. Greg Child related a tale to me about doing a one-pitch route in Yosemite with Yabo. When they tossed a coin to decide who would lead, Yabo lost and followed the pitch, safely belayed by Greg to a foot ledge 100 feet above the ground. When it came time to rappel off, Yabo gripped the rope in his palms and lowered himself down, hand over hand, rather than safely descending the cliff using his rappel device.

"Why did you do that? You could have fallen and killed yourself," Greg had asked when he'd joined Yabo on the ground.

"I had to make up for not leading this pitch," Yabo answered.

Every moment had to be extreme for Yabo. In the face of his antics, I vacillated between being afraid for him and afraid for myself.

The Sunday evening after his back-to-back solos of Leave It to Beaver, Yabo begged me to give him a ride to LA. Pleasant small talk filled the space between us as we drove to Yabo's destination, but when we got there he refused to get out of my car. Yabo was incorrigible and he just sat beside me, with the same brooding expression that I'd seen so many times before. He reminded me then of a rapidly building thunderhead, getting blacker and blacker till it explodes into a tornado.

"If don't get out of my car, I'll take you to the police station. I don't have time to deal with your craziness today."

This didn't move him either, so I wheeled the car around and drove onto the highway. I explained that it wasn't fair of him to use emotional blackmail tactics on me, but my words failed to reach him. As we sped along the freeway at sixty miles per hour, Yabo began opening the car door and threatening to jump out. Shouting at him to snap out of this madness, I exited the highway and headed for the Fullerton Police Department. I parked the car, and just as I opened the front door of the police station, I saw Yabo walking briskly down the street, then he ran away.

"Can I help you, miss?" a police officer asked when he saw me pausing on his threshold.

"No. Everything is all right," I replied.

"Are you sure?" the officer asked, unconvinced.

"I hope so. My friend is very upset and he just ran off. You might want to look out for him."

I found out later that after Yabo jumped out of my car, he began running out into traffic trying to kill himself until he was finally picked up by the police. After being held in a mental hospital for twenty-four hours, he was released and he returned to Dean's house.

Such behavior begs a question: Why did Yabo become so fixated on me?

Though Yabo had several male friends in the climbing scene, he had few female friends. A quirky character like John Yablonsky was at a disadvantage in finding a girlfriend. When Yabo and I established our platonic yet sincere connection, it was a new experience for him. Few people had ever taken him or his values seriously before, let alone a woman. This is why Yabo saw me as his soul mate.

Yabo had appeared on the climbing scene a few years before me. When he first arrived in Yosemite, in about 1973 at age sixteen, he was so timid, so bedraggled and socially awkward, that the climbers he attempted to befriend shunned him. Yabo stuttered. Yabo was unwashed. Yabo wore his greasy hair so low over his forehead that no one could see his eyes. Yabo was strange. At first, admitted John Bachar, who would eventually become one of his best friends, everyone would run away from Yabo as they headed out for a day of climbing, leaving him alone in the woods. But on the rocks he proved himself to be a natural, and gradually he was accepted into the cliques of climbing.

But perhaps abandonment is the key to understanding the demons that drove Yabo. He was born in Los Gatos, California, and his mother had deserted the household when he was about five years old. Yabo's knowledge of his mother was nearly nonexistent. By all accounts she was an unstable woman whose surviving family members suspect she had a drug or alcohol problem. She had allegedly carted Yabo around California in a transient lifestyle before handing him over to his father, Sam, and then disappearing forever. It seems that the primal wound of losing his mother never healed in Yabo. His hyperactivity and his unruly temper as a child (he punched a hole in a wall of the house in his teens) made him a handful for his teachers and for Sam. Regarding Yabo's father, a man of Russian-Jewish origins who ran the Los Gatos movie theater and who died in 1999, the facts are unclear. Yabo spoke of a man capable of such anger that he once chased him into the yard and hurled a shovel at him that clanged against the fence just as Yabo was making his escape over it. Even more troubling, he talked of his father repeatedly rubbing in the fact that his mother had left Yabo because she did not love him. Yet, according to Yabo's younger half-sister Eva, it was Sam who enrolled Yabo in a climbing class in 1968, and it was Sam who drove to Yosemite to persuade Yabo to come back to attend his graduation at Los Gatos High. Her portrait of her father is of a stern but caring man, giving enough to be a regular babysitter for other families in town.

Yabo's problems were many. To those who knew him, his pain was undiluted. A deep, depressive sense of hopelessness pervaded his self-image. Some who knew him well say he was plagued by his inability to live a normal life and hold down a job that would make his father proud. He often borrowed money from Sam. And though his stepmother was a model mother to him, Yabo still suffered from never knowing what became of his birth mother, or why she gave up on him.

Though Yabo used the home in Los Gatos as a base after he quit high school at age sixteen, he spent most of his time on a Kerouakian road trip punctuated by climbing. During these years he never had much money or employment. He hitchhiked the highways, visited climbing areas, flirted with drugs, and smoked cigarettes whenever he could scrounge them. Only climbing grounded him to something tangible, and for this he frequented his local crag, Castle Rock. On the sandstone boulders he developed massive strength and endurance. Of his young days climbing there, Yabo once said, "I was a really unhappy kid . . . climbing was a way for me to exert my energy in a positive manner. It was also a way for me to find the strength within myself to deal with all the problems in my life."

Balancing Yabo's advances against my ongoing relationship with John was always a challenge, but when I met Karen on the track team I realized that I'd found the perfect woman for Yabo. When I introduced them, they hit it off immediately, and within a short time they were living together. It was a relief to see Yabo with a woman and happy, though in order to be with Karen as much as possible—since she was now the object of his obsession—he sometimes hung around with our track team. I recall Yabo piling into a college van with the all-women's team to attend a track meet. It was touching to see Yabo singing along with all the girls to a pop song on the radio. I had never seen him so natural, so happy. At least for a while after that, Yabo faded from my life.

The relationship between Anna and me had, by the end of the track season, grown beyond the roles of athlete and coach. Our hard training throughout the season had paid off. I had performed my best ever in both the 1,500- and 3,000-meter track events at the California State Track and Field meet, and against all odds our team miraculously won the state championships. By spring of 1983, I had been offered partial scholarships at three different universities in the LA area. One of these was the University of Southern California, which offered a master's program in physical therapy. Though I was interested in continuing my education in physical therapy, the tuition alone was more than I could afford, even with a partial scholarship. The extra time required for training and track meets meant that I would not have the time or energy to work and study. Over the past four years while John was launching his writing career, I had worked hard to support us both while going to school, studying, and running. I was so busy that my beloved weekend climbing trips became less frequent. I missed the freedom of going rock climbing, yet I felt the necessity of working toward what I thought would be my future career.

As for John, he was working at his writing, but he wasn't able to make a living from it yet. In his writing John told stories that were a mixture of fact and fiction, and they brought out his naturally comical side. His tales captured people's attention because they were entertaining and extravagant, but sometimes this bigger-than-life influence of Hollywood jarred with my more literal approach to life. At the age of twenty-two, I didn't know much about intimate relationships, but I could feel our lives drifting apart.

A series of events in the summer of 1983 shaped the final chapter in our lives as a couple. As so often in the past, it was a phone call that started the changes, this time from the writer David Roberts, who called from the East Coast to propose interviewing me for a new outdoor magazine. He'd seen a photograph of me climbing in a Patagonia catalog. In the photo I was grinning, a playful expression on my face, while dangling one-armed from a difficult crack called Insomnia at California's Suicide Rocks.

The photo had caught David's attention and he sold the idea of doing a story about me—a young female climber with a reputation for winning the Survival of the Fittest competition and for getting up hard routes. The chance to be written about was flattering, but I was even more enticed by the free airline ticket to New York, which lay a two hours' drive from the Shawangunks, a complex of quartzite cliffs near New Paltz and a place I had heard so much about. These rocks were as vital to American climbing history as Yosemite Valley, and the chance to visit them was a welcome break from school, work, and track events.

At the same time, John was preparing to go to Borneo for a three-month overland traverse through the jungle. Ironically, the photographer who'd shot me on Insomnia Crack, Rick Ridgeway, was the mastermind behind John's Borneo trip. Rick had sold the Borneo adventure to RJ Reynolds, the maker of Camel cigarettes, and after meeting John on the weekend of the photo shoot Rick had pegged John as the perfect man for the job.

At that point, John and I were at a crossroads. His career as a professional adventurer and writer was about to come of age, while I was focused on finishing my college education. Change was in the air, and while John was packing for Borneo and I was packing for New York, I found the courage to confront my feelings with him.

"I'm no longer happy in this relationship. I think it would be best if you found a place of your own when you get back from Borneo."

My soul ached as I said these words, and I was disappointed in myself that I could not explain more fully to John what had changed between us. I thought of my parents' divorce, and the way I had found it hard to communicate my feelings then too. I had a lot to learn about confronting difficult emotional issues, but I knew that moving on would allow both of us to grow.

He looked at me as if he'd been expecting this moment for a long time. In the moments of silence between us, I think we both saw the four years of our lives together flash through our thoughts.

"Just promise me you'll always be my friend," he said.

"Of course I will," I uttered with tears streaming down my face. We stood in the hallway and held each other for a long time.

True to our promise, John and I see each other whenever I pass through Santa Monica. He is married to Mariana, a Venezuelan schoolteacher, and they have two daughters. Shuttling between dual homes in Venice Beach and Venezuela, John works as a writer. His books have sold nearly a million copies.

Chapter 10

Heading East

Manhattan throbbed with people and traffic. From the window of my Midtown hotel I stared out at a man-made canyon of steel and brick, thinking about John, who was by now somewhere in the jungles of Borneo. He felt far away, and not just geographically. For the moment, I couldn't quite imagine what my life would be like without him. But the anonymity of the crowded street below seemed strangely inviting, and I realized that this opportunity to discover a whole new climbing area and culture couldn't have come at a better time. A call from David Roberts down in the hotel lobby snapped me out of these thoughts. He had come to interview me for *Ultrasport* magazine, but instead of sitting down with a tape recorder and a notepad, David insisted that we have lunch and just talk.

"I'll take you to the Algonquin Hotel. That's the restaurant where

James Thurber and other *New Yorker* writers held their famous round table discussions," David said as we entered the street.

"Who is James Thurber?" I asked.

"You don't know?" David said with a note of surprise as we slid into a taxi. David was a mountaineer and Harvard graduate who had become immersed in literature. I remembered seeing his book *The Mountain of My Fear* on Chuck's bookshelf. It was the story of the tragic first ascent of the west face of Alaska's Mount Huntington, during which David, one of four climbers on the expedition, had lost a close friend. I listened with fascination while David explained the New York writing scene to me, and I noted with embarrassment that another bit of common cultural knowledge had eluded me. It confirmed my suspicion that I spent so much time climbing and training that I missed many other aspects of the world around me. But here I was, in New York because people had noticed my climbing accomplishments, and I was grateful for the opportunity to expand my experiences.

In David I found a fine interviewer because he understood that a rock climber is most at ease on the rock, not at a literary luncheon. The next day, we left New York and headed for the Shawangunks, where he planned to interview me while I climbed with some of the local experts. As we neared New Paltz, the town closest to the Gunks (the abbreviated name climbers give to this area), I was astonished to see that there were farms and forests a relatively short drive from the densely populated city. At the cliff, David introduced me to Rich Goldstone, who would take photographs of me, and to Russ Raffa, with whom I would climb.

"Rich used to be a gymnast," Dave explained. "In the 1970s he put up some hard routes here. And Russ is one of the best climbers in the Gunks right now."

I was immediately struck by Russ's piercing brown eyes. He had the good looks of a model and an athletic build. As we went from climb to climb on my tour, I felt comfortable around him. His self-confidence— an endearing cockiness, really—and his sharp wit kept me laughing all day. He told me that he had recently quit his job at a real estate investment company in New Jersey and had moved to New Paltz to find more balance in his life between climbing and work. In New Paltz he lived a short drive from the Gunks, which he regarded as having some of the best rock climbing in the world.

When I laid hands on our first route, called Cascading Crystal Kaleidoscope, I found myself in agreement. Oxides and lichens had painted the cliff with a riot of reds, greens, and yellows; sharp edges perfectly shaped for the fingers peppered the walls; and tiers of roofs jutted out over our heads. Out West, I had been raised on a diet of granite, but here, on the quartz conglomerate of the Gunks, I discovered that a different texture of rock could offer me an entirely new world of climbing.

The Gunks had their geologic origins four hundred million years ago when ancient sands had been buried, squeezed, and heated into a layer of glasslike quartzite. After the quartzite had emerged from under the earth, erosion and weathering had shaped the outcrops into forms with layers of horizontal cracks and ledges that climbers found perfect for swarming over. And, I learned that first day, the tiny cracks and splits

Making the first free ascent of Tweazle Roof (5.12d) in the Gunks.
(MARK ROBINSON)

in the rock were ideal for placing a wide variety of nuts, Friends, and other types of removable—or "natural"—protection devices. It was a traditional climber's paradise.

For our next climb Russ suggested another 5.10 called Matinee, known to locals as being tricky to protect as well as technically challenging. As I sailed up it, I noticed that a small crowd of climbers had gathered below to watch the girl from California. After Matinee, Russ said, "You haven't fallen on a climb yet. Perhaps you should try something a little more challenging." Clearly, I was being tested. It is something of a ritual that visiting climbers are toured from climb to climb until a route is found that utterly humbles them. Climbers even have a special word, "sandbagging," which refers to this custom of consciously setting others up on climbs that are known to be difficult, scary, or both.

"Ah, I know a route that will be a challenge for you," he said with an ironic edge to his voice.

Foops had been climbed by a physics professor named John Stannard in 1967, and had a rating of 5.11c. It was a roof as horizontal and as smooth as the ceiling of a living room. When I arrived underneath this looming overhang, clinging to the thin seam that snaked along its underside, I found that I was too short to reach the good hold at the roof's lip. I spent the next two hours going up and down trying to figure out a sequence of moves that would get me to the lip. By the time I made it through this section, I was physically thrashed. Climbing in the Gunks, I was learning, was as difficult as it was exhilarating. Russ seemed pleased that I had succeeded on Foops, but gratified that I had found it hard.

At the end of the day our group joined a gathering of local climbers at the Uberfall, an open space beside the cliff that is surrounded by oaks, maples, and dogwoods. A Saturday evening wine-tasting party had become something of a ritual. Bottles that had spent the day chilling in a natural spring nearby were decanted into plastic cups, while the crowd mingled and discussed the affairs of the world and engaged in bawdy humor. A university professor dressed in wildly patterned polyester pants, Maurie Jaffe, told me he had brought the wine.

"This fine bottle of wine meets our price limit of less than two bucks a bottle," he boasted.

With climbing friends in the Gunks; (left to right) me, Barbara Bein, Kevin Bein, Gary Garrett, Mark Robinson, and Russ Raffa. (MARK ROBINSON COLLECTION)

"This one's decent, Maurie," offered his friend Peter. He held his plastic cup up to the light, gargled a mouthful of budget cabernet, then said, "It has the smoky, subtle undertone of a sulfur plant."

I met other climbers that evening who would, in the coming years, become lasting friends. Among them was Russ Clune, a globe-trotting climber who would visit nearly every rock-climbing destination on the planet; Laura Chaiten, a New Jerseyite with a rollicking sense of humor who was Russ's former girlfriend; Elliot or "Elrod" Williams, one of Russ's best friends and the person with whom he started climbing; and Barbara and Kevin Bein, an inseparable pair of Ivy League graduates who pursued a life of climbing and traveling. Kevin had been dubbed "mayor of the Gunks," due to his perpetual presence at the cliff and to his intimate knowledge of the climbs. Barbara had a Twiggy-like build, yet she climbed nearly as hard as her muscle-bound husband. I remember their house in New Paltz as being littered with dumbbells and free weights and smelling strongly of garlic from the DMSO horse liniment that Kevin rubbed into his ever-aching and overtrained elbow tendons.

After that first day in the Gunks, the wine leaving us a little tipsy, we slung our backpacks over our shoulders and headed down the trail to the car. As we walked, David pointed out a couple of routes that Fritz Weissner had pioneered in the 1930s, when he and his buddies first discovered the great climbing potential in the Gunks.

"Who is Fritz Weissner?" I asked.

"You don't know who Fritz Weissner is? He's one of the most famous mountaineers in the world! He climbed routes here, using hemp ropes and soft iron pitons, that are still considered tough today. He made the first ascent of Devil's Tower in Wyoming and he nearly made it to the summit of K2 back in 1939!" David's words tumbled out of his mouth as he tried to educate me. Several times that day, his eyes had gone wide when I had shown my naïveté about climbing history. When I later learned more about the legendary Fritz Weissner, I realized that not knowing about him had been a glaring omission, but tonight I was impatient with my teacher. Perhaps it was the wine.

"Dave, I'm tired of you criticizing me for my lack of knowledge. I didn't learn about climbing from a book. I learned about it by doing it!" I blurted out.

David raised his eyebrows and smiled, probably figuring he had just gotten the perfect *bon mot* he needed for his story. As for Russ, years later he would tell me that when he heard my quip to David that day, he knew he was starting to fall in love with me.

Life moved quickly for me after that. Within a month I had piled all my belongings into my VW van and had driven across the country to New Paltz. I enrolled at the State University of New York at New Paltz, where I would finish my bachelor's degree in biology. And Russ and I were inevitably drawn together from that first day onward, beginning a relationship that would challenge us as people and as climbers.

Russ grew up in a suburb of New York City where everything moves fast: fast food, fast deals, and fast talking. At Northeastern University in Boston he studied Islamic civilization and Sufism. Realizing that employment opportunities in his field were limited, he accepted a job working in real estate after graduation. Russ discovered climbing at the relatively late age of twenty, but he quickly became obsessed with the mental and physical nature of rock climbing and moved to the Gunks so that he could spend every free moment on the cliffs.

There were many aspects of Russ that I admired. Where I would avoid conflict whenever possible, he had chutzpah to spare. I found his direct and audacious nature both lovable and maddening. Some days we seemed to be perfect complements to one another, other times our basic outlooks on life seemed to be diametrically opposed. As a salesman Russ always worked toward "closing the deal," and sometimes this assertive manner clashed with my accommodating tendencies. Yet I naturally began to rely on Russ to be my protector, as it was he who dealt with situations or people I felt uncomfortable with. Perhaps I deferred to his greater experience of the world, as he was over eight years my senior.

By 1984 he had become my constant companion, although at first our relationship was rocky; I moved into, then out of, then back into his home before we made up our minds. Yet when we were together we were happy simply sharing life's basic pleasures, from running the old carriage roads around the Gunks with our Akita dog, Apollo, to breakfasting on bagels and coffee over the *New York Times* in the mornings. Russ had a humorous take on the human condition, and he could be as stubborn as me. Yet I felt greater empathy from him than from any man I had, to that point, ever known. Trying to understand each other, we often explored each other's past and how it related to our behavior. I felt that Russ's assertive nature was primarily due to growing up in an urban environment and culture, where time is always at a premium. We concluded that my family environment had shaped my ways. As a child I had learned to be self-reliant and was content to entertain myself instead of competing for my parents' attention with so many siblings around me. When my parents divorced, I had immersed myself in another world—a world in which climbing ultimately became my defining sense of reality. Russ and I both understood, however, that though I might suffer from tunnel vision in some facets of life, when it came to climbing, it was precisely that ability to focus single-mindedly that enabled me to climb fiercely hard routes.

**Russ Raffa on
The Pit and the
Pendulum (5.11).**
(SANDY STEWART)

My climbing took a turn in a new direction during those years in New Paltz. Having learned to climb on the granite formations of the West, I had little experience climbing routes that required placing protection in small, horizontal cracks or using double ropes to avoid rope drag on climbs that followed a zigzag itinerary past large overhangs. Climbing with Russ, I learned a lot about the technical aspects of placing protection, but what inspired me most was his mental ability to push his limits on difficult, poorly protected routes. One of his most impressive performances occurred on a climb called To Be or Not To Be, where he demonstrated the mental control necessary to make hard, bold leads. I had already experienced boldness with Yabo, but climbing with him had been a schizophrenic experience. Russ, by contrast, climbed with a cool head and a calculating mind.

To Be or Not To Be had become a war of attrition for the Russes Raffa and Clune. It was one of those poorly protected routes on which a fall could result in disaster, so they would try it only when they felt they had the nerve. But rather than place a bolt to bolster their confidence, they were willing to try the route again and again until the day when they got the gumption to climb onto the dangerously unprotected face that regularly stopped them. And besides, in the Gunks there was a strict rule: no bolts. If you couldn't protect a route with removable gear, you were left with the choice of either climbing it solo, with minimal protection, or top roping it. But top roping a new route, by anchoring the rope from above, was considered cheating.

They had already made several attempts to climb this route on prior occasions, when one day I went with them and they offered me the first shot at leading it. I climbed up about 20 feet before I could place a few small wired nuts in a crack, then I carefully negotiated my way past a difficult section of face climbing. Thirty-five feet up I reached a horizontal crack, where I placed a camming device called a Friend, which was my first and last secure piece of protection for another 20 feet or so. Above that, the moves became increasingly difficult as the holds were less abundant. I climbed a few feet above the Friend and reached the point where the boys had retreated on earlier attempts. I looked at the upcoming sequence of moves, then back toward my last piece of protection way below my feet. My arms were pumped. A fall would be bad from above. I thought, *If it doesn't feel right, don't go,* so I carefully climbed back down to my last piece of protection.

"Lower me," I called, deciding it was too dangerous to continue up.

Clune went up next. He climbed a few feet past the Friend, then he too hesitated.

"Take! I don't want to go for it. I'm coming down."

In typical Raffa style, Russ prodded Clune by saying, "Why don't you take a short fall onto the Friend to test the system?" His idea was that this would show us how safe the protection was. However, there was a risk: Clune was so high above this last piece of protection that he might come close to hitting the ground. But Clune had a daring streak that ran deeper than that found in most climbers, so he gritted his teeth and jumped off. The Friend held his fall and the rope stopped him just five feet above the ground. This meant that a fall from only a few feet higher would result in a ground fall. Clune's bold jump was a significant contribution to what happened next.

"The gear looks good to go. Now it's your turn," Clune said to Russ with a sarcastic grin.

Russ was familiar with the bottom section of the climb and when he arrived at the point where Clune had jumped, he seemed focused and determined. In the days leading up to this moment he had been climbing at his best. He moved at a controlled pace into the crux, then he assessed the holds by climbing up and down into the hard section a couple of times.

"Okay, here goes," he finally said.

He climbed onto the virgin face with calm and confidence. My heart raced in my chest and my palms sweated as he led up and out from his protection. The key section took him just a couple of minutes to climb once he committed himself to it, but weeks of mental preparation formed the backbone of his ascent. At the top of the pitch he let out a scream of victory. Russ has always regarded this route as one of his best. Maybe it was not the hardest thing he had climbed physically, but mentally it was a bold leap into the unknown. One mistake and he might have been lying broken at my feet.

A few months later I peered over the edge of oblivion on another first ascent, named Yellow Crack Direct. This climb started up an existing 5.11 route named Yellow Crack that had been first free climbed by Henry Barber. "Hot Henry" was one of the most prolific American free climbers during the seventies, having done first ascents all over the world, from the eastern United States to Yosemite, Colorado, East Germany, England, and Australia. As was characteristic of Henry's style, Yellow Crack had a reputation as being poorly protected and scary, and our new variation (which took a straightened path up the wall, hence the "Direct" appellation to the name) offered even less protection. In addition, it appeared that it would be considerably harder. Russ went up first to feel out the new terrain. He climbed up to a point 40 feet off the ground, then lowered down from some nuts he had placed in a crack.

"The climbing looks really hard up there. You want to give it a try?" he asked me as he untied from the rope.

"Sure, I'll give it a try. But what happens if I get past that overhanging section and there's no crack to place protection in above?"

There wasn't an answer to that question, and I did not expect one.

We knew that if there wasn't any protection up there, a fall would be serious, maybe even fatal.

When I arrived at Russ's high point, I made sure the nuts he had placed were securely lodged in the crack, then I scanned the rock for holds that would lead me through the yellow-colored bulge ahead of me. After touching a few of the flat finger-edges in the vicinity, I envisioned the sequence of moves I'd need to make, then I went for it. As soon as I pulled past the crux section and stepped into a shallow corner in the wall above, I realized that my worst fears had become reality. There was no crack in which to slot a nut. I was now in a critical position where I had to decide whether to continue higher or try to climb back down. The difficulty was about 5.12c, a level that was near the limit of my ability at the time. In my tired, anxious state, I knew I would likely slip off if I tried to climb down. The only way down was up.

I looked down toward my last piece of protection and saw that it was way below my feet. Russ held the rope carefully. Beside him were our friends Clune and Jeff Gruenberg, who stood there watching me intently. Up until that moment, I had felt as though I'd been fueled by the synergy of our group, but now, notwithstanding the concern evident in their expressions, I felt very alone. I needed to apply all my concentration to survive the next few minutes. I took a few deep breaths and concentrated on relaxing the muscles in my forearms, then I committed myself to the next few moves. Time seemed to stand still. I felt the silence radiating from those below. No one dared offer any suggestions of where I should go. They knew that to divert my attention could be disastrous.

Around a corner, on the face above me, my fingers read a handhold like Braille. I eased my weight onto a tiny edge, then I pulled my body a move higher. Precarious holds kept appearing, and I bent my body into whatever position was needed to keep me on the cliff. Finally, I reached a large ledge that marked the end of the climb and uttered a sigh of, "Thank God!"

Some time later, Russ and I would take to the foot of this climb a reporter from the *New York Times* Sunday magazine, who was writing a story about me. "It was one of the boldest leads I have ever seen," Russ would say proudly. "I tried leading it. I knew you had to totally commit to doing the moves, otherwise the chance of surviving would be minimal. Those are the moments that really stand out—when you see someone totally on the edge."

But another friend of ours at the interview, Mark Robinson, shook his head. "It's not satisfying to watch someone risk their life. Though there was a time I might have thought so."

"Those *are* the most satisfying moments," Russ insisted again to the reporter.

"They're the most intense," Robinson replied, "but satisfying? I definitely disagree."

Although the exhilaration of such high-risk ascents was real, I too was becoming unsure just how much further I wanted to press my luck on the bold climbs of the Gunks.

A new route called Vandals marked a turning point in my climbing style. I became involved in this route by chance one day when I was hiking along the carriage trail, looking for some friends to climb with. When I looked through the red, orange, and yellow fall foliage toward the cliff, I noticed Russ Clune, Jeff Gruenberg, and a talented young climber named Hugh Herr at work on a new climb. On the cliff above them they had rigged up a strange complex of ropes.

"What are you guys doing up there?" I asked.

Clune invited me over. The creative rope work was designed to protect what was turning out to be a very hard and—because of the no-bolts rule in the Gunks—poorly protected new route. My friends had rigged up a system of protection using two different ropes connected to a couple of skyhooks delicately balanced over flakes. Tied into both ropes and belayed from them with equal tension, a climber could have some measure of security while trying the hard moves. Nevertheless, Clune would later sprain his ankle on one of his many attempts on Vandals, when he fell off high up, ripped out the small wired nut from its precarious position behind a flake, and slammed onto the rock face below.

Clune, Gruenberg, and Hugh Herr were all top-notch climbers, but the most visible among them on the cliffs was Hugh, who wore two artificial legs made from metal rods. Several years earlier he and a friend had gotten lost while descending from a winter climb of Mount Washington in New Hampshire. A nor'easter had hit the mountain with a blizzard of Siberian ferocity. By the time rescuers got to the lost team, they were on the verge of death. One of the rescuers had been killed in an avalanche, and Hugh's legs had frozen up to the knees. After losing both legs and going through years of rehabilitation, Hugh was back on the crags, climbing harder than ever. Hugh even turned his adjustable artificial legs to his advantage, cranking them taller so he could reach holds that would have formerly eluded his reach, or to experience being as tall as a basketball player for an evening on the town.

Vandals, which we rated 5.13a, was the hardest climb I had done up to that point, but its value to me was much more than just another hard pitch. On one of the days that we tried this climb, as I took another

The infamous Vandals route in the Gunks (5.13a). (SANDY STEWART)

turn trying to get past a large roof, I suddenly got fed up with the repetitive process of doing a particularly painful, shoulder-twisting contortion. After falling on this move numerous times and stressing my muscles and tendons, I had an idea that verged on heresy. Instead of following the strict rule of traditional-style climbing and lowering back down to the ground to start again, I decided to rest my weight on a piece of protection and hang under the roof to look around for any hidden holds that might get me through the next bit of climbing. The disapproving term climbers gave to the tactic of hanging on the rope to practice a move was "hang dogging," but frowned upon or not, this suddenly seemed like a logical approach in free climbing this route. In one moment I had, to some degree, thrown out years of climbing philosophy. But at the same time I felt that climbing had progressed to the point where this tactic was reasonable. The subtle advantage of hanging on the rope to figure out the crux moves gave me the added information that helped me learn and eventually succeed on the route. The old style of climbing suddenly seemed rigid, limited, and contrived. Hang dogging had expanded my vision of what was possible.

The shift from traditional climbing to the more gymnastic form known as "sport climbing" was a trend that was quickly sweeping across the country. Tony Yaniro, an American, had experimented with hang dogging as early as 1979, when he did the first 5.13c in the world, Grand Illusion, a grueling roof crack on a crag in the Sierras. By the mid-1980s another American, Alan Watts, was rappel bolting and hang dogging on his new routes at Smith Rocks in Oregon. Other climbers on other cliffs were trying the new style too.

As arcane and harmless as it may have been to climb in this new manner (a nonclimber would find it hard to see much difference between hang dogging and traditional climbing), it fueled a bitter controversy. In some places climbers who had spent years as climbing buddies fell out over questions of this changing style. On the new sport routes, the faces were so hard to climb and so strenuously difficult to protect by placing bolts on the lead that many climbers began placing the bolts while hanging on a rope placed from above: hence the term "rap-bolters." Those who upheld the old ways of traditional climbing began to denounce the hang dogging and rappel-bolting sport climbers as faithfully as McCarthyites had denounced communists in the 1950s.

Meanwhile, hang doggers called their critics the "rock police." In one of the more publicized clashes between the ethical camps, two famous Yosemite climbers who had been practically blood brothers got into an ugly brawl when one removed the bolts that the other had placed by rappel on a new route. Who was right? Who was wrong? Was this kind of antagonism beneficial to anyone?

By 1986 this weighty issue had come to a head. I took part in a debate about ethics at the American Alpine Club's annual meeting in Denver, Colorado. Representing the hang doggers were Christian Griffith, Todd Skinner, and Alan Watts. Many people were shocked to hear Christian predict that the hardest routes in the future would be artificially created with chisels and glue. Yet it was already happening in France, where a few famous sport routes had been chipped. On one level these great routes were paragons of our sport. On the other they were atrocities. But in my mind, the difference between hang dogging and chipping holds on a climb was considerable; these were two completely separate issues. It seemed obvious to me that chipping holds to "free climb" a route goes against the very essence of free climbing—to get up in "pure" style, without altering the rock or using artificial means to pull yourself higher. But to use bolts and hang dogging techniques in order to free climb otherwise unprotected faces also seemed like a legitimate style. Either way, posters of these new bolted sport routes and those who created them decorated shops, vans, and the bedrooms of aspiring climbers.

The representatives of traditional style at the "Great Debate," as the Amercian Alpine Club called the discussion, were John Bachar, Ron Kauk, and Rob Robinson. I was assumed to be a traditionalist, since I had done so many "trad" routes. But since I had "dogged" on the crux move of Vandals, I was, in fact, caught in the middle. For this reason I was a little embarrassed when Yvon Chouinard, the president of Patagonia, handed me a T-shirt to wear while I sat on the panel, facing the audience. The shirt showed a cartoon of Satan hanging from a rope clipped to a bolt. THE DEVIL IS A HANG DOG read the caption. Other shirts visible in the audience read SPORT CLIMBING IS NEITHER. When it was my turn to speak, Jim McCarthy, the moderator of the debate, grilled me about my use of hang dogging techniques on the first ascent of Vandals. A lawyer by profession, Jim interrogated me as if I were on trial. The court found me guilty of hang dogging, but I didn't feel guilty. I had found a logical way to push the levels of difficulty higher and I enjoyed the learning process. And that was where my interest in climbing lay. In time, these sport climbing tactics would become widely accepted as they opened up a whole new dimension to the sport.

Though the debate between trads and doggers grew heated during the 1980s, the American Alpine Club, of which Jim McCarthy was president, organized an exchange visit of climbers between France and the United States. The French Federation of Mountaineering were the hosts, and Russ and I were two of four Americans invited on the two-week trip in June 1986.

Our tour began on the sandstone boulders of Fontainebleau outside Paris, then we hit the limestone of Le Saussois, Verdon Gorge, and the famous pocketed limestone cliff called Buoux. The French were keen to show off their top routes on these cliffs. Chouca (5.13c, or 8a+ under the European rating system), Le Minimum (5.14a/8b+), and La Rage de Vivre (5.14a/8b+), first climbed by the brothers Marc and Antoine Le Menestrel, were some of the hardest sport climbs in the world.

France swept me away on that first visit. I could identify with many aspects of the French lifestyle and culture. I appreciated the tradition of taking a two-hour lunch break to enjoy a fresh, home-cooked meal with family or friends versus American McFast food, old stone houses versus cinder block condominiums, the standard six-week yearly vacation period versus two weeks, and the relaxed attitude of life in southern France versus the fast pace of America.

I had never climbed on limestone before this visit. I was amazed at how fluid and dancelike the movement could be on this ornately featured rock. Pockets and edges provided in-cut handholds on even the most overhanging faces, and this produced wildly acrobatic climbs. In addition, all the routes were bolted in such a way that there was rarely a chance of getting hurt from a fall. Instead of worrying about risk, the climber could focus on pure difficulty. Seeing this new sport climbing style didn't make me reject the traditional values I'd learned in America, but it intrigued me. I understood that the Europeans had the perfect terrain on which to push the limits of difficulty in this gymnastic form of free climbing.

Yet for all that I liked about France I sometimes found the French to be much more chauvanistic than the easterners I lived among. One famous French climber who later became a friend, Jibé Tribout, flabbergasted me one day with an offhanded comment. While drinking café au lait and discussing free climbing standards across the world, out of the blue Jibé sputtered, "A woman will never flash a 7c."

His meaning: women are not good enough to waltz up to a route of 5.12d difficulty (the American equivalent of 7c) on their first try without falling off. I was speechless at this blatantly absurd bit of chauvinism. At the time Jibé had made his declaration, no woman had accomplished that feat, but within three years' time I would shatter Jibé's claim. His statement, and others he made just like it over the coming years, would help inspire me to make some of my most important climbs. I suspect that deep down Jibé knew that his quips to me were like throwing down the glove—a challenge to a duel. After all, a climber like Jibé, who did the first free ascent of a 5.14a in America, would know that nothing makes a climber work harder than a good challenge.

Near the end of my French tour, while climbing in the Verdon Gorge, I met an Italian climber named Marco Scolaris, the organizer of the first international free climbing competition, which had been held in Italy the year before. I had just finished climbing Take It or Leave It, a route of 5.12d that followed a series of small pockets in a steep wall. After I arrived at the top of the route, Marco walked over to introduce himself.

"I have not seen a woman climb a route so hard!" he said.

I was flattered, though I felt that the climb had been well within my abilities. By now I was accustomed to being judged not just as a climber, but by my gender.

Marco then told me about the new craze in European climbing: competitions. He described the very first international climbing competition, which had been held on a natural limestone cliff and where climbers from all over Europe had come to be challenged in a test of pure difficulty. Whoever climbed the highest won a cash prize. The second annual Sport Roccia contest would be held at the picturesque country town of Arco, near Milan, later that summer. All the best climbers would be there.

"Lynn, you must come to this competition next month. There is only one woman who climbs strong like you, so maybe you could win."

"Who is that woman?" I asked Marco.

"Her name is Catherine Destivelle. She's French. She won the Sport Roccia last year."

And so began a new phase of my life: professional competition climber.

Chapter 11

Into the Arena

Minutes after Russ and I stepped off the plane in Milan, we were seated in a red Maserati, speeding toward the town of Arco, a two-and-a-half-hour drive to the northeast. Marco Scolaris had arranged my passage from America to the second Sport Roccia competition, though I wondered if I'd survive to compete as our driver threw the coupe around the winding shoreline of Lago di Garda. Russ and I gripped the edges of the backseat and stared bug-eyed as we passed a row of cars on a blind curve inside a dark, narrow tunnel. The driver's elderly mother, seated in the passenger seat, barely reacted to the lead-footed driving of our escort; she was more interested in cooing over the opulent lakeshore villas along the way.

In Arco we settled into a room at the Albergo Cattoi, a quaint family-style inn where we ate a delicious meal served by Marisa and

la mamma, who communicated in foreign words and friendly gestures, since none of us spoke a common language. After lunch we
headed to the tourist office to register for the competition. Marco
welcomed me, then handed over an entry form and the list of rules
for the competition.

"How much is the prize money?" I asked him, scanning the paper-
work.

"I don't know, but the winner of the men gets a new car."

"No car for the top woman?"

Marco shrugged off my pointed remark. "Ask him," he said, nodding toward the head organizer of this competition.

"I can't speak Italian. Can you ask him for me?"

Marco conveyed my question to the organizer, and this man's quick
reply caused them both to break out laughing.

"What was his answer?"

"He said that the women would be paid an equal prize if they climb
without their tops on."

While these two reveled in their humor, I stood speechless, wondering what kind of *casino*—a bit of Italian slang suggesting a chaotic
debacle—the Arco contest would be.

Blue skies and a beating sun greeted day one of the competition. As I
hiked to the base of the 900-foot limestone cliff on which the climbing
would take place, I heard fragments of several different languages from
among the hundreds of spectators covering the hillside. Around us,
there were signs that a small forest had been felled to provide better
viewing. The cliffs had also been manicured for the event. To create
routes of exactly the right difficulty, holds had been chiseled into the
rock or modified with glue, while platforms had been bolted onto the
face on which the judges and camerapeople could stand to observe the
climbers. Marking the vertical course were boundary lines of red and
white tape, and the banners of several sponsors dangled down the rock.
Some twenty-two centuries before, the Romans had filled the
Colosseum with gladiators, lions, and ill-fated prisoners and slaves. It
looked to me as if this crowd were gathered to see a *circus maximus* of
the vertical, and that the contestants, who looked awkward and nerv-

ous, were about to engage in battle. For me, this scene was completely different than the "pure" climbing ethics and generally solitary sport I was used to in America.

Marco Bernardi, one of the celebrated Italian free climbers and technical organizer of the competition, explained the rules to me in broken English. The competition would take place on two consecutive weekends, he informed us, the first event here in Arco, the second the following weekend in Bardonecchia. In Arco on this first day we had three routes to climb with only a ten-minute break between each climb. We had nine minutes to complete each route, and we could all watch each other compete throughout the day. Later events would have more rigid rules that kept climbers in isolation areas away from the wall so that they began a climb knowing nothing about it, making for a pure on-sight ascent. In principle, I liked what I heard. This was the dawn of a new era in climbing, and though many of the top European climbers, including Catherine Destivelle and Patrick Edlinger, had initially decried the idea of turning the sport into a competition, many of these protesting climbers came to the Sport Roccia event in 1986. I too was curious to check it out and meet this gathering of climbers from all over Europe. Despite our differences in culture, we were bonded through our shared passion for climbing.

For a few hours I sat on a rocky hillside, watching climbers move up the wall, and noticing that some climbers who had done very hard routes were nervous wrecks in front of a crowd and fell off quickly. Then I heard my name called over a bullhorn. A wave of apprehension and excitement hit me. I would now find out what it was like to compete on the rock.

I stepped up to the wall, tied into a rope, took a deep breath, and began climbing the first route. Ten feet up I encountered a steep bulge with a few hidden holds chiseled in the rock. I made an aggressive lunge to a good hold at the lip, then climbed quickly to the top. The ten-minute rest before the second climb was just enough time for me to untie from the rope, walk to the next route, and tie in again. The route felt easy and I solved it quickly. But the third route had thin, technical moves, and I climbed slowly. A few feet from the end, the judges ordered me to stop climbing. I had run out of time.

The climber who followed me was the Frenchwoman I had been

Making the final lunge to the chain in Arco, Italy. (MARCO SCOLARIS)

warned about: Catherine Destivelle. Catherine began climbing very rapidly up the rock until she arrived at the first overhanging bulge, where she made a false move and fell. The rules stated that we were allowed to try a route again if we fell, provided the second try remained within the nine-minute time limit. Catherine lowered from her fall, pulled the rope, and hopped onto the route again. This time, she made it to the top. She climbed the next two routes without a problem.

Catherine and I, and several other climbers, were now qualified for the finals, slated for the next day. The route we'd have to climb was rated 7a+, or 5.12a in American grades. This time we had only one chance to try climbing the route on-sight (without watching any other competitors), and we waited in an isolation area. When my turn came to climb, I made it to the top of the course without a hitch. Catherine was the last of the women to climb and when she made it to the top too, we were tied. I assumed we would compete on a superfinal route and I itched to square off with the champion of the last Sport Roccia in a one-on-one contest. But the judges had other ideas: there would be no superfinal, they announced. Although it seemed illogical to me, I found that I had lost more points for running out of time than Catherine had lost for falling. The judges valued speed over style, and they pronounced Catherine Destivelle the winner of the first stage of the competition in Arco.

This way of judging a climb contradicted my traditional American climbing heritage, of which the first rule was don't fall, and where care and technique were qualities that could save one's life. But, I realized, competition climbing was an entirely different strategy than rock climbing, and to win I would have to adapt. Moving slowly and certainly over each move caused me to eat into my allotted time. Catherine, on the other hand, had climbed like a flame, burning brightly with energy, but risking that she'd flicker out if she made an ill-considered move. She and I had very different styles, and each style had merit. As an alpine climber, her style was to climb quickly up and down the mountain. My style as a free climber was to slowly assess every move, sometimes shifting up and down until I found the right sequence to climb up without falling.

The following weekend in Bardonecchia we gathered for phase two of the competition. This time, I fell on one of the semifinal routes, but Catherine climbed all three without falling. This put me so far behind her in my score that I ruled out my chances of winning. Nonetheless, I felt mentally ready to give my best effort on the final route.

When I stepped onto the wall, I realized that I was on the hardest route of the entire competition. But even though I was certain I could not win, I kept pushing myself up the rock with an attitude of "never give up." After making it past two difficult crux sections, hanging on to tiny edges of rock, I grabbed the concluding hold seconds before my time expired. I had on-sighted a route of 5.12b.

Next it was Catherine's turn. To my surprise she fell twice, then ran out of time on her third attempt. When the judges counted our points, they found that my on-sight ascent had brought us to a tie. An announcement was made: Lynn and Catherine would compete on a superfinal route. We would be competing on the same route as the men's superfinal.

Catherine and I entered the isolation tank yet again. We knew very little about each other and I could not speak more than a few words of French. We simply exchanged looks of uncertainty. All I knew about her was that whenever I had picked up a climbing magazine over the past few days, there had been Catherine, in a photo, an interview, an article, or an advertisement, being touted as the best woman climber in the world. In America in 1986 there were no professional climbers and the media cared little about climbing. I was able to make a meager living through my rock climbing guiding service in the Gunks. But here, sitting beside me, was a woman who was adored by the European climbing press and who was being paid by equipment and clothing companies for doing what she enjoyed.

Catherine's boyfriend, Lothar, joined us in the isolation area, and the two of them studied me carefully while I stretched out on the grass and began practicing a few gymnastics exercises. Lothar, a salt-and-pepper-haired man who was several years Catherine's senior, had an intimidating presence. He'd made a fortune from a successful clothing company that he'd owned, and now he was free to spend his time climbing, skiing, and managing Catherine's career. Lothar chattered continually on a walkie-talkie while in the isolation area, like a general commanding his troops. Russ, who was my only ally at this contest, had flown home a few days earlier to resume his work as a sales rep. Under the gaze of Lothar and Catherine I felt doubly alone.

Minutes before Catherine and I were to compete, an announcement was made: there would be no superfinal. Catherine was the winner. My mouth gaped open at this change in rules. Even Catherine appeared surprised.

Before we had gone to the isolation area, we had been asked to climb one of the routes in front of the judges. On this route they had rated our style and speed, giving us points for each. In what seemed to me like a capricious whim, even a breach of the rules, the organizers had decided to select a winner from this display, rather than acknowledge the fact that I was the only one to do the final route. (By today's standards, the winner is the one who performs best on the final route.) Again they had favored speed over style. I had more style points, but Catherine was faster, and this earned her first place.

I walked away from the Sport Roccia feeling that the rules of the competition had been changed to favor the big star and her sponsors. The fair thing to me, to Catherine, and to the audience would have been to have a superfinal. Though the rules had been disregarded, I didn't blame Catherine. She seemed sincere, and it was obvious that she was passionate about climbing.

Catherine Destivelle was born in 1960 in Algeria to Parisian parents who were climbers themselves. They introduced her when she was five to the gymnastic boulders of Fontainebleau, a famous climbing spot outside Paris, and by age fourteen she was frequenting the Alps. Just as I had cut my teeth on the big walls of Yosemite—typical for an American climber—Catherine came to climbing in a classically French way: armed with an ice ax. She made ascents of snow and ice routes on the frigid north faces of mountains like the Ailefroide and the Olan, then at age seventeen she made a seven-hour ascent of the vertical and technical American Direct on the Petit Dru, a granite spire that rises above Chamonix. For several years afterward she quit climbing to pursue a career as a physical therapist, and she even tried her hand at gambling for high stakes in all-night poker games. But an invitation to enter the French version of Survival of the Fittest changed everything for her. Her exposure on television caught the attention of a filmmaker, Robert Nicole, and he cast her in a climbing film called *It's Dangerous to Lean Out*. The film, which aired in 1985, chronicles Catherine's ascent of Pichenibule, a spectacular sport climb in the Verdon Gorge. Rated 7b+ (5.12c), it was, at the time, the hardest route climbed by a woman in France. The film made Catherine a celebrity athlete in France and opened the door to enough sponsors so that she could climb full-time. Her victory at the first Sport Roccia contest made her an even bigger name, but a week after the contest she was in Chamonix traveling across a glacier and she fell 130 feet into a crevasse, fracturing her back and pelvis. By the second Sport Roccia—where she and I competed against each other—she had recovered.

Though Catherine was the most publicized female climber in the competition circuit of the mid-1980s, I sometimes wondered if her spirit did not lie elsewhere. After Arco we didn't meet again in a competition for quite a while. Instead of defending her title of "best woman rock climber" at the contests of the next two years, she traveled to places like Mali in western Africa, where she helped make a film about the cliff-dwelling Dogon people. Even her remarks about contests indicated that her heart was not in it. "I don't like competing even when I win," she told one journalist in 1993, while to me she once confided,

"Lothar enjoys these competitions much more than me." In an interview from the book *Beyond Risk*, she said of competition, "Competition is not the same as climbing. I get nervous. I don't like people watching me when I climb."

When I drove into Grenoble a year and a half later, I saw posters of Catherine plastered over walls and billboards. It was late 1987, and I had entered the city's first International Indoor Climbing Competition. The posters advertised the contest as if it were a rock concert. This time, Catherine would be competing, and the media was tireless in reporting that she was in town, given that they hatched the notion that the two of us were engaged in a grand rivalry. But the contest got off to a bad start.

On the first day of the event, several climbers were disqualified for making a blunder that was really the fault of the course setters. At a point on the route, the holds had been placed so close to the boundary that nearly every climber adopted a position that forced them to "flag" their leg outside the red marking tape. Although they were not placing their foot on anything at all and their legs were only brushing beyond the boundary marker, they were immediately disqualified and told to stop climbing. But not Catherine, whose foot crossed into no-man's-land three times on the way up. I saw nothing of this, being sequestered in the isolation room, but after I climbed, I found Russ in the audience.

"What's been going on out here?" I asked.

"A lot of people have been disqualified for stepping out of bounds, but not Catherine."

This preferential treatment had not gone unnoticed. Many of those who'd been disqualified had lodged protests, and Catherine herself had offered to drop out. But under pressure by the media and sponsors to see their poster child compete in the big event, the judges had turned a blind eye to Catherine's mistake. Protests were ignored and Catherine entered the finals.

Setting the course for a competition is an art in which the climb should become increasingly difficult all the way to the top, so as to slough off competitors at different levels. Ideally, only the strongest and most efficient climber, if anyone, should complete the final route. But on the night of the finals, Andrea Eisenhut, Catherine, and I all made it to the top. The rules stated that the only competitors allowed into a superfinal round were those who were tied in points. Although Catherine had been permitted to compete in the finals despite having stepped out of bounds, her score had suffered and she had fewer points than Andrea and me. But instead of ruling her out of the superfinal, the organizers told us of a sudden rule change that kept Catherine in the final showdown. This produced a flurry of protest, and a huddle of competitors and judges gathered below the wall.

"What do you think?" a judge asked Andrea. "Should Catherine be allowed in the superfinal?"

"No," she said firmly.

Andrea confessed to me, "It would be unfair to change the rules to favor Catherine, especially after what I saw last night. I was walking around the stadium looking for the office to register for the competition and I didn't know that you weren't supposed to go in there. When I opened the door and walked in, I saw several people hanging around the climbing wall. One of those people was Catherine, and she was bouldering around at the base of the wall. As soon as they noticed me standing there, one of the organizers said, 'Hey! You aren't allowed in here.' I don't think it's fair that she should get special treatment. What do you think?"

"I'm disappointed that Catherine won't be in the superfinals, but the only fair thing to do is to abide by the rules," I conceded.

Within minutes another announcement was made: Catherine would not compete in the superfinal. Since I was the only woman to climb to the top of the superfinal route, I was declared the winner, yet the victory was bittersweet. I felt unsatisfied with the poorly placed boundary markers, the constantly changing rules, and the circumstances that prevented Catherine and me from competing against each other on a challenging route fair and square.

It was not until January 1988 that we got the chance to face each other again, in Catherine's hometown of Paris, at a competition held at the Palais d'Omnisport at Bercy. This multisport palace was a massive, high-tech stadium that could even be converted into a lake with a wind generator for windsurfing competitions. The wall was a towering, abstract fortress designed by a climber-sculptor named Jean Marc

Blanche, and the contest drew a crowd numbering in the thousands. A huge video screen over the stage allowed spectators to see close-ups of the faces of competitors, who were videotaped as they climbed. This was the splashy heyday of the sport climbing competition era. Such an extravagant outlay of effort and money for a climbing event would rarely be matched.

As I sat in isolation, I tried to chat with Catherine and engage some of her halting English, but she seemed shy and distracted. Perhaps her reputation and the pressure that comes with it was overwhelming her. Sport climbing had become a form of entertainment and she was its photogenic rock star whether she wanted to be or not. I held no grudge against her for the episodes of the past competitions. Rather, I admired her talent and good fortune. In between competitions on plastic walls she climbed on beautiful limestone cliffs in the south of France. She had become the first woman to climb the grade of 5.13c on a famous route called Chouca, located in Buoux on a bulging wall of limestone called Le Bout du Monde, or "the edge of the world."

On the final round at Bercy the contestants stepped onto the stage one by one. Catherine bounded up the wall well past the other women's highest point, then she slipped and fell. My turn came. The bright lights, cheering crowd, flashing cameras, and movements of judges on the fringe of the climb were distracting and bizarre, but I shut them out of my mind and focused on my performance. As the murmur from the crowd rose to a crescendo, I knew I must have passed Catherine's highest point. A few moves from the top, my foot slipped just before I latched my fingertips around a big hold, and I fell. Though I had climbed the highest of any woman to win this competition, it wasn't until the following year, at the second annual Bercy competition, that I felt truly satisfied by with my performance. That night, the men's and women's final route would share the same finish and I would be the only person, man or woman, to climb to the top.

Although I spent large chunks of time in Europe during this period, important things were happening at home, the most significant of which was my marriage to Russ. On October 22, 1988, Russ and I tied the knot in New Paltz. The wedding and reception were attended by two hundred of our friends and family. As something of a joke after the real ceremony, Russ set up a photograph of us suited up in our wedding finery and climbing harnesses, taking our vows while dangling over the top of a cliff at the Gunks. While Russ and I hung from the side of the cliff, our friends Jim McCarthy, Mark and Susan Robinson, Jim Nolan, and Bob D'Antonio stood on the summit with the climbing guidebook in hand reading our "vows." The picture appeared in *Bride* magazine, and the caption read, "Wedding on the rocks." I laughed off the double meaning with a nagging concern. Already I knew that marriage, for us, would be a challenge. Russ and I had very different outlooks on the world, but our lives were so intertwined that I couldn't imagine my life without him.

As a couple we decided that I would continue pursuing my career as a competition climber and Russ would continue to work as a sales representative in the outdoor industry. For the next two years I threw myself into the competitions circuit, shuttling between America and

Wedding on the rocks in the Gunks with our friends Jim Nolan, Susan and Mark Robinson, Jim McCarthy, and Bob D'Antonio.
(CHRIS BONINGTON)

Europe, climbing rock whenever possible, and working for the climbing hardware manufacturer Chouinard Equipment, for whom I traveled around presenting slide shows about climbing. My winnings from competitions financed my peripatetic lifestyle, yet sometimes the money disappeared from the pockets of the organizers before it reached the hands of the winners. In 1988 in Marseilles—a city famous for being the French capital of organized crime—the checks paid to the winners bounced both times they were issued.

America's first International Sport Climbing Competition was held in the summer of 1988 at Snowbird, Utah, a ski resort in Little Cottonwood Canyon in the Wasatch Mountains above Salt Lake City. The alpinist and entrepreneur Jeff Lowe had brought the competition to the United States, persuading resort owner Dick Bass (a Texas oil millionaire and the first man to climb the Seven Summits, the highest peaks of each continent) to let him build competition routes on the concrete wall of Snowbird's multistory luxury hotel. ABC Sports covered the contest, and their main interests were the perceived rivalry between Catherine and me, and also the uncertainty over who would dominate the men's title. Among the French were several competition-tough men, like Patrick Edlinger, Jibé Tribout, Didier Raboutou, and Marc Le Menestral. Although the American field was untested, many favored Ron Kauk, the ruggedly handsome Yosemite climber who had a knack for climbing hard routes with finesse and calm. His quip "John Wayne never wore Lycra," made at a bouldering contest he'd won wearing Levi's, had been intended as a jab at the climbers who wore the harlequin-patterned Lycra tights that were popular back then, but which have since thankfully gone out of fashion. Though he was a dark horse at Snowbird, few doubted that he had a chance at the trophy.

The big showdown between Catherine and me almost became a big letdown when she fell low on the semifinal climb, scrapping her chance of entering in the finals. Since she and I had always dominated the field whenever we'd competed together, this final showdown was anticipated to be an exciting event. This was the first organized climbing competition of its caliber in America and, unfortunately, it was not without problems. To my dismay, there were last-minute rule changes and controversies even on my home turf.

I was sitting in the Snowbird lodge with Russ and Jim McCarthy when Jeff came over and announced that a review of videotapes of Catherine's climb, and also of the climb of my old friend Mari Gingery, had revealed something surprising. The tapes, he said, showed that Catherine and Mari were, in fact, tied. The tape of Mari's climb showed her hand reach out and touch a hold that was out of bounds at exactly the same point where Catherine had fallen. The judges had noticed Mari's mistake and had allowed her to continue climbing and to qualify for the final competition. But by disqualifying Mari at the point where she reached out of bounds, she and Catherine would tie for sixth place. Possibly out or pressure to create tension for the TV show, Jeff decided to allow both women into the finals, expanding the field of finalists to seven. With Catherine back in the competition, this event would certainly be more exciting to watch.

On the day of the finals, I felt strong and mentally prepared. This 120-foot-high climbing wall was an exercise in endurance, the type of climbing I feel most comfortable doing. But soon after starting up, I became aware that the course setters had chosen to create difficulty by spacing the holds far apart. Instead of having to puzzle out moves from a complex of holds, progress on this wall of cement and plastic often depended on long stretches or jumps. This did not favor my height, and I found myself gripping the plastic blobs in awkward positions at full stretch. Forty feet above the ground, I came to an impasse where I couldn't reach the next hold, so I crouched up against the concrete and hurled myself upward. But instead of latching on to this hold, my fingers missed the target and I went flying backward with the rope wrapped around my leg. As I fell, I could hear a collective murmur of disappointment from the crowd. When I stopped, I was hanging upside down and my head had come a millimeter from bashing into the wall. I was just as surprised as the audience to fall where I did, and I felt a sense of inner betrayal between my mind and body for not collaborating more accurately for that move.

Mari came out of the isolation area next, and she fell at the same place I had. Then came Catherine, climbing nervously up the first section of the route, and pausing at the point that had spat Mari and me off. The tension in the air was palpable when Catherine arrived at the make-or-break move of the contest. After testing the move a couple of times, she stretched her arm toward the hold, gritting her teeth. Her back and arms quivered with muscle tension. She stretched her arm up and when her fingers crept over the top of the hold, she hung her weight from it and began to pull up. Applause rose from the crowd, then an instant later she fell off, but by climbing one move higher than Mari and me she had won America's first International Sport Climbing Competition.

After the women's event, the men performed. There was a feeling of expectation in the audience, a sense that someone had to climb all the way to the concrete summit, up and over the bulging wave-shaped feature that had been engineered to hang over the top of Snowbird's Cliff Lodge Hotel. But one after another, the best male sport climbers of the day plummeted. Climbers dealt with their failure differently. Some screamed and thrashed like children throwing tantrums. When Ron Kauk unexpectedly slipped a mere 10 feet up and was lowered to the ground, he untied the rope from his harness and dropped it onto the ground with a gesture of distaste, as if it were a stinking cigarette butt. Marc Le Menestral seemed to be in it for pure enjoyment as he shot up the wall in leaps and bounds, shouting, "Fun!" and "Great move!" As I watched the contest, I overheard the French climbers around me speaking cattily about whatever contestant was about to walk onto the stage next. Palpable rivalry existed between Patrick Edlinger, who was from

Getting ready to lunge on the final route at Snowbird, just before I fell. (BETH WALD)

southern France, and the Parisian climbers. Just as Catherine's reputation had been crafted by magazines and films, the media had created a cult around Patrick, and it seemed to me that his countrymen were jealous. Some of that cult had been spawned by his stylish winning performances in contests; some of it came from a film called *Life by the Fingertips,* in which he calmly free soloed a difficult climb in the Verdon Gorge in bare feet. His flamboyant dress, immaculate physique, and flowing shoulder-length blond hair gave him the look of a warrior-savage in that film, and the Frenchmen seated around me took delight in finding as many ways as they could to call Patrick a poseur. But none could deny that Patrick was a gifted climber.

"Hush!" Jibé Tribout loudly whispered in French to his friends as Patrick began his climb. "The king has commenced!"

Their guffaws turned to silence, then admiration, as Patrick floated gracefully and effortlessly past the high point of every climber before him. I felt goose bumps run over my flesh as I watched this performance of total excellence, and I felt the audience bond together with a common sense of awe. Patrick was the last to climb that day, and he was the best. As he climbed through the final bulge to the top, the sun broke through gathering thunderclouds and shone down brightly, bathing him in golden light. People who were in the audience that day still speak of that afternoon when Patrick won Snowbird. Performances like that are hard to forget.

By 1989 I was ranked number one in the women's sport climbing field, having won almost every competition I had entered since 1986. By that time, the young, talented climber Isabelle Patissier had moved into Catherine's position as my strongest contender. At the competition in Nîmes, held in an ancient Roman coliseum, Isabelle Patissier won her first International Climbing Competition. In the summer of 1989, the first World Cup contest in the history of the sport would be held in Leeds, England, and I felt good about my chances of winning it. But events at Buoux that day prevented me from ever competing in Leeds.

But if I were offered the chance to go back in time and retie the knot that slipped through my harness that day on the Styx Wall at

Competing in Lyon, France, in 1989. (PHILIPPE FRAGNOL)

Buoux, and thus avoid the fall that nearly ended my life, I'd say, "No, I accept everything as it is." Life has repeatedly shown me that the most difficult experiences are the ones that evoke the most meaningful lessons.

During the months I spent recovering in New Paltz I thought hard about what I wanted to do with my life. Deep down, I believed that there was a reason I had survived the fall, and that reason had something to do with the path that climbing had set for me. I began to feel that I was destined to do something more meaningful with my life than such a self-serving activity as climbing. I didn't know how this would take form or when I would do it, but I felt sure it was coming. For the moment, my obvious talent lay in competing, and I felt compelled to continue in that direction.

I had been fortunate to escape with no injury worse than a dislocated elbow. But my climbing buddy, Dr. Mark Robinson, warned me not to take such an injury lightly. Once the swelling subsided, I began the process of recovery with simple coordination exercises and massage, while paying attention to any sensations of pain or stiffness. The quality of "listening to my body" made the biggest difference in my healing process. When I began my rehabilitation process, I could barely bend my elbow. Six weeks later, I was back on the rock.

But it wasn't my body that needed to be retrained after I started climbing again. It was my mind. While I climbed up the rock, I felt fine, but when I leaned back to be lowered down from a route, fear struck me with a powerful surge. Only patience and acceptance got me through my shell-shock. After a month my fear subsided and all that remained of the incident at Buoux was a small tear in my pectoral muscle and a pea-sized knot of scar tissue on my buttock. Today, my memory of the fall seems like a distant dream.

I returned to the competition circuit just three months after my accident, starting with the second Snowbird contest. Although I'd had a consistent string of victories across Europe, a win on my home turf had so far eluded me. When I slipped off the wall to come in second behind the French climber Nanette Raybaud, I realized that I had lost because I'd been more concerned about winning than climbing my best. "Choking" was a term I had learned long ago in swimming, later on in gymnastics, and I was reminded once again about the importance of having the right attitude and state of mind.

A month later I had refound my form, winning competitions in both Arco and Lyon. The women's superfinal in Lyon was between the legendary Italian Luisa Iovane and me, and it was held on the same final route as the men. When I slipped off near the top, I heard later that Jibé Tribout had lowered his head and muttered, *"Merde."* Having climbed higher than him on a route rated 5.12d, I would have come in third place in the men's field. Three years earlier he had told me that such a feat would be impossible for a woman.

After winning the third annual competition at the Palais d'OmniSport in Paris in January 1990, I headed to a crag in the south of France called Cimaï. I had been thinking about trying to climb a route of 5.14a for several months, but at that time there was not a single 5.14a in America. Moreover, no woman had ever done a climb of this grade before, though Isabelle had climbed a 5.13d called Sortilege, also at Cimaï, and I had done the first free ascent of Running Man at the Gunks, also 5.13d. Although 5.13d was only one level below 5.14a, the added difficulty was a significant leap. I felt capable but by no means certain of success. The 5.14a that I decided to try is called Masse

Hanging out with the accomplished climbing couple Luisa Iovane and Heinz Mariacher after competing. (BETH WALD)

Critique. This route ascends a prominent, slightly overhanging lime-stone wall, and its first ascentionist had been none other than Jibé Tribout. After completing the climb, he had allegedly proclaimed in predictable style, "No woman will ever be able to climb this route."

My first day of effort on Masse Critique was humbling. I couldn't do all the moves on the route, and I had to use the rope and protection bolts for aid while working my way up the face. But the process of working through the moves stimulated the concentration and visuali-zation techniques that I had learned as a gymnast. In order to maximize the use of each hand- or foothold, I imagined a perpendicular line drawn from the hold, indicating the exact direction I needed to push or pull for maximum leverage against gravity. Like a drummer who needs to coordinate her hands and feet with specific timing in order to create music, I focused on coordinating the push/pull forces between my hands and feet to create fluid movement up the rock.

As I tried the route more and more, moves that had seemed impossi-ble on one day became feasible the next as my body and mind worked in sync to make one section of the climb flow into the next. By the fourth day I had figured out the entire sequence of moves and I was able to free climb the route in sections, but only with long breathers while hanging from the bolts. It helped me to mentally rehearse the route several times each day. Every time I imagined myself going through the moves, I made sure to imagine myself going all the way to the top. I found that the most effective times for replaying the moves through my head were immediately after climbing, in the quiet hours of the evening, such as while relaxing in the bathtub or before falling asleep. After a few days of work on this route, I had programmed the entire sequence of moves together in my mind.

After a week of effort and repeated attempts, I lowered to the ground one afternoon feeling a painful throb coming from the tendon of the finger on which I wore my wedding ring. Later, when I tried to slip my ring back on, I discovered that my finger was too swollen. Suddenly I found myself thinking of my marriage, and with a profound shock it occurred to me that Russ and I were rapidly drifting apart. In the last

**Perfecting the moves
on Masse Critique.**
(PHILIPPE FRAGNOL)

few years I had been so focused on climbing, training, and traveling to competitions that I had ignored the real direction in which we were headed. I sat on a boulder near the climb, massaging my finger and wondering what to do. I realized that in the next few days I would have to conclude my efforts on Masse Critique and fly home.

The next morning—the ninth day since I had embarked on Masse Critique—I woke with a strong feeling that I would succeed. I drove to the crag with a few close friends, tied into a rope, and stepped onto the wall. I passed each crux section as if in a trance. I made sure to wait for the right moment of positive feeling before committing to action, but once committed I was conscious of only the flow of movement. By the end of this 80-foot route my lungs felt huge in my chest and I could feel the lactic acid accumulating in my forearms, but I was determined to follow the vision that I had rehearsed so many times in my mind. One final move, and then I arrived at the top of the route. I had broken the 5.14 barrier, and it felt like a dream come true. But soon thereafter, the trance was broken and it was time to head home.

A few days after my return to New Paltz, Russ and I decided to spend a week together in Florida, where we could hang out on the beach, swim in the ocean, and stay with his parents, who had rented a condominium for the month. I had been climbing in France for six weeks and this vacation was a chance to relax and catch up. One night at dinner, as the evening wore on, I made a joking remark about the mountain of laundry I had found sitting on the floor beside the washing machine when I had returned. It appeared that Russ had not done a single wash the whole time I'd been away, and I found it humorous. But Russ's mother took my comment as a jab at her son.

"You know, you can be replaced!" she said in her strong New Jersey accent, looking directly into my eyes.

The words stung me, and reduced all of us to silence. After the Raffas left, I found myself waiting for Russ to comfort me, or at least make light of his mother's snide remark. He said nothing, leading me to wonder if his mother was right. In retrospect, his mother's comment highlighted the fact that there was a growing lack of mutual support in our relationship.

I knew we spent too much time apart—we rarely even went climbing together anymore—but we each had our own careers. In years past, Russ and I worked together as a team. I often traveled and worked with him during the selling season and Russ was my ally at the climbing competitions. But over the past few years, we had spent increasingly less time together and our paths in life began to diverge.

After a few months at home, I returned to France for the continuation of the 1990 World Cup season. It was at this time that I began climbing with the American Robyn Erbesfield, a twenty-seven-year-old woman from Atlanta, Georgia. As the only representatives from the "American team," we ended up renting a house together, surrounded by vineyards in the Provence region of France. Together we trained for the competitions, climbed on the cliffs, and, on rest days, played Hacky Sack in the meridional sunshine. Our life in the countryside seemed simple and centered. I enjoyed strolling through the open markets in the local village, filling my straw basket with fresh fruits, vegetables, and cheeses (many of which I had never seen in America), and then later taking the time to prepare and share well-cooked meals, a daily ritual

Robyn Erbesfield training at Orgon, France.
(PHILIPPE POULET)

in France. When I started learning the language, I found it humbling to have to resort to communicating like a child again. But like a child, I became more attentive to my sense of intuition while listening and communicating in this foreign culture. I completed my immersion by reading children's books like *Le Petit Prince, Asterix* comic strips, *La Liberation* newspaper, and listening intently to radio programs and French music while driving.

I enjoyed living and climbing in France, but I was ready to retire from the competition circuit and begin a new direction in my career and personal life. One evening in the fall of 1990, after I had been in France for several weeks, I called Russ from the house in Provence that Robyn and I had rented.

"I've done enough of these climbing competitions," I said. "I enjoy the lifestyle of traveling and climbing, but I'm not interested in competing much longer."

There was a pause on the other end of the line. "Well, I think it's interesting to have an international life," Russ said.

But the truth was, we were not sharing this "international life." It was clear that we had different views regarding what it means to share a life together. At that point, we both realized that regardless of whether or not I stopped competing, our lives had drifted so far apart that it was unlikely we could rebuild the life we once had.

While preparing for the last three events of the World Cup season, I found it hard to concentrate on climbing. It was no surprise that at the next World Cup event in Nuremberg, Germany, my foot slipped off the first hold and I was disqualified. Though I had not even climbed one move up the wall, both feet had left the ground and my slip counted as a fall. In an ironic twist, Lothar was the judge who informed me of my disqualification.

"You know, Lynn, a rule is a rule," he said. After all of the rule bending of the past to favor Catherine, I had to laugh.

Following my disqualification, I went to my hotel room and phoned Russ to tell him what had happened. As we talked, I found the courage to confront the issues we had been avoiding. We both knew our marriage was in trouble and that it probably wouldn't last. The conversation was depressing, and it left me with a fatalistic feeling about our future as a couple. Later that evening, during a TV interview in Munich, the host asked, "Why did you slip in this competition?"

Caught by surprise, I blurted out the truth: "I'm having problems in my marriage."

Only two competitions remained in the season, in Lyon and Barcelona, and even if I won them both and Isabelle came in second place, we would be tied for first. When I asked the president of the organization that ran the competitions what he'd do if we tied, he said, "We will cut the trophy in two."

A few weeks later in Lyon, the superfinal showdown between Isabelle and me turned out to be one of most memorable performances ever in competition. After completing the final route, I was led into the isolation area, where I noticed Isabelle talking to one of the male competitors who had just finished climbing the men's final route. After they had been talking together for several minutes discussing the moves of a climb, one of the organizers announced that the men and women should be separated, since Isabelle and I would be competing on the same climb that the men had just finished climbing. Regardless of whether or not Isabelle had been discussing the moves of the superfinal, this incident served to reinforce my own intent to climb to the top of this route. With all odds against me, I realized that this was the perfect opportunity to demonstrate the power of positive thinking. Out of seventeen men who had competed on the final route, only François Legrand and Didier Raboutou had climbed to the top.

Isabelle climbed first and because she was a native of Lyon, the crowd cheered enthusiastically as she climbed. From the isolation area, I heard thundering rounds of applause as Isabelle made her way up the wall. Several minutes later, I heard the roar of the crowd burst in a collective "Aahhh," and I assumed Isabelle must have fallen off. I was the last person to climb. Before I began my climb, Lothar, who was one of the judges during this competition, said to me, "You are allowed to traverse right at that first roof," and he pointed up to the first giant overhang on the wall.

I wondered why he said this, but I figured I would make my own decision about which way to go when I got there. As it turned out, I chose to climb straight up over the roof rather than traversing out right like all the other competitors had done. As I swung into the initial moves over the roof, I heard a loud murmur from the crowd. But as soon as I pulled over the lip and found a position to rest that no one else had discovered, the crowd roared again with loud cheers and stomping feet. At the end of the route I made a spectacular lunge to grab the final hold, and when I was lowered to the floor, it was amid wild cheering from the audience. Robyn stood waiting for me at the base of the climb to give me a big hug, and even my father and his wife were there to share in this victory.

The final event of the 1990 World Cup series was held a month later, in Barcelona, Spain. Distracted by my problems at home, I climbed poorly, yet I got higher on the route than Isabelle, who came second. Just as I had predicted, she and I had tied for first in the overall scores for the World Cup. This led to a last-minute flurry by the French to see if they could change the rules to award first place to Isabelle. The judges demanded that I give them a urine sample that they immediately tested for drug or steroid use. I tested negative. Isabelle and I were then declared cochampions of the 1990 World Cup, but at the award ceremony she refused to stand beside me on the podium, preferring to remain in the audience pouting and complaining that she alone should have been the winner. Isabelle, a head-turningly pretty woman, had a talent for being petulant and bratty at competitions. At Nîmes she had stunned the audience when she had paused during her ascent on the semifinal route and turned in the direction of a family caring for a crying infant. "Take that baby out of here," she had shrieked.

After Barcelona, the UIAA representative from France (the UIAA being an international climbing organization that oversee matters from contest controversies to setting standards for the strength of ropes) kept up the pressure and protested our cochampionship, insisting that Isabelle be declared the sole World Cup winner. After dealing with all this petty nationalism, I was as weary from the emotional toll of competing on the World Cup circuit as I was of the bad sportsmanship, rule bending, and monumental egos that infested the competitions. Once this fiasco was over, I wandered through the cobblestone streets of Barcelona thinking about my return home.

The weeks I spent back in New Paltz were stormy. Russ and I seemed like strangers to one another, and though we worked hard to come to a better understanding, we both knew that our marriage was on the rocks. The notes of the psychologist we saw during this troubled time are revealing: "Both of you seemed to be living a very nonintimate life together," he wrote in his report. He described me as being "detached and emotionally controlled." He observed that Russ made "few demands" of me for intimacy and closeness. Regarding my issues, he noted that I was "not willing to make the kind of changes that would have been required on your side of the relationship, partly as a result of your perception that this relationship could not give you what you needed." To me, it was clear that our values and the way we related to people were essentially incompatible.

By spring 1991 our marriage was over. New Paltz no longer felt like the right place for me. However, I have maintained a connection to friends in New Paltz, including Russ, and we still get together occasionally to visit and climb in the Gunks.

On March 2, exactly one year after my ascent of Masse Critique, I checked ten boxes containing my belongings onto an airplane in New York and flew to the Nice airport. All through the flight I thought about Russ and my heart was heavy. I knew I would miss him, but from this day forward we would be heading on separate paths. I was beginning a new phase of life by moving to the country where I had nearly died only a few years before but with which I had fallen in love. I had no idea where this path would lead, but I chose to take a leap of faith. I remember pausing in the airport when I arrived, hearing the radio announce the end of the Gulf War. I too felt as if a war had ended, a war that had been waging inside myself and that had finally come to a peaceful end.

I settled in the Lubéron region of Provence, because of its proximity to world-class climbing areas like Buoux, the Verdon Gorge, and a dozen other crags, and because of the community of French friends I had grown to know in the surrounding villages. The landscape of this part of France spoke to something deep inside me. On autumn days when the crisp *mistral* wind cleared the air and the golden sunlight soaked into the cliffs, vineyards, and centuries-old stone houses, the world resembled an oil painting by an Old Master.

In the summer of 1991, I funneled the winnings of my competitions into the purchase of a 150-year-old stone farmhouse in the village of Grambois in Provence. The charm of my new home, with vaulted ceilings and three-foot-thick stone walls, was not without complication.

Just about everything needed repairing, from the crooked doors and shutters to the aging electrical system to the leaking roof. I added hand-crafted wood cabinets in the kitchen, renovated the bathroom, replaced the carpet with oak floors, painted and plastered the interior, and built an artificial climbing wall in a room with a vaulted stone ceiling. Not everything could be fixed, however. Rising damp crept through the stone walls, and the primitive septic system backed up in my front yard. But the renovations served as a kind of therapeutic contemplation for me, and even though I sometimes felt like a slave to this house of stone, my home in the Lubéron was a solid base between all my travels. My sense of well-being among friends and neighbors in the area grew more profound over time. My neighbors taught me how to take care of my garden, make household repairs, bake fresh bread, and make confiture from the fruits of my cherry tree. The "Auberge de Lynnie" also became a stopover for a constant flow of climbers on the international climbing circuit. Some nights at dinner parties, every person in the room was from a different country.

In my place in the French countryside, I felt a sense of freedom. Most of the time, though, I was alone in a big, empty stone house. But this aloneness was good. I was solely responsible for my choices. Every morning upon waking to the sounds of birds flitting through the fruit trees, I was conscious of a process of renewal on every level of my life. Even though the end of my marriage had been traumatic and I missed my family and friends in America, I knew that my close relationships would always be with me no matter where I lived. I felt that I lived at the intersection of many cultures, and rather than feeling like an American expatriate in France, I felt like a citizen of the world.

Yet I did go through periods of emotional doldrums and the lowest of these times was surely during that first year in 1991. One morning I was sitting in my unfinished home, nursing a sprained ankle that I had twisted in a bouldering competition and looking out the window at the charred forest where a huge fire had come to within a few miles of my home. As I slit open a batch of mail, I came across my airmailed copy of *Climbing* magazine, sent to me from America. It contained a shocking piece of news: Yabo was dead.

I had not seen Yabo for two years, but I had received a few letters from him and I had heard reports that he had started climbing again, after giving it up for a while. In his letters he talked optimistically about diving into the competitive side of the sport and becoming a professional climber, though I doubted he had the composure or personality to make this leap. In Snowbird in 1988 he had entered the contest but had climbed stiffly and nervously, and he had not done well. After a lifetime devoted to rock climbing, Yabo sensed that the sport was leaving him behind, and this made him unhappy. Some of my friends told me that he envied the kind of climbing life I lived. In the end, Yabo had become confused by the game of competitive climbing, and his desire to succeed at this was at odds with his spirit as a traditional rock climber.

Sometime around 1990 Yabo had met Jean Milgram, a climber living in the San Francisco Bay Area. As with other women in his life, Yabo focused every attention on her, until inevitably the pain of his troubled youth and his sense of hopelessness flowed to the surface in a way that Jean found disturbing. She helped Yabo find work, she loaned him money so he could keep climbing, and she even arranged for a psychologist to meet with him, but although she loved him, she could not cope with Yabo's inner conflict. Finally she told him that they should stop seeing each other.

On hearing this, Yabo plunged into a dark, irrational, and destructive mood that grew worse over a period of several days. At Jean's suggestion, Yabo drove up to Yosemite to go climbing for a few days, but he was too upset to focus on climbing. Instead he carved Jean's name into his stomach with a piece of broken glass, then he drove straight back to the Bay Area. When Yabo arrived at Jean's house, he insisted that she go with him for a ride in his van. He then drove to the east side of the Sierras, to an old climbing haunt called Dead Man's Summit, where he threatened suicide and made ominous statements like, "If I can't have you, no one will." Later, he came up with the idea that he would be reincarnated in the child that he wanted to give Jean. After Jean persuaded Yabo to take her home, she called the police.

"I've seen this kind of situation before. One or both of you is going to wind up dead," advised the streetwise officer who came to Jean's house to settle Yabo down.

On the last night of Yabo's life—September 4, 1991—he returned to

Jean's house in a state of anguish and became violent when she reiterated that she could not be his mate. Years later, Jean told me about that night. She described how Yabo had wrapped his hands around her neck and started choking her, then abruptly stopped. It was as if he had shocked himself with the realization that he might be capable in a moment of passion of killing the person he loved most. He chose, at that point, to take his own life. Yabo lay down on Jean's bed, held a pistol in his trembling hand, and pointed it to his head. Jean, who had run out when he released her, said that as she reentered the bedroom, she had just a moment to look into Yabo's eyes. Before she could say or do anything to stop him, he pulled the trigger.

Yabo's death, at the age of thirty-five, stunned me and many other climbers in America. He had been a close friend, and I felt sad that I could not have done more to help him. In the wake of his death, a legend grew. Climbers who had never met him extolled his wild solos in campfire and barroom tales, and the myth painted him as part manic-depressive, part mystic. An obituary in *Climbing* magazine written by John Long was more realistic. John suggested that Yabo's grief "was simply from ignorance of the proper proportion of things, his balance and sense of scale thrown off by problems beyond his control." For a while, spray-painted on a concrete freeway overpass in Boulder, Colorado, were the words, YABO LIVES!

This period also coincided with the loss of another dear friend and free climbing legend, Wolfgang Gullich. Wolfgang was one of the few professional climbers I knew who had been successful in integrating his climbing and professional life in a harmonious way outside the realm of competition. He was a rock climber and adventurer who traveled to many beautiful places around the world.

The morning preceding his fatal automobile accident, Wolfgang had taken part in a radio interview in Munich. During this interview, the radio host asked if Wolfgang viewed his exploits in climbing as being particularly dangerous or life-threatening. Wolfgang responded that while taking risks in climbing, he was usually highly conscious of his actions. Ironically, he finished by saying that driving on the Autobahn can sometimes be more dangerous than climbing, due to the monotony of routine and lack of attention. Shortly after this radio interview, Wolfgang was killed when he fell asleep at the wheel and crashed while driving back to his home in Nuremberg.

Wolfgang was a great climber and a wonderful human being. One of the qualities I most appreciated about Wolfgang was his sincere, compassionate nature. He was an approachable person who rarely declined requests for interviews and appearances. His pursuit of pure technical difficulty helped raise the standards of difficulty worldwide. He was the first person to climb a route rated 5.13d, in 1984. The following year, he did the first free ascent of Punks in the Gym in Australia, which was one of the first routes rated 5.14a in the world. He continued his trend in breaking new barriers when he became the first person to climb a 5.14b and a 5.14d with his first ascents of Wall Street in 1987 and Action Direct in 1991.

I found out about Wolfgang's accident while on a climbing trip in the

Wolfgang on Action Direct, the first 9a (5.14d) in the world.
(THOMAS BALLENBERGER)

Frankenjura in Germany. The next day, when they turned his life-support machines off, I didn't feel like climbing. But after considerable reflection, I decided that the best way to commemorate his death would be to carry on the positive inspiration that his life stood for. It was at this time that I began to contemplate the more profound significance of my own life-jolting experience of falling nearly 80 feet to the ground at Buoux. This acknowledgment, which began as a grain of conscious-ness, was beginning to mature and take form. One of my goals on the rock had been to climb a 5.13b on-sight and I was determined to do it on this particular day as a kind of personal dedication to Wolfgang.

That afternoon, a small group of us decided to climb at a crag called the Student, which was one of Wolfgang's local crags in the Frankenjura of West Germany. From the moment of our arrival, I felt an incredible sense of inspiration and confidence. I warmed up on a few classic routes and eventually found myself at the base of a climb called Simon, which happened to be rated 5.13b. Before attempting this climb, I cultivated a quiet, receptive mental state. I was ready to go for it with relaxed confidence. As I began climbing, each move seemed to flow naturally and I hardly felt any accumulation of fatigue in my forearms. When I eventually made it to the top without a fall, I felt a deep sense of emotion and peace, knowing that the quality of my performance was greatly inspired by Wolfgang's spirit as a climber and human being.

When I lowered back to the ground, my friends Jibé Tribout and his wife, Corrine, were so silent, they seemed more surprised than me. It wasn't until we were hiking back down the trail that Jibé finally asked, "Was that the first 5.13b you've ever done on-sight?"

I responded with a simple, "Yes," and I didn't even bother to rub it in that he had once said that a woman would never even "flash" a 5.12d.

After competing nearly constantly for six years, I decided that 1992 would be my last year on the World Cup circuit. The competition life had been good to me: by the end of my career, of thirty-eight contests I would enter, I would win twenty-six of them. And the cash prizes and sponsorships had allowed me to live the life I wanted. But as the game of competition evolved and the way of life became more consuming, I no longer felt a sense of freedom pursuing this style of climbing. Even at the competitions themselves, competitors spent most of their time sequestered away in "isolation," waiting for the moment to climb. Sometimes we would be captive for as much as twelve hours before climbing a single route. Like in most other highly competitive sports, the price of victory meant conforming to a rather restricted experience in life. Though I had a lot of fun and learned a great deal during these years as a competitor, I began to feel that too much of my energy was invested in climbing, training, diet, and traveling to the next competition.

Since that first chaotic Arco contest in 1986, a new generation of climbers had entered the arena, and, like the gymnasts of my youth, many of them were adolescents. As the sport turned increasingly toward youth, the culture of training for competitions changed also. Many contenders spent the majority of their time training on artificial walls crammed into their basements, and were seldom seen out at the cliffs. It was a joke among competitors that the hardest climbing moves ever done lay in these basement gyms. I rarely trained on such walls because being out on the rock is what has always inspired me the most.

Knowing that it would be my last year to compete in Arco, I was motivated to climb my very best. For me, Arco was the Wimbledon of rock climbing. Each year thousands of animated spectators gather to watch the best sport climbers in the world perform. When I arrived at the top of the final route, marking my fifth and final victory in this "Rock Master" event, I felt a peaceful sense of completion.

Although I was feeling strong and motivated toward the end of the competition season, I didn't win the next World Cup competition in Nuremberg. It seemed like an ironic twist of fate that once again I would be disqualified due to a technicality regarding the rules. According to the rules, we were required to clip into the last carabiner while hanging from the final hold of the route. Unfortunately, when I arrived at the top of the route, I was in such a state of relief and excitement that I did the natural thing and grabbed the top of the wall to steady myself before clipping into the last carabiner. This oversight led to my disqualification and eliminated me from competing in a superfinal with Robyn Erbesfield.

This event, and my experiences at the last few World Cup events of the year, served as confirmation that competitions were no longer my place. Even the style of climbing on these artificial walls seemed to correspond less and less to my own natural style of climbing. On natural rock, I learned to adapt my personal dimensions to its subtle features. Since artificial walls are inherently limited in form and feature, they offer less freedom of expression. The style I had developed through years of climbing on rock was maladapted in this realm of competition and I wasn't interested in conforming. Just as I had as a young gymnast, I felt an increasing resistance toward the structure and artificial constructs associated with competition. In keeping with my own spirit of spontaneity and intuitive feeling, I preferred to plan my sequences while climbing rather than preplan them by inspecting the route with binoculars as many competitors did. I tried my best to ignore the allotted time limitations and maintain my natural climbing style. But this wasn't necessarily a strategy that rendered victorious results in competition. At one of the last few competitions of the year in Saint Polten, Austria, before I could make the last few moves to the top of the route, the judge called out the remaining seconds of time. At that point, I knew that my "time" in competition was winding down.

By the end of the second-to-last competition for the 1992 competition circuit, held in Laval, France, I knew I would not win the World Cup. It was evident that my friend Robyn Erbesfield had already amassed enough points to secure a victory. Ever since Robyn and I had first climbed together, I knew that she had the talent and drive to be my successor on the World Cup scene. We had even talked about the day when she would stand on the first-place position on the podium, holding the trophy. Robyn had worked hard to achieve her vision and I was happy we could share a mutual sense of completion on that day.

Although I did not win at Laval, I was nevertheless given an award that carried sentimental meaning for me. Catherine Destivelle presented an award to me in honor of a famous writer named Alfred Jarry who had grown up in the town of Laval. This writer had invented a character that he named the Ubu. The trophy itself was a small sculpture of this funny-looking creature, with a cone-shaped head that was meant to symbolize positive vision toward the future and concentric circles on its belly signifying creativity and inspiration. This award was a fitting confirmation of the sentiments I felt at that moment, as well as a gesture of camaraderie from Catherine.

After Catherine retired from competitions in 1990, she had thrown herself into alpinism with verve. She made a free ascent of Trango Tower in the Karakoram Mountains of Pakistan—on which she climbed rock pitches of 5.12 at nearly 20,000 feet—as well as first ascents of a few other new climbs in the Himalayas with her husband, Erik Decamp. But perhaps her most significant achievement was her winter trilogy involving solo ascents of the three biggest north faces of the Alps—the Eiger, the Bonatti route on the Matterhorn, and a twelve-day solo of a big-wall climb on the Grandes Jorasses. I admired the way she had returned to the kind of climbing that inspired her the most. Although I did not want to head into the mountains like her, I felt the need to step out of the bright light that shone on competition climbing and return to my own roots: rock climbing.

The final World Cup competition of the 1992 season—and the last big comp of my career—was held in Birmingham, England. As a parting gesture to the last seven years of competing, I wanted to give this competition my best effort and climb to the very top of the wall. The course setters by this stage of the game were making the final moves of the climbs diabolically hard, often in the 5.13 range of difficulty. You had to earn the final hold, fight for it. Waiting in isolation, I sensed the nervousness of the other competitors as they went through their rituals of stretching, rubbing down the edges of their shoes to increase the friction, and listening meditatively to tunes on their Sony Walkmans. But I felt relaxed knowing that I was at the end of a personal era.

The walls separating the isolation room from the stage on which the climbing wall was mounted were thin, and the reactions of the crowd to each of our performances filtered through. When a climber reached the top of a route, there was tumultuous cheering. Minutes after Robyn began climbing, we heard the chorus from the audience murmuring a sad "Aaahhh," so we assumed she must have fallen low down on the wall. Then it was Isabelle Patissier's turn to climb. She stood up and left the room, wearing socks over her rock shoes to protect the stickiness of the rubber on their soles while walking to the base of the wall. Long minutes passed, telling me that she was high on the route. Then I heard a sudden "Ahhhh" from the audience. Isabelle had not reached the top of the course.

My turn came. I walked onto the stage, examined the wall for a minute, then I went for it. The moves on this route were technical, out of balance, and strenuous. It seemed like the course setters, who were Brits, were giving me a taste of the routes they had been raised on. On nearly every move I had to contort myself into awkward positions that seemed so likely to toss me off the wall that I sometimes had to lunge between holds. I shook the fatigue out of my forearms while clutching tiny edges at the lip of the final overhang, and then I searched deep in myself for one last bit of power and concentration. I threw myself to the final hold, clipped the carabiner, and then suddenly my trance was broken by the loud cheering from the audience and an overwhelming sense of elation.

Winning this final contest meant a lot to me, even though it was Robyn who would hold the World Cup trophy that night. I was happy to have made a wholehearted effort one last time in competition as a way of celebrating the end of an era and the beginning of a new direction in life. As I untied from the rope after being lowered to the stage, Robyn came striding toward me. Her big beautiful smile and her outstretched arms, which she wrapped around me, were worth more than any trophy.

"Lynn, you are awesome!" she said as she gave me a big hug.

Her gesture of good sportsmanship and friendship capped the end of my competition career in the most positive way. Robyn would go on to win the World Cup over the next three years. She married the French sport climbing champion Didier Raboutou, and they now have two children together. But as we left the stage in Birmingham that night, arm in arm, and I looked back to the artificial wall standing tall among a battery of floodlights, I felt a sense of completion. My experiences in the arena had been good, but I felt no regrets as I turned and walked away.

Chapter 12

Freeing the Nose

After my career in climbing competitions, I returned to my roots as a rock climber, and I headed back to the cliffs that nature had made. After succeeding on Masse Critique, I knew that if I expanded my vision of what was possible, I could probably do an even harder climb. But rather than directing my efforts toward climbing a route of a higher technical grade, I wanted to expand my capacities on climbs with sky above my head and space below my feet. The idea of combining a high level of technical difficulty on a climb of big-wall scale began to take shape in my mind.

On one of my visits back to California in the early nineties, I met up with my friend John Long. While talking about climbing and my future plans, John said, "Lynnie, you should try making the first free ascent of the Nose on El Cap. It's one of the last great problems in American free climbing."

The Nose Route on El Capitan

Summit Overhangs

Changing Corners

Camp VI

Glowering Spot

Camp V

Great Roof

Camp IV

Boot Flake

Texas Flake

Jardine Traverse

Dolt Tower

Stove Legs Crack System

Sickle Ledge

3rd class climbing to start of first pitch

Of course! John was right. This was just the kind of challenge I was looking for. The Nose route follows the most prominent line right up the center of the biggest granite monolith in Yosemite Valley, and is perhaps the most famous big-wall route in the world. Climbers had been trying to free it for several years, but a few sections of the wall presented immense difficulty and had stopped all comers cold. Although it had been years since either John or I had done the route, we both remembered clearly that the crux problems consisted of thin cracks and delicate face climbing. John pointed to my fingers and said, "Those little fingers of yours will be the secret weapons on the Nose."

With my background as a traditional climber, combined with all my experiences on various types of rock over the years, I realized that this would be the perfect challenge.

A year passed, in which I shuttled back and forth between America and my home in France. Then, in 1992, I happened to cross paths with Hans Florine, who casually asked me if I would like to do a one-day speed ascent of the Nose with him. Hans was one of the leading speed climbers of the day. In competitions he often won the crowd-pleasing speed events in which two climbers race each other, and the clock, up a wall of moderate difficulty, hitting a bell at the end of their route to signal their arrival at the final hold. Hans had transferred that ability onto the rock, and the pure crystalline granite of the Nose had become his playground. By August 1992, Hans had made seven ascents of the route, and I had confidence in his ability to figure out the best strategy in solving time-consuming maneuvers like the King Swing pendulum. Speed ascents of the Nose are not done in the same style as free ascents because they involve a mixture of free and aid climbing techniques—an "anything goes" approach. To climb nearly 3,000 feet of El Cap granite so rapidly, a climber generally uses aid to pull past difficult sections. Though we clocked a time of eight hours and forty minutes, my main objective was not about speed. As we raced up the wall, I tried to imagine what it would be like to try free climbing past the notorious Great Roof, as well as the other sections that had never been free climbed. By the top of the route, I knew that I had indeed discovered a magnificent challenge. Perhaps I would never succeed in free climbing the Nose, but being back in Yosemite on one of the most beautifully sculpted cliffs on earth would be worth an effort as grand as the route itself.

The first climber to put serious effort into free climbing the Nose was a Californian named Ray Jardine. A space-flight mechanics system analyst by profession, Jardine had spent his free time living in Yosemite between 1970 and 1981. With his thick beard and horn-rimmed glasses, Jardine looked like an eccentric professor, but his powerful physique and his mind-set of pushing the limits of climbing difficulty by adopting new tactics made him a controversial figure among Yosemite climbers, some of whom did not agree with his style. Jardine drove the grades of crack climbs into the 5.12 range, and later he pushed grades even higher when he made the first ascent of the Phoenix, a 5.13 crack. To achieve this he ignored the prescribed styles of the day, and it was Jardine who first brought the issue of hang dogging to public attention. Jardine's creativity in finding ways to make harder climbs possible led him to other innovations such as the piece of gear he called the Friend, an ingenious spring-loaded device designed to expand inside a crack. He eventually sold the design to a British company and these camming devices have been so successful that nearly all climbers use them today, in one derivation or another.

In 1981 Jardine decided that a free ascent of the Nose would be his masterpiece climb, and for four months he set about trying to accomplish it. But instead of coming away with a masterpiece, Ray Jardine created a great controversy—some say an atrocity—over which he ultimately left Yosemite and stopped climbing.

Jardine did not call the route he wanted to free climb the Nose. He referred to the general area of rock around this section of El Cap as the Southwest Buttress, and he envisioned a route that he called Numero Uno that would link together sections of the Nose with new lines or with parts of an adjacent aid route called Grape Race. The result, he hoped, would be a route up the great face that went entirely free. Before him, climbers like Jim Bridwell, John Bachar, and Ron Kauk had freed the most obvious cracks on the Nose. What remained to be freed were several sections of aid climbing and pendulums (where a climber rigs up gear to swing across a blank section of rock), the Great Roof, and a few other wildly steep sections of climbing near the top. Jardine found featureless rock just before the famous King Swing pendulum that connects the upper and lower sections of the wall. Looking through a tele-scope set up in the meadow, he noticed a row of holds heading toward another crack system, on Grape Race. If he could just span this 35-foot section, he would be able to overcome the first of the major obstacles in freeing the Nose.

"After several days of working on the traverse, I determined that it was a lot harder [than 5.11—a grade that was at the upper end on the scale of difficulty in those days]. So I bought a cold chisel," Jardine told writer Eric Perlman in a *Rock and Ice* magazine interview in 1995.

Using logic that most climbers find hard to justify, Jardine "tooled" several holds into the rock by striking the chisel with a hammer to chip away small edges for his fingers and toes. The traverse he manufactured allowed him to climb sideways across the rock into Grape Race. The dif-ficulty was 5.12a. Without chiseling, many climbers, including myself, believe that the traverse may have been possible, but at a much higher grade. Jardine has since admitted he was appalled at his own workman-ship, because the holds he created stood out as being blatantly man-made.

"Was I committing a moral injustice or making a little bit of history?" he asked rhetorically in his interview in 1995, adding, "My vision was for a moderate route up the Southwest Buttress of El Cap. I wanted to make it not of the highest standard but of the highest meaning. After I realized that enhancing face holds was not the way to go, I quit the project—I knew its time had not yet come. Progress demanded that the route go free, but I lacked the technology to contrive the necessary holds."

Though Jardine's vision may have been ahead of its time, he failed to recognize that the spirit of free climbing is about adapting one's per-sonal capacities and dimensions to the natural features of the rock, not the other way around. Jardine left Yosemite in 1981, leaving the Nose to be freed by others.

It was not until 1991 that two talented free climbers, Brooke Sandahl and Scott Franklin, resumed the challenge. They free climbed across Jardine's traverse to make progress far up the wall, but the Great Roof stopped them. When they arrived underneath the Great Roof, they dis-covered that it was soaking wet and therefore too difficult to try climb-ing without aid. The following year, Brooke returned to Yosemite to continue his effort with Dave Schultz. Though they failed to free climb two key sections of the route, their vision helped pave the way for some-

Simon Nadin waking up on the Camp Five bivy ledge on the Nose. (LYNN HILL
COLLECTION)

one to come later and make the first all-free ascent of the Nose. Their
most significant breakthrough was the new free variation they created
on the last pitch, up the spectacular overhanging headwall where
Harding had spent fourteen hours placing fifteen pitons and twenty-
eight bolts on the last day of his historic first ascent of the route in 1958.

Returning to El Cap felt like coming home, I realized as I headed up the
wall on my first attempt to free the Nose, in 1993. Some twenty years
had passed since my first view of this grand monolith, when I had come
on a camping trip to Yosemite with my family. Later it had been a rite
of passage when I struggled my way up the Nose with Mari and Dean
in 1979, climbing the route using aid during our three-day ascent. Then,
thirteen years later, I had made a speed ascent with Hans Florine in just
over eight hours. Now, at age thirty-three, my mission was to free climb
every inch of this legendary 3,000-foot rock formation.

My partner was a British climber named Simon Nadin, a tall man
with a soft voice and a sunny-faced complexion, whom I had met at a
World Cup competition in 1989. That year, Simon had entered his first

competition; by year's end he was the first World Cup champion in the history of the sport. I felt at ease around Simon and respected his understated personality. As a climber, he had bundles of natural talent. In addition to being a good sport climber, Simon was used to doing bold, naturally protected routes in England. Simon, like me, had served an apprenticeship in traditional climbing style as opposed to sport climbing alone. When Simon and I had had a chance encounter at Cave Rock, on the shore of Lake Tahoe, we discovered our mutual desire to try to free climb the Nose. Though Simon had never climbed a big wall, I trusted him to be my partner on this towering cliff where swallows and peregrines swooped. Within an hour of our meeting, Simon had postponed his return flight to Britain. Five days later, we were already two-thirds of the way up the wall, sleeping on a ledge beneath the Great Roof.

We woke up on our bivy ledge 2,000 feet above the ground with the first rays of light spilling into the valley. As we looked down from our

Royal Robbins on the Great Roof in 1960. (TOM FROST)

perch, the giant pine trees on the valley floor appeared like small heads of broccoli. Despite our airy position and bright sunshine illuminating the day, I didn't feel a sense of lightness. Getting to this point had taken us two days, and now, on our third day on the route, the force of gravity was weighing on us heavily. We were twenty-one pitches up the wall, and we had climbed eighteen hours without pause the previous day, finally quitting at midnight. The fatigue from all that free climbing, and the backbreaking work of dragging up two ropes, a heavy rack of gear, and a cumbersome haulbag, made us wake feeling tired and fuzzy-headed. As I looked at the Great Roof looming above my head, I felt my swollen hands throb with each beat of my heart.

The Great Roof pitch begins with a corner shaped like an open book with a crack at its center. The rock to either side is smooth, and the width of the crack at times pinches down to a quarter of an inch. The corner rises straight up for about 100 feet, but then it begins to tilt to the right, leaning over until it becomes a large roof shaped like a breaking wave of granite. To free climb it, a climber must surf sideways on smooth, featureless rock with his or her fingers jammed into the crack above. We knew this was one of the longest pitches of the entire route and its impressive architecture appeared unrelenting in its continuity. To make matters worse, the intensity of the midsummer heat radiated from the rock, making our skin ooze with perspiration.

"It looks like you get the first shot at leading the Great Roof," I said, handing the gear over to Simon. We had been swinging leads all the way up the wall.

"I guess I'll give it a try," he said softly in his adorable English accent.

Simon looked graceful as he cruised up the first three-quarters of the pitch, lay backing and jamming his way up the crack that split the center of the right-facing corner. But just before arriving under the Great Roof, his progress came to a distinct halt.

Simon slumped his weight onto the rope and shouted down to me, "The crack is too thin. I can't even find a way to hang on up here."

Watching such a talented climber become increasingly frustrated with each unsuccessful effort, I couldn't help but share his sense of disappointment.

"You might have a better chance at this pitch than me," he shouted before lowering back down to the belay and turning the lead over.

This was the section that John had in mind when he pointed to my small fingers and said they would be my secret weapon. Ironically, my height of five-foot-two is often a shortcoming on the most difficult face climbs, where there are inevitably moves with long reaches between holds, but on the Great Roof it appeared that the tables were turned and perhaps my small size would be an advantage.

When I arrived at the first difficult section below the roof, I immediately understood why Simon was having such a hard time hanging on. Though I was able to wedge my fingertips into a few small openings in the crack, the face on either side was utterly devoid of features to stand on. At one point, the only edge of rock I could use to stand on was located at shoulder height and I needed to make a powerful kick just to get my foot up onto this hold. Underneath the roof itself, I had to duck my head down inside the curl of this granite wave, while wedging two fingertips of each hand straight up into the crack above my head. In order to keep my feet from skating off the smooth surface of the rock, I needed to maintain a perpendicular angle with my feet pressed flat against the vertical wall below. Moving from this rock-surfing position involved strenuous yet delicate tai-chi-like dance steps to coordinate finger moves and foot shuffles. After trying countless combinations of hand and foot sequences, my strength and concentration were nearly spent. I knew it would be possible to free climb this pitch, but I wasn't sure I would have enough strength to do it that day. I didn't have the luxury of coming back another day, nor did I have the energy to refine the sequence any further. My only hope of free climbing this pitch on my next try was to perform each move with as much grace and finesse as possible. I lowered down to the belay to rest before giving it my best effort.

After a twenty-minute rest, I started up again feeling surprisingly strong and fluid. But as soon as I began the most difficult series of moves, my timing was off and my body position faltered. I thrust my fingertips into a small opening in the crack just as my right foot popped off the face. In the next instant, I was airborne, then the rope caught my fall and I swung sideways into the corner. I hung on the rope, panting, with 2,000 feet of air below my feet, and then I lowered back to Simon.

"One more try. I'll do better next time," I said, voicing my mantra of hopeful determination.

While I rested, a team of Croatian climbers passed us. They moved quickly, climbing in traditional aid style. Down on the meadows I noticed that the pines were casting long shadows. We had limited energy and daylight left. Either I would make the first free ascent of this pitch on my next try, or we would have to abandon our all free attempt and finish climbing to the top.

While resting at the belay, I looked across the valley at the face of Middle Cathedral. On its mottled wall I noticed a play of shadows form the shape of a heart. I have always noticed the symbols around me, and this heart on stone reminded me of the values that have always been most important in my life and in climbing. My own development as a climber has been an extension of the experiences, passion, and vision of others. For me, free climbing the Great Roof was an opportunity to demonstrate the power of having an open mind and spirit. Though I realized that I could easily fall in my exhausted state, I felt a sense of liberation and strength knowing that this was an effort worth trying with all my heart. I had a strong feeling that this ascent was a part of my destiny and that somehow I could tap into that mysterious source of energy to literally rise to the occasion. I said nothing to Simon of my private thoughts, and when I returned to the roof, I realized that this was the moment of truth.

This time, as I began the most difficult sequence of moves, I could feel my strength waning, but willpower alone seemed to fuel me past the move where I had fallen on my previous attempt. Inches before the end of the traverse, my foot slipped off the face again and I began tipping backward. Because I had crunched my body into a tight and awkward position under the roof, my head butted into the ceiling above me, unexpectedly steadying me. I propelled myself onward, extended my right arm as far as I could, and shoved my fingers into a small slot. I composed my breathing for a moment, then focused on making a few final moves onto the belay ledge where one of the Croatian climbers stood staring at me wide-eyed. He had just witnessed the first free ascent of the Great Roof and he was as surprised as me at what had just taken place. Simon shouted up some words of congratulations, then came up the pitch using aid.

Simon didn't need to say anything for me to understand the disappointment he felt in having failed to free climb the Great Roof himself.

Years later, I read an interview in which Simon spoke about his feelings watching me free climb the Great Roof that day:

"One more attempt was all the dwindling light would allow. I tried hard to stay cheery and not upset Lynn's concentration. Dejected that I had failed at the first obstacle, the consolation of just doing the Nose wasn't enough. Lynn's free ascent of this pitch was inspirational. She had been on the edge, feet popping off several times but somehow summoning up enough reserves to complete it."

The hard climbing was not over yet, though. There was one more pitch above Camp Six called the Changing Corners that had never been free climbed, and it had a reputation among the few who had tried it for being "reachy," meaning that the key holds were far apart. I knew that there was a good chance I would not be able to find an alternative way to make it past this blank section of rock.

Sensing that Simon needed a bit of cheering up, I said, "I think you'll have a much better chance of free climbing the pitch above Camp Six. Brooke told me that this section involved a long reach with virtually nothing in the way of intermediate holds. There's a good chance that you'll be able to free climb it and I won't. If that's the case, we may be successful in making the first free ascent of the Nose as a team."

In retrospect, I don't know if my comments inspired or intimidated him. Simon merely nodded with a look of mixed emotions as he prepared to climb the next pitch. We climbed a little higher that evening, finally bivouacking on the ledge at Camp Five.

The next morning we organized our gear and shared our last food: one-half of an energy bar and one date each. We started ahead of the Croatian climbers, and it was Simon's turn to lead up a difficult pitch called the Glowering Spot. It turned out to be a horrendous way to start the day. This pitch follows an incipient crack to the left of a grass-filled corner that throws the climber into a frenzy of technical stemming and shallow finger jams. Rated 5.12d, and protected by small wired stoppers that are tedious to wiggle into the crack, Simon was grunting with fatigue by its end. As I climbed up behind him, struggling to stay on the rock without slipping, one of the Croatians appeared behind me, aid climbing upward, right at my heels.

Having climbed twenty-eight pitches, we arrived at Camp Six at eleven-thirty A.M., tired but hopeful of being able to continue our free ascent. Brooke Sandahl had already tried to free climb the pitch above us a year earlier by deviating to the left of the original line, up a steep face, then back right across a blank section of rock. I went up first to check out the crux moves and was quickly discouraged. Getting across the crux section involved reaching out to a tiny hold a full arm-stretch away, with nothing on the sheer face below to stand on. Taller climbers could stand on a small crystal of rock on the face, but this hold was located so low down on the face that I wasn't able to reach the crucial hold with my arms spread apart in a nearly iron-cross position. After a few tries, it was obvious that the mechanics necessary to make this move were not going to work for me. Simon went up next. Though he was able to make it past the first reachy move, he was stopped by the next section, which involved an acrobatic jump to the right. After a few tries, he too determined that the moves were too difficult in his tired condition.

As a last resort, I tried climbing up the original line that nearly all climbers had followed for the previous thirty-five years. This way climbed a shallow, flaring corner to our right. The walls to either side of this feature were smooth, and little in the way of a crack split the corner itself. The climbing was desperately hard and our spirits had been withered away by hunger and fatigue. We had only a few hours of daylight left to make it to the top, so we reluctantly decided that we had no other choice but to abandon the all free effort. We had made a valiant effort to free climb this route, but a mere 10-foot stretch of blank rock had foiled us.

Over the next few days, which I spent at a family reunion in Idaho, I thought of the moves that had stopped us. Getting up those few feet had seemed so improbable, but after considering the possibilities from a fresh perspective, I was convinced that it was worth giving it another try.

The following week I returned to Yosemite with my friend Brooke Sandahl, a talented and passionate climber with an understated manner who turned out to be an ideal partner on this landmark ascent. Brooke revealed to me that when he was a young boy learning to climb with his father, he had looked at pictures of the Nose route and thought, *One day I'm going to free climb that route.* Brooke was eager to try it again himself. We hiked nine miles to the top of El Capitan, rappelled down to the pitch above Camp Six, and set to work on this enigmatic section of climbing. Brooke focused on trying his own face climbing variation; I focused on climbing the original line. Climbing up this corner demanded an ingenuity of movement that I had rarely ever encountered. We spent three days working on this pitch, and by the end I had pieced together a sequence of moves that went together like a crazy dance. I had invented a wild tango of smears with my feet, tenuous stems, back steps and cross steps, lay backs and arm bars, and pinches and palming maneuvers. Ironically, instead of being stopped by the reachy variation, I discovered that the original route turned out to be much better suited for a person of my body dimensions.

September heat dogged us, but I was able to climb this pitch with only one fall. Brooke was not successful on his variant, but seeing how close I was to success, he was keen to join me in our effort to make a free ascent of the entire route from bottom to top. When we returned to the Nose a few days later, we were well stocked with food and water,

**Brooke attempting his
variation of the
Changing Corners pitch.**
(LYNN HILL)

and we both felt a sense of harmony in this magical place. When we arrived at the Great Roof, I went up once to familiarize myself with the moves, then made a successful free ascent on my first try. Next Brooke gave it a try for the first time since his ascent in 1991 when the crack was soaking wet. Though he felt it was possible for him to free climb this pitch, he knew that it would be too hard to do that day, so we continued climbing up to our bivy ledge at Camp Five. At the end of the same day, I led the Glowering Spot pitch while I was still limber from the day's climbing.

The morning of our final day, I woke up on the ledge at Camp Five and opened my eyes to look straight up the giant dihedral at the last several hundred feet of the climb. There, above, was the Changing Corners pitch that would make or break our free attempt. I had just dreamed that I had free climbed this pitch, and I felt a strong sense of excitement about what was soon to unfold. The weather was cool and I felt relaxed.

Brooke put me on belay and I started up knowing I would have to link the complex set of moves together exactly the way I had imagined them over the past several days. To get up the Changing Corners section, I had worked out a maneuver involving a bizarre contortion that seemed like a disappearing act. Using a carefully coordinated sequence of opposite pressures between my feet, hands, elbows, and hips against the shallow walls of the corner, I turned my body 180 degrees around.

"That looks like a contortion only Houdini would make up," Brooke yelled up as I spun around from my double-arm-bar contortion. When I reached the belay, I felt a tingle of disbelief run through me. Though we had several pitches to go, none were as hard as this one. Rating the difficulty of such a pitch is almost impossible. Even after having done it, I would say the most accurate grade would be to call it "once, or maybe twice, in a lifetime." I rated 5.13b/c, but it could have just as easily been rated 5.14b. Scott Burke, who spent 261 days over a three-year period in an effort to free climb this route in 1998, was quoted as follows in *Climbing*: "'There are no holds,' he said, claiming difficulties of 5.14b. If his grade holds, The Nose sports one of the hardest free pitches in Yosemite and in America and ranks as the hardest free climb of its size in the world."

Brooke shouted up a stream of congratulations, then he turned serious. "Looks like a storm, we better punch it all the way to the top today."

A dark wall of clouds was rolling in overhead leaving a few raindrops in its wake. Nothing is more miserable than being caught in a rainstorm on El Cap. It takes only minutes for the cliff to become a sheet of water and for hypothermia to set in.

The last pitch before the summit was one of the most exciting pitches I've ever done. With nearly 3,000 feet of exposure to the ground on an overhanging wall with 5.12c face climbing at the lip of a bulge, this was a spectacular way to conclude such a monumental climb.

Brooke and I bivouacked on the summit, curled around a campfire next to Mr. Captain: a venerable old juniper tree that was gnarled from centuries of lightning strikes and winter blizzards. The storm passed by and the evening sky was bright with stars and a fulsome moon. We huddled around the fire, relishing its warmth, laughing and reliving the most powerful moments of our climb. I felt a rush of emotion knowing that the combination of both of our dreams and efforts had led us to

Celebrating with Brooke Sandahl on the summit of the Nose after our all-free ascent in 1993.
(BROOKE SANDAHL COLLECTION)

this historic moment. Though Brooke had climbed all but two sections free, he admitted that he was glad not to have completed the entire route free. He felt that free climbing every pitch would have taken away some of the mystery of this great climb and might have left him with a sense of emptiness about what to do next. But that night as we fell asleep under the bright stars, we both felt a sense of completion—as though everything we had ever done had led us to this summit.

Ever since Warren Harding's 1958 ascent, the Nose has been used by climbers as a benchmark to set and measure standards. The first one-day ascent in 1975 set a precedent for speed, and as years went by, climbers whittled the time down from fifteen hours to an impressive four hours and twenty-two minutes, a record set by Peter Croft and Hans Florine in 1992. This record held until 2001, when Dean Potter and Timmy O'Neill established a new speed record of an incredible three hours and twenty-four minutes. The next obvious challenge was to repeat a free ascent faster or in better style. "Perfect style" would mean a free ascent with no falls, or in climbing lingo, an "on-sight" ascent. No doubt someday someone will do this. But the idea of making an all free ascent of the Nose *in a day* represented a new free climbing challenge in a class of its own.

The idea of attempting such a challenge myself was the result of the merging of several thoughts that had been lingering in the back of my mind. I had often thought about making a film that would convey the history and spirit of climbing, and after talking over various ideas with a French film producer I had met at a film festival near Grenoble, we both agreed that the Nose would be an ideal subject. Rather than simply document another free ascent of the Nose, I wanted to add a greater dimension to the challenge: to free climb the Nose in one day, as opposed to the four days it took with Brooke, would offer a completely new challenge unlike anything I had ever done. It represented a "marathon linkage" and would demand all of the physical, mental, and emotional capacities I had developed over twenty years of climbing. The additional challenge of making a film of this ascent would require significant effort, but even if I failed to free climb the route in a day, it would be a story worth sharing.

Planning on a midsummer ascent, I started training in early spring. I ran and climbed nearly every day, increasing the intensity of my efforts on a weekly basis. Because I was preparing to free climb a thirty-three-pitch route, I needed plenty of endurance and a high level of power; the most difficult sections of the Nose begin after nearly 2,000 feet of climbing. As I practiced going the farthest while expending the least amount of energy, I discovered a new consciousness in my climbing. I learned to appreciate how subtle shifts in my attitude could greatly affect the quality of my movements. By focusing on maintaining a "soft grip" and a "relaxed face," I was better able to relax all the muscles not necessary for each movement. By observing my breathing patterns, I discovered that while reaching in stretched-out positions, it was helpful to inhale in order to gain extra lift, and conversely, while making powerful or dynamic moves, it was helpful to exhale air in a quick burst or to make a karate-style grunt. I focused on maximizing the use of momentum in order to move quickly through awkward body positions or to jump between holds instead of wasting precious strength. Conversely, I practiced minimizing all excess movement to arrive at a "still point" before committing to a delicate move. Throughout the months of training, I practiced an attitude of acceptance; no matter what the situation presented, I made an effort to remain patient and relaxed each step of the way. My intent was to pay attention to my intuitive sense and follow the natural intelligence of the body. When I made this shift in emphasis, my whole approach changed.

As for my climbing performance, I wanted to be fit enough to climb 5.13b on-sight after climbing all day long. While training in the Provence region of France, I spent some time climbing in the Verdon Gorge. This deep chasm of limestone in the mountainous region of the south was an excellent place to train for technical, multipitch rock climbs. The local climbers in the Verdon told me about an ideal route to test my skills. Mingus was a sustained twelve-pitch aid route that had never been fully free climbed. Local experts figured it would go free at a rating of 5.13. My goal was to do the first free ascent of this route in a day. The idea of climbing the entire route on-sight was an ideal, but I didn't expect to do it. But when I did in fact make the first free ascent of this route without a fall, I knew that my training had been effective and that I was ready to begin to try free climbing the Nose in a day.

I knew free climbing the Nose in a day would require a monumental effort, but I had underestimated how much more complicated it would be to make a film during this process. To make matters even more difficult, I found out on the day I was leaving for Yosemite that the American coproducer, who was supposed to help organize the film project with the French film team, had backed out. At that point, I assumed the responsibility of not only doing my best to free climb the route, but to manage all of the myriad logistics of coproducing this documentary film. When I happened to cross paths with the man who had been slated to be the coproducer at a trade show in Salt Lake City, his question to me was, "Do you really think you can do this?"

His comment was disturbing. At that point, I had no idea how much effort would be required to deal with the numerous technical, interpersonal, and logistical issues involved in climbing and filming. Already, from the beginning, it seemed like anything that could go wrong, did go wrong. On the first day of filming, both the soundman and the cameraman refused to rappel down from the summit to film, because they were intimidated by the exposure of 3,000 feet of air below their feet. Several other people whom I had counted on for help also bailed out at the last minute. Then there were technical problems with the camera, dead batteries, and other minor dilemmas to resolve. Whenever I was faced with another unexpected problem, I kept reminding myself, *It's all part of the climb. I must accept whatever happens and keep moving forward.*

The one person I could always count on was my climbing partner, Steve Sutton. I had known Steve since I was a teenager and his good humor and helpful attitude comforted and supported me. Steve was also a veteran of numerous wall climbs and was able to follow each pitch at breakneck speed while carrying all our food, water, and supplies in a small pack on his back. Despite my intention to maintain a positive attitude under all this pressure, I was exhausted by the time I was ready to begin my climb.

In retrospect, it's not surprising that my first attempt at free climbing the Nose in a day was unsuccessful. I began my climb on a particularly hot August day, and when I arrived under the Great Roof at twelve-thirty in the afternoon, it became painfully evident that I had made some crucial errors. After twenty-two pitches of climbing, I had run out of chalk, we were nearly out of water, and the intense heat of the midday sun had all but drained my energy. My hope of free climbing the Nose in a day faded rapidly as I spent the next five and a half hours trying to free climb past the Great Roof. After my fifth attempt, I had spent nearly every bit of strength I had left. At six P.M., I was obliged to abandon my all free ascent and continue climbing to the top. I was so exhausted and my skin worn so thin from jamming my hands and feet into cracks all day long that just getting to the top using aid required a painful effort. By the time we reached the summit, at around nine P.M., I was feeling so completely thrashed that I began to doubt my ability to ever realize this goal. But despite my feelings of discouragement, I couldn't give up the effort.

On September 19 at ten P.M., I started up the route again, this time with no film crew in sight. Guided by the radiance of a full moon, Steve and I climbed pitch after pitch through the peaceful night. After arriving at Camp Four at around eight-thirty in the morning, I dozed off for what seemed like about ten minutes. Suddenly I woke up and noticed the sun just beginning to come around the corner. It was time to resume climbing while it was still cool under the Great Roof. I felt strong and confident on the lower section of the pitch, but then realized I was at the limit of my capacity as soon as I began the crux series of moves. I could

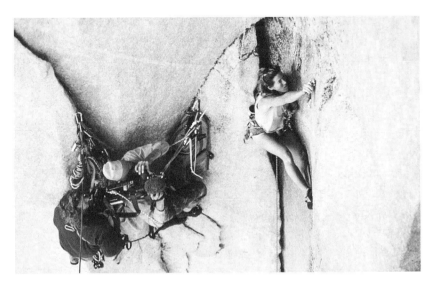

Jim Bridwell and Jean Afanassieff filming me on the Nose just before the Changing Corners pitch. (HEINZ ZAK)

barely fit my fingertips into the small openings in the crack and my feet felt ready to skate off the glassy smooth wall underneath the roof. Knowing that I could easily fall off at any moment, I had faith that I could make it only if I kept moving. So instead of stopping in the middle of the roof to clip into a key piece of protection, I risked it and kept climbing.

At ten twenty-five A.M., I was very happy to be standing at the belay, having made it past the Great Roof on my first try in perfect style. But there was more difficult climbing to come. I began the notorious Glowering Spot pitch at high noon, during the peak heat of the day. This turned out to be the scene of one of the scariest moments of my climb. When I arrived just below the crux section, I placed a small wired stopper in the crack, but just before launching into the most difficult series of moves on the pitch, this crucial piece of protection fell out. With the ledge within striking range below should I happen to fall, it was obvious that climbing farther without any protection would be a dangerous choice. In order to retrieve this wired stopper, I would have to down climb a series of difficult moves to my previous protection and thereby expend more energy than I could afford. Fortunately, I discovered a perfect slot to place one of my two remaining pieces of gear and continued climbing past the crux. With only one more cam left to protect the upper section, I was committed to doing a long run-out to the belay. Having persevered through those nerve-wracking moments, I was more than happy to make it to the belay without falling.

An hour later Steve and I were below the crux Changing Corners pitch. By now the rock was way too hot to consider free climbing under those conditions. We decided to rest on the Camp Six ledge for several hours until El Cap went into the shade. We were both exhausted, and we stretched out on the small shelf of rock, trying to conserve our precious reserves of energy. Steve looked out at all the air around us, shimmering with the heat radiating from the rock.

"You know, Lynnie, we could base-jump from this ledge," he said, alluding to one of his newfound passions where one parachutes off a high cliff or tower rather than from a plane. "The idea of just jumping off and flying through the air is tempting, don't you think?"

"At this point, I prefer to make a free *ascent* rather than a free *fall*," I said.

"I have a feeling you're going to make this free ascent, Lynnie," Steve said, as encouraging and as confident in me as ever.

While lying on the ledge in a half-asleep state, I thought about the various people who inspired me throughout my life. These thoughts helped me cultivate the faith and energy I needed to persevere. For me, this ascent represented a kind of performance art to demonstrate the values I believed in. My belief in this effort was what allowed me to access a source of energy much greater than my own. I thought of what I had learned from a seventy-year-old Chinese chi gong master whom I had met in France earlier that year during a martial arts workshop. At the end of the weekend, this Chinese master asked me to arm wrestle with him. As hard as I tried, our hands remained upright and locked in an impasse. Then he asked me what I was thinking about. I told him that I was concentrating on bringing my hand down to the table. When I asked him what he was thinking about, he said that he was focusing way beyond the table, toward an infinite source of energy. I noticed that his eyes were transfixed into space as if in a trance and that I felt an impenetrable wall of force in his arm. Afterward, we discussed my goal of free climbing the Nose in a day and he said, "When you are on the wall, try to imagine a force of energy that begins in the center of the earth and extends beyond the summit toward infinity."

While resting at Camp Six, over 2,500 feet above the ground, I felt as though the force of gravity had magnified as I climbed higher. But by imagining a powerful source of energy that extended beyond the summit, I sensed that I could flow upward in its current.

By five-thirty, most of the pitch was bathed in shade and I was anxious to give it a try. As I launched into the first series of difficult moves, with my arms stretched out in an iron-cross position and my feet splayed out on tenuous friction holds, I realized that the rock was still radiating with heat. I could already feel my grip beginning to slip. I matched both hands together on the inside corner of the smooth arête, then delicately wedged my fingertips into the tiny crack and pivoted my body around into the corner. As soon as I began working my fingertips higher up in the crack, I suddenly slipped off and dropped onto the rope. This was my first fall of the day and I was disappointed to have ruined the chance to make a perfect no-falls ascent. I rested at the belay for twenty minutes, then fell again on my second attempt. As I began the opening moves on my third try, my foot slipped off while making only the second move. Concerned that my free ascent might be foiled once again, I realized that I needed to regroup and change my attitude before giving it my final attempt.

As I rested at the belay, I glanced out across the valley to Middle Cathedral and saw again the familiar heart-shaped shadow that had inspired my successful ascent of the Great Roof the previous year. The shade line had risen up the wall, underlining the point of the heart. This was the ideal moment to give it my last full-hearted effort. After making it past the first strenuous move and into the insecure corner, I brought my foot up high on the smooth edge of the arête while pinching the corner with the palm of my hand. Since my lack of patience in waiting for the rock to cool had already cost me dearly, this time I knew that it was critical to remain patient and not rush into the next crucial "Houdini" move. This time the sequences flowed together, and even though my ascent had been marred by three falls, I was extremely happy to finally make it on my last try. Free climbing this pitch in such a fatigued state had required a greater effort than any climb I had ever done before.

I found myself below the last two pitches at nightfall. Though my muscles felt slow and heavy, I was confident that I could muster the energy to climb the last strenuous pitch of 5.12c. Wearing a headlamp to see through the darkness, I reached out to the edge of a bulge above me. When I latched on to this hold and let my feet swing out from the face below, I felt an alarming sense of fatigue in my arms. Then I focused my attention on a tiny edge on the face above. In the next instant, I lunged upward and caught the edge with two fingertips. More hard moves came at me out of the night. At the final bulge I was so drained of strength that I had to leap for a hold in a hit-or-miss style. It seemed that the dwindling battery power of my headlamp matched the fading strength of my arms. I arrived at the summit after twenty-three hours of climbing.

Jim Bridwell and Hugh Burton were there to meet us at the top, their headlamps shining a path of light out into the night. My mind swirled in an otherworldly state, yet I felt an underlying sense of peace and serenity. In my dreamlike trance, I knew it was not possible to comprehend all that I had just experienced on this journey. In fact, it has taken me years to fully digest what took place that day.

In the years since my free ascent of the Nose, it has given me great sat-isfaction to see other climbers expanding the possibilities of free climb-ing on the big walls in Yosemite and other more remote big walls around the world. Several more free ascents of other routes on El Cap have been done by the Huber brothers, Heinz Zak, Tommy Caldwell, and Beth Rodden, but the most impressive performances have been by Yuji Hirayama and Leo Houlding, who did nearly perfect on-sight ascents of the Salathè Wall and El Niño, respectively.

When I returned to climb the Nose again in the year 2000 (though I never did an all-free ascent again), I looked at those crux pitches in amazement. Just getting up this gigantic wall of rock using aid requires an incredible amount of energy and determination. Revisiting this route and remembering how hard it was to free climb those crux pitches made me realize how much power can be accessed with the right atti-tude and motivation. Ralph Waldo Emerson said long ago, "What lies behind us and what lies before us are tiny matters compared with what lies within us."

Chapter 13

Full Circle

Several months after I free climbed the Nose in a day, I fell into a state of postclimax depression that left me feeling aimless and empty. Just as Brooke had predicted, my vision had taken me to such an extreme effort that once I succeeded, I felt an equal but opposite reaction. Though I knew I would never have the desire to climb a route more difficult than the Nose, I realized that the highs of climbing are addictive and that my appetite to grow and discover new challenges had risen to a new level. The question was, what next?

The Nose had given me the taste for free climbs of a grand scale. The next logical step would be to do other long free climbs in the alpine realm. After Chuck had died on Aconcagua in 1980, I knew I would never get into high-altitude mountaineering. But the idea of rock climbing on the beautiful cliffs that are found on the flanks of some mountains appealed to me. Living in France, whose long and rich history of mountaineering is embedded into its climbing culture, I knew many climbers who courted such ambitions. One such aspirant was Frenchman Hugues Beauzile.

I came to know Hugues in 1993, when he invited me to a party that is thrown every year at a popular cliff in the south of France called Claret. The party, replete with spotlights to illuminate nighttime climbing, and a hundred-foot bungee jump strung from the cliff, was a birthday celebration for the honorary father of this crag, Lucien Bèrardini. Lucien lived nearby in Montpellier and was famous for his first ascent of the south face of Aconcagua in 1954, the very same route on which Chuck had died.

Lucien, an energetic man in his sixties, was like a father to Hugues. In 1989 Lucien had shown Hugues the then-unexplored cliff above the village of Claret. The pair of them, and their friends, had put up scores of sport climbs on the cliff, making Claret one of the most popular winter crags in southern France. After rock climbing for only four years, Hugues decided to set his goals on more challenging alpine-style routes, just like his good friend Lucien. Without much knowledge or proper equipment, Hugues set out to do a winter ascent of the Walker Spur route on the Grande Jorasses. Fortunately, the night he arrived in Chamonix, he happened to meet a local climbing guide named Fred Vimal, who gave him some equipment, a bit of advice, and showed him some pictures of the route. Though Hugues suffered from cold wind, bad weather, hunger, and thirst, and ended up with minor frostbite on his fingers after his ascent, he was pleased with his first experience in the realm of alpine climbing and it fueled his appetite for more.

Hugues had ambitious plans, and he realized that he needed to gain more big-wall climbing experience, so Lucien proposed a trip to Yosemite. Hugues and Lucien did the Nose route on El Capitan with only eight liters of water between the two of them. In order to make faster time, and get to water sooner, Hugues climbed forty-eight hours straight through the day and night. When Lucien fell asleep at the belay, Hugues made sure to pull the rope gently as he led upward so as not to wake him up!

His next project was a solo ascent of the Thomas Gross route on the west face of the Petit Dru. Again, he was partly inspired by Lucien, who had done a first ascent on the same wall in 1952. One day, while talking to another local guide from Chamonix, Hugues found out that the Thomas Gross route had never been repeated. Apparently this route had a reputation as intriguing as Thomas Gross himself. On the epic first ascent, Gross, a Czech, had hauled all manner of gear, including his guitar and a large frying pan for cooking the onions he was fond of. Gross led a hedonistic life of climbing walls across the world, then he mysteriously dropped off the map in the mid-1980s while traveling in India.

Hugues made two epic attempts on the route before finally succeeding. On his first attempt, he sprained his knee and dislocated his hip before he even got to the base of the route when he jumped out of a steep couloir to escape a dead-end impasse. On his second attempt, while leading the second pitch of the route, he pulled off a big, loose block and he ended up slashing his leg to the bone. But Hugues went back, and after making a harrowing nine-day ascent through two snowstorms, his ascent of the Thomas Gross route received plenty of attention in the climbing press. A photo of Hugues, taken by a mutual friend and photographer who happened to be flying by while Hugues was on the route, appeared on the cover of *Vertical* magazine. The article about his climb depicted Hugues as the "Rasta of the mountains" because he wore a mane of dreadlocks gathered like a fountain on top of his head. Hugues, however, never let drink or drugs pass his lips.

At the time that I met Hugues, he was planning his first high-altitude trip. Perhaps not surprisingly, it was to the south face of Aconcagua, and his partner was to be Lucien. The climb was to be a fortieth anniversary celebration of the first ascent. Before they left for South America, Hugues and I had a conversation in a café in Aix-en-Provence. As we spoke about mountains and climbing, I fiddled with a ten-franc coin. Hugues talked about his dreams of climbing with me in places like Trango Tower in Pakistan and the Eiger in the Swiss Alps. Using the coin as a metaphoric instrument, I pushed it toward the edge of the table.

"I could continue pushing toward the extremes, but I'm afraid that if I go too far, I'm going to fall off the edge," I said.

Before the coin toppled onto the floor, Hugues quickly snatched it out of the air and placed it back on the table.

With Hugues at my house in France. (HEINZ ZAK)

"Why are you interested in doing extreme routes in the mountains?" I asked.

"I find great satisfaction in tapping into a kind of elevated state of consciousness during those crucial moments of difficulty. The greater the challenge, the more inner strength I'm able to access," he said.

I understood this. But deep down I felt that Hugues was bound to step over the edge someday. He was young and felt invincible in the face of risk. He seemed to possess the spirit of a benevolent warrior and I worried that, like Chuck, he might not come back from Aconcagua.

In January, Hugues headed down to South America with Lucien. Meanwhile, I set off on a slide-show tour across the United States. One morning, I woke up disturbed by a strange dream. In this dream, I looked down from the sky on a huge snow-covered mountain. A cross lay flat against the snows near the summit. White lights surrounded the cross. I felt an inexplicable sense of peace emanating from this scene, then I woke up. At first I didn't know what this dream meant, but later that morning I thought of Hugues. I called a friend in France to find out if he knew anything about the Aconcagua expedition.

"Hugues has not been seen for a week," my friend explained.

"Lucien had refused to join Hugues on the ascent, since the conditions were too dangerous, but Hugues decided to solo the route. Lucien warned Hugues not to go saying, 'You are going to kill yourself up there.' He went just the same."

The next day, while driving to Salt Lake City airport with my brother Tom, I pledged that if Hugues died up there on that mountain, I would never pursue alpine climbing. When the plane arrived in New York later that day, my old friend Russ Clune picked me up at the airport. In the car, he grew somber.

"I'm sorry to tell you this, but I received a message for you about your friend on Aconcagua," he said.

I felt a painful sensation dart through my chest. I knew what was coming; I had known all along. Only now rescue teams had brought back the official news. Hugues had died of exhaustion after spending eleven days climbing the south face. His death had come on the same day as my dream of the white mountain and the cross. I would later learn that Hughes had died on exactly the same route and probably within only a couple hundred yards from the place where Chuck had died. A few years later, when reading Reinhold Messner's book *Free Spirit*, I had an eerie sense of déjà vu when I found this account of Messner's summit day on the south face of Aconcagua:

About twenty meters below (the summit) fluttered some shreds of material. They hung from the corpse of a dead climber who lay there on his face among the stones, as if he had collapsed and had not found the strength to prepare for death. Now he seemed to be part of the stones, a red mound amongst the rocks. I saw how he did not get up again. He moved no more, only the storm tore at his clothes. Perhaps he had been a good mountaineer, perhaps he had wanted only to sit down. At such heights a stumble could mean death. I did not allow myself to sit down, I had to go on. Suddenly a white cross emerged in front of me. It was about a meter high, made of aluminum and twisted by the wind. I was on top.

Had my close friendship with Hugues provided me with a moment of contact with him during his final moments when he hovered between life and death? I'll never know for sure, but Hugues's death, like

Chuck's, confirmed my fears about the mountains. But there was another realm in the climbing world midway between the icy realm of high-altitude mountaineering, where the wind could suck the life out of a person, and the smaller cliffs in the valleys below.

One such place lay in the distant Pamir Alai region of Kyrgyzstan, a former Soviet satellite state in Central Asia but now an independent republic. There, in the remote valley of the Karavshin River, were cliffs of a scale greater even than those found in Yosemite, and with a mild climate. Russian climbers had been visiting the area for two decades, putting up routes on the best big walls, but with the end of the Cold War and the relaxation of relations with the Soviet Union, it was suddenly possible for Americans and Western climbers to travel there.

In 1995, I joined the North Face climbing team as a professional climber. Almost immediately the company proposed a "team" expedition made up of all its sponsored climbers. Kyrgyzstan's Karavshin Valley was chosen as the destination. Knowing that the weather conditions during the month of July would be stable and warm and that we wouldn't encounter much snow or ice on these routes reassured me. It was also comforting to know that my companions would be among the most accomplished alpine climbers in America: Alex Lowe, Kitty Calhoun, Jay Smith, Conrad Anker, Greg Child, Dan Osman, and the photographer Chris Noble. All of them had climbed peaks from Patagonia to the Himalayas. If I wanted to learn about the mountains, then I'd be in good company.

Before heading to Kyrgyzstan I had already done a few alpine rock climbs in Chamonix with my friend the French alpine guide François Pallandre. With him I learned to appreciate the pristine beauty of climbing in the Alps. Though cold weather and the objective dangers of the mountains kept me on edge, I began to understand why Chuck and Hugues had been so enchanted with the beauty of such heights. In Chamonix, François and I would catch the gondola from the valley floor, then ski down into a range of fanglike spires. We'd climb all day on beautifully textured granite, then we'd ski back down to town via the Vallée Blanche. Coincidentally, François had also been climbing in the Karavshin region a few years earlier. When I told him that I had a chance to go there, he showed me spectacular photos of the peaks we'd be climbing and assured me that it would be a worthwhile experience.

Our team flew from California to Tashkent, the capital of Uzbekistan. There, we met our Russian hosts, packed our supplies into a helicopter the size of a school bus, and flew across the border into Kyrgyzstan. Below us the land was dry and barren, then we crested a mountain ridge in our Mi-8 chopper and touched down on a meadow beside the Ak Su River. This would be our base camp. The helicopter flew off, and as we pitched our tents, a Kyrgyz yak herder rode up on his horse and gave us a friendly, grinning welcome to his valley.

"*Ak Su,*" the horseman said, pointing to the river. This word, our Russian base camp sentry Misha explained, meant "clear water," in the language of the seminomadic Kyrgyz people. "*Kara Su,*" the horseman said, pointing over the ridgeline, and over the enormous triangular wall of granite called Peak 4810. The other river valley, the horseman said, was called "black river," and was not so sweet to drink.

For the month we'd be in this valley we would be without radio contact with the outside world. Such isolation made me feel vulnerable. If someone got hurt, we'd be days from medical care. But my companions were used to living and climbing in the most remote places. Alex Lowe was a ferociously fit individual whose climbing had taken him all over the world. He'd guided people up Everest, he'd climbed the hardest ice routes in the United States and Canada, and he had an appetite for climbing and for exercise so insatiable that his friends nicknamed him the Fiend. Conrad Anker was a seasoned veteran of Alaskan and Yosemite big-wall climbs who, when not climbing, liked to paint watercolors. Jay Smith had climbed new routes on mountains from the Cerro Torre group in Patagonia to Alaska. With a drooping mustache and silent-type disposition he embodied the tough mountaineer image, and when I learned that he trained Navy SEALS in mountain techniques I was not surprised. Kitty Calhoun, with her trademark southern drawl and explosive laugh, was America's most accomplished female Himalayan climber, having summated Dhaulagiri and Makalu, both 8,000-meter (26,000-foot) peaks. A veteran of a dozen Himalayan expeditions, Greg Child had stood on summits like K2, and three months earlier he had been atop Everest. The expedition's daredevil was a stylish free climber named Dan Osman, or DanO, as his friends nicknamed him. Dan had developed his own sport: rope flying. Something of a cross between parachuting and bungee jumping, it involved tying into an ordinary climbing rope attached to the top of a cliff and leaping off in a swan dive. After falling hundreds of feet, when the stretch in the nylon pulled tight, he came to a bouncing stop. And last but not least was Chris Noble, the expedition photographer, who in addition to capturing adventure images around the world had climbed high peaks like Pumori in Nepal.

On my first climb in the Karavshin Valley, I teamed up with Greg for a new route on Peak 3850—so named because its summit stands 3,850 meters (12,630 feet) above sea level. Our route followed obvious cracks up a tombstone-shaped wall. Though the climbing was never too hard, loose blocks poised along the way forced us to tread carefully. On our second day on the wall, the rope strung between Greg and me flicked behind a block and dislodged it from its perch. We both had less than a split second to see it toppling toward Greg.

"Whoa, that was close," he shouted after the fifty-pound block narrowly missed his head. Then he carried on up the wall as if nothing unusual had happened.

I didn't mind the usual challenges of big-wall climbing, like dragging the heavy haulbag, sleeping on park-bench-sized ledges, or even the long hikes with heavy packs, but the possibility of getting hurt or becoming stranded on this indifferent wall of rock during a thunderstorm made me feel uneasy. Unlike on most free climbs, where I feel more in control of my situation, here I was surrounded by the unpredictable.

After three days of climbing, Greg and I reached the summit. We rested for a while on the spike of rock that formed the top, then we began looking for the way down. Steep walls dropped off on all sides. Getting down was going to be a long, complicated process, I realized. We rappelled over the edge, our rope dangling from a cluster of aging Russian pitons. Then we continued rappelling and climbing down for another thousand feet into a steep gully that led to the valley floor. All the way down this gully, there was constant movement as melting snow dislodged small rocks. As stones came rocketing down all around us, it seemed as if Peak 3840 were alive.

"Stay close to the wall. Don't go out into the center of the gully," Greg advised, just as a volley of rocks battered the snow slope in front of us.

**Climbing Perestroika
Crack on the Russian
Tower in Kyrgyzstan.**
(GREG CHILD)

I heeded his advice, following him as he ran from boulder to boulder, as if hiding from enemy fire. Seconds after I crossed an open patch of the gully, a grapefruit-sized missile clattered past me and exploded against the cliff.

"Is it always like this?" I asked.

"You get used to it," Greg responded.

I wasn't convinced that I would ever get used to such hazards, but after a few days of rest, I was curious to try another route. This time Greg and I decided to free climb the Perestroika Crack on a peak called the Russian Tower. Russians had climbed the route during the Mikhail Gorbachev years, and my friend François had done it a few years earlier, calling it one of the best climbs in the valley. He'd climbed it in "team free" style, which meant that only the leader free climbs each pitch, leaving the second climber to remove the gear and carry the pack while following the pitch on jumars. This style is fast and logical for the mountains when time is of the essence, but for me, as a climber focused on aesthetics rather than summits, it lacked the beauty and rhythm of a continuous stream of free climbing. After free climbing the Nose in a day, I wanted to feel the satisfaction of moving over stone for thousands of feet.

François had given me his sketch map of the route, or a topo, as climbers call them. While lounging around base camp, Greg and I studied the map and scanned the wall with binoculars.

"Most of the climbing up there is 5.10 or 5.11. There is only one pitch rated 5.12b. Let's try it all free, with each of us leading and/or following free too," I suggested to Greg.

"Sure, I'll give it a shot," he answered. I detected a hint of skepticism in his voice, as if to say that he thought we would be biting off more than we could chew on this enormous pinnacle of granite.

We started out from base camp at one-thirty A.M., scrambled up a gully, and arrived at the base of the wall at about four. By sunrise we had climbed the first four pitches and had arrived at the top of a notch where Chris Noble and Dan Osman were sleeping. They were waiting for us, ready to take pictures of Greg and me climbing the striking crack that split the wall above for the next 500 feet. As I paced past Chris, I noticed that my headlamp was fading.

"Can I borrow your headlamp battery? Mine is fading fast and I have a feeling I might need a fresh battery up there," I said, sensing that night may come before we saw the summit.

The day sped by as we climbed pitch after pitch. We "swung," or alternated the leads. We had made it past the most difficult "crux" pitch by dusk, but as darkness set in, we were still a long way from the top. Hanging from the side of the cliff, I pulled the topo map out of my pocket.

"This shows that we have four pitches to go to the summit," I said.

Greg craned his neck out into the dark sky and looked up. "Nope," he said with certainty. "Your topo is wrong. It's a lot farther than four pitches. We'll summit at dawn."

"I think we'll be on top soon," I insisted optimistically.

I was convinced that we had only a couple of hours of climbing to go, but the evening turned out instead to be a long night. Just after sundown I got lost on a blank face when the crack I was climbing pinched down to a seam. Climbing by instinct, I felt my way across the wall and eventually found another crack system to our right. Then Greg found himself leading a poorly protected, overhanging roof crack that was dripping with water.

"What have I done to deserve a wet, off-width roof by torchlight at 2:00 A.M.?" Greg yelled down to me.

From the belay I shouted back, "Only you know the answer to that."

I heard a series of grunts, then the echo of a slap as his hand dived onto a ledge that marked the end of the pitch.

"That was another close one," he said when I joined him.

At that point my goal of free climbing the entire route seemed contrived and senseless. Ever since I had started climbing, I had believed that the style by which one got to the top was more important than the summit itself. But here I saw that simply getting up without incident or injury was the most important thing. Even so, I couldn't stop myself from trying to free climb every move of this climb. Greg had the sense to give up his effort to free climb the entire route at two A.M., when he began jumaring whatever pitches I led to speed things up. At three he suggested that we stop and sleep for the night.

"I'm too cold to stop moving and we don't even have a ledge to sleep on. At this point, it would be easier to keep going than to stop," I pleaded.

Greg shrugged, yawned, and continued up. We had no food, and our only warm clothing consisted of sweaters, light rain jackets, and bivouac sacks. Soon I began slipping into a dangerously sleepy state at each belay. The only thing that kept me awake was the chill wind and constant rope tangles I had to sort out. During the wee hours of the night, we heard the thunder of a giant rockslide across the valley. A cascade of sparks tumbled down the wall, and the gunpowderlike smell of smashed rock wafted toward us. As the sun crept over the mountain crests across the valley, I made the last few moves to the summit. Greg joined me at the top, shivering and numb-footed.

"You were right, we did top out at dawn. But at least we can rest in the sun for a few hours," I said sheepishly.

We had been moving continuously for twenty-eight hours and our bodies were trashed. It was a relief to take off our rock shoes. We curled up in our Goretex bivy sacks and slept for three hours. By midmorning it was warm enough to emerge from our fabric shelters and begin our long descent. Acres of rubble led down a gully behind the Russian Tower, and my legs trembled with fatigue as we slogged downward hour after hour. I watched in amazement as Greg seemed to hurl himself down this jagged and rocky slope, sliding on his heels through the scree. He was able to make fast progress using this technique—called glissading—but his brutal approach went against my sensibilities as a free climber. In order to avoid falling or spraining an ankle, I took my time to place each foot in the most secure position possible. The downside to being careful was that it was slow. On the other hand, Greg was reveling in his ability to race down this unstable terrain.

"I'll never make an alpinist out of you if you insist on all this control and precision. That's fine for 5.14, but in the mountains you've got to learn how to slide and grovel. Yahoo!" he screamed, then he was off in a cloud of dust.

If the arduous and dangerous descents of those climbs left me feeling out of my element, then events on my next outing three days later left me feeling horrified. Alex, Greg, Conrad, Dan, and I were near the summit of a spectacular thirteen-pitch route on a peak called, in Russian, Ptitsa, or the Bird. By midafternoon a storm encircled us. Amid booming thunder, we started down from the needle-sharp summit. Five hundred feet below the top I felt a stinging sensation traveling up my spine.

"Get down low. Curl up in a ball," Greg shouted.

A buzzing sound, like a swarm of bees, passed overhead. My hair stood on end.

"What's going on?" I asked.

"Electricity," Alex shouted. "Stay put! Or you might get electrocuted."

The crackle of atmospheric electricity disappeared, and we stood up and hurried down off the rock formation and onto the shoulder of a steep snow slope. My companions seemed accustomed to scrambling unroped on steep snowy terrain, but I worried about the consequences of a slip. A fall here would be fatal.

"Can we rope up?" I asked Greg, before realizing that we didn't even have a way to anchor ourselves to the face.

"Too slow. We need to get out of this electrical storm before someone gets zapped," he said.

Greg handed me an ice ax and told me to follow in his steps, which he stomped out in the snow for me. Just when I thought we had reached a safe position, Conrad, who was behind us, shouted, "Watch out!"

I looked up just in time to see a white wave. Avalanche! A heavy raft of snow slid into me and wiped me off the face. I jabbed the pick of my ice ax into the snow, but it slid through the soft, sun-warmed surface. I slid for 80 feet until I stopped, inches from a crevasse cutting across the slope. For the others this seemed par for the course, but for me it confirmed everything that scared me about mountaineering.

After this experience I felt like just relaxing for a few days, but with six days left before the helicopter was scheduled to arrive and take us back to Tashkent, we had just enough time to do one more climb. The biggest wall in the valley was called Peak 4810 and Alex was itching for a chance to climb it. I had always respected his ability and judgment as a climber, and his enthusiasm was infectious. So when he proposed that we climb this route together, I couldn't pass up the opportunity. Alex had a photograph of 4810's west face that some Russian climbers had given him. Three aid routes scaled this 4,000-foot rock face, but we planned to make the first all-free ascent of this wall. This time I acknowledged that speed was essential and that "team free" style was the most logical approach to this climb. The leader would climb each pitch free and the second would jumar up behind, carrying all our supplies crammed inside a large backpack. To move fast, we took a minimal supply of gear and water, hoping to find enough snow on the bivy ledges to scavenge for water along the way. "Light is right," Alex always said. To this end, he suggested, "Wear your sneakers, not your hiking boots, Lynn." But a few days earlier, one of my sneakers had floated away while I was washing them in the river. So the lightest choice meant heading off to the cliff wearing one sneaker and one hiking boot.

After hiking four hours down the Ak Su River and marching over a pass to the next valley, we met a local Kyrgyz family who shared some flat bread and yak yogurt with us. Our communication was limited to simple words and gestures, but it was evident that our curiosity about this nomadic family was matched by their curiosity about us Westerners. After our brief pause we continued hiking for another two hours before the base of the west face came into view. We spent a restless night sleeping at the base with the silver-gray, massive 4,000-foot wall looming above our heads. At first light we were awake, crossing a snowfield and then a big crevasse before reaching the base of the cliff. We didn't know exactly where any of these three routes began, so we decided to start up the only obvious-looking crack system that started from the ground. Alex led the first pitch following the crack up to a ledge, then it was my turn to lead the second. We knew that we were on some sort of route when we found a small bolt on the face, but it wasn't clear where the line went from there. Perhaps the Russians had used this bolt to pendulum over to another crack system. But our intent was to free climb up this wall, so I decided to climb up a natural dike formation that cut diagonally across the face to our right. As I began the

Alex Lowe resting on our first bivy ledge on Peak 4810. (LYNN HILL)

delicate friction moves up this dike, I realized that there would be no protection for at least another 30 feet.

"It looks run-out and pretty dicey," I yelled down to Alex. "But I think I can free climb up this way."

I continued up, but climbing with a pair of rock shoes that were a bit too big and carrying two ropes and an assortment of heavy gear made me feel awkward. The thought of falling and getting hurt way out in the middle of these mountains reminded me to proceed with full attention. By the time I was able to place a solid piece of protection in a crack another 40 feet higher, I was already pumped, and it looked like the climbing above was even steeper and more strenuous. After making a few powerful moves over a small roof, I was relieved to find a perfect belay ledge. This was only the second pitch of the route and I was already feeling intimidated by what else might lie ahead. Next it was Alex who had to lead a steep section of wet rock with little protection. If he had fallen on the first few moves, he would have landed on me. But I felt confident in his ability and he proceeded as though this kind of climbing were commonplace for him. Most of the time we were padding over the rock, half lost, relying on instincts that years of climbing had bred in us. It was as if an internal compass guided us toward the natural weakness in the rock. After we had climbed five pitches up the wall, Alex arrived at the belay and asked, "Where is the haul line?"

"It was clipped in here at the anchor. Didn't you tie into the other end?"

"No, I don't tie into the end because it causes too many rope tangles."

Either I had not clipped the rope in to our belay or Alex had accidentally unclipped it in his haste. Whatever the case, we had dropped our vital second rope. Without it, getting down the mountain would be much more risky. Instead of being able to tie a pair of 150-foot-long ropes together and rappel in 150-foot stretches, we'd have to double our sole rope through the anchors, and make 75-foot rappels. This would require more time and more gear. We might find ourselves stranded between available anchors. To go on would be like embarking across the Sahara on a jeep safari with no spare tire.

"Should we go up or down?" Alex asked.

"Up," I said.

"Yes! That was the right answer," he said, punching the air with boyish enthusiasm.

Neither of us wanted to relinquish the climb at that point, so we climbed on. Strangely, once we had committed ourselves to this course, I felt relaxed. I felt comforted by the fact that Alex was totally confident, and fast as a greyhound on this terrain.

We reached the summit at two P.M. of the third day. The sun blazed over the Karavshin Valley, and the hiss of the river making its way down the stony slopes filled the air. Standing on top, Alex beamed with unadulterated joy. In an old tin can crammed in a crevice on top, we found a "summit register" of climbers who had passed here before us. Russians and Britons had been up here in previous years, and just a day earlier, our friends Jay, Kitty, and Dan had summited after doing a new route on the south face. Lacking a pen, they told us later, they'd used the point of a knife like a quill, dipped in blood from a scratch on Kitty's knee, to write their brief, odd-looking entry. Their blood-letter gave a brief description of their new route and concluded with the words, "Life is kaif." Our Russian base camp hosts had taught us this local expression—*kaif*—which meant that life is good. We were living the "high life" in Kyrgyzstan, and as I stood on top of that grand peak looking at the higher snow-covered mountains that divided where we were from Tajikistan, I felt a wave of goose bumps race across my skin.

I knew this would probably be the highest peak I would ever climb and that it was time to come full circle in my life. I thought of Hugues, Chuck, and many other people who had been a big part of my life. I had gone as far toward the edge as I was willing to go. Even though for me the spirit of climbing has always been linked with the insatiable curiosity to learn and grow, I realized that I didn't need to try bigger, longer, or more difficult routes to achieve this end. I could do more with less. It was clear to me that the further I went toward the "extreme," the further I was from achieving a harmonious balance in my life. Although I had achieved my personal goals in climbing—winning the World Cup, freeing the Nose, confronting my fears of the mountains—my lifestyle as a professional climber had also made it difficult to maintain a stable personal life.

Though I enjoyed living in Europe, and still spend a lot of time there, I sold my house in France the following year and returned to the United States, figuring that I would have a better chance of finding stability between climbing, personal relationships, and future career opportunities.

As the years went by, more and more of my friends and acquaintances in the alpine climbing world lost their lives. Dan's daredevil stunts finally got the better of him in 1998, when he fell more than a thousand feet to his death while attempting the highest rope-jump of his career. Dan often did his stunts on camera, and I had watched videos of him doing risky things like speed climbing without a rope up a 400-foot cliff in just over four minutes. On that free solo he lunged to a hold and missed, but he'd saved himself from a death fall by catching himself by one arm on a lower hold a millisecond later. His final stunt—the longest rope-jump ever tried—took place on a cliff near the Leaning Tower and Bridalveil Falls in Yosemite. He had jumped off this forma-tion numerous times, and with each jump he'd lengthen the ropes so that he could fall a little farther. His goal was to make a jump of 1,000 feet. His system was cleverly and painstakingly worked out so that he would fall down the entire face and stop just before reaching the ground. But on his final jump of the day, fate had it that the rope broke at its weakest point: the knot.

While sitting on a plane reading about his death in *Climbing* maga-zine—DanO was on the cover—I struck up a conversation with a young boy sitting next to me. The youngster was curious about the daring fel-low in the photograph, so I read the text aloud.

"On November 23rd, DanO stood atop Yosemite's Leaning Tower and prepared for his biggest rope jump ever—over 1000 feet of free fall. He called friends in Tahoe on his cell phone, and kept it on so they could hear him jump. He let out a wild laugh, counted aloud, 'Three, two, one,' then yelled, 'See ya!' DanO's friends on the phone heard the wind roar as he approached terminal velocity, and then nothing."

"Cool!" the boy said.

"I don't think that was so cool. This guy *died*!"

This kid's reaction made me realize just how far over the edge our sport had been pushed. Climbing now had to be "extreme" in order to get any attention from the press or from sponsors. Risk takers, even when killed doing stunts that could only be called folly, were now the heroes in our image-driven society. Dan was a sweet, kind, and child-like person with a reckless streak a mile wide. Things that seemed insanely dangerous to most of us were day hikes for Dan, and things that were exciting for the average climber bored him. He lost perspective of how unforgiving his stunts could be, and this killed him. This attitude was completely at odds with my own motivation for climbing. For me, flirting with death was not necessary. I was content with the challenge of free climbing as a means of finding peace and harmony in my life.

In Kyrgyzstan we all saw that Dan would someday step too far over the edge. During the electrical storm, while we were cowering from the threat of being fried by a lightning strike, Dan strutted around the ledge complaining that he had bees buzzing inside his helmet. Greg, Alex, and Conrad had warned Dan to get down or he might be electrocuted. Wishing to escape this situation quickly, we had abandoned a rope which had been tied to the needle point apex of the Bird. Since this summit was a perfect lightning rod, we had no qualms about leaving it. When the electricity eased off, we headed the rest of the way down, but Dan had waited until we were ahead of him, then soloed back up to the summit to retrieve the rope. "I didn't want the mountain or the weather to beat me," he later explained to us all when we reproached him for risking electrocution.

Alex had been particularly hard on Dan about his actions at the summit. Had Dan been struck by an electrical discharge, the rest of us would have had to climb up and help him down, dead or alive. More lives would have been placed at risk. Alex had admonished Dan, and he and Greg had told him that they would not climb with him after that episode, for fear that he'd do something irrationally dangerous. Dan sat despondent, uncomprehending of why no one could understand his need to confront and fight the elements.

Then, in 1999, Alex himself was killed in an avalanche in Tibet, while skiing under the 8,000-meter (26,000-foot) peak Shishapangma. Alex, by this stage, was at the height of his powers as a mountain athlete. Several high-profile expeditions with films and web sites attached to them, on peaks like Great Trango Tower in Pakistan and Queen Maude Land in Antarctica, had featured him as a star. Alex was one of the best alpinists in the world, and he made reasonable decisions while climbing, yet he spent so much time in the mountains that the odds were becoming inevitable that someday he would be in the wrong place at the wrong time. The avalanche that buried him broke loose from the top of Shishapangma, 6,000 feet above, and swept down the mountain face in less than twenty seconds. Alex, the climber, cameraman David Bridges, and Alex's frequent partner Conrad Anker ran for cover as thousands of tons of snow roared toward them. Conrad veered in one direction, Alex and David ran the other. The difference between death and survival was a few paces. Conrad dived behind a hump of glacial ice, then dug his ice ax into the snow. Wind and ice blocks pummeled him. When the maelstrom was over, he immediately called out for Alex and David. No answer came. Conrad had lost two friends—one of them his best friend—and Alex's wife, Jenny, and his three young boys had lost a husband and father. Yet in a hopeful and sweet twist of life, two years after Alex's death, Conrad and Jenny are married and Conrad has shifted the focus of his life from the mountains to helping to raise the boys.

Though the tragedies of Dan and Alex, and of Chuck and Hugues before them, touched my life and saddened me, I never felt a need to give up climbing. My foray into the realm of alpine climbing confirmed my preference to stay true to the form of climbing I've always loved most: free climbing. Instead of pursuing more extreme adventures in cold, unstable places, I chose to broaden my experiences in the world. During my travels over the past several years I've climbed on beautiful and often remote rock walls in Morocco, Vietnam, Thailand, Scotland, Japan, Australia, and South America, as well as all over Europe. I also spent time living in Italy, where I climbed on the grand walls of the Dolomites and many other classic climbing areas with my dear friend Pietro Dal Pra, one of the best climbing partners I've ever had. During our adventures together, I learned about the rich history of climbing in the Dolomites, as well as how to speak Italian, and reconnected with many other friends in Italy—the place where my life as a professional climber began.

In the summer of 1999, on an all-women's climbing expedition to Madagascar on which I was the leader, I found myself sitting on top of a 2,000-foot rock formation in the Andringitra Mountains located on the island's southern highlands. Sitting beside me were my partners

Nancy Feagin, an American rock and mountain expert, and Kath Pyke, a traditional rock climber from England with many first ascents to her credit. Getting to the top of this equatorial summit on the fourth-largest island in the world, located off the southeast coast of Africa, had offered new challenges for all of us.

Behind us lay weeks of strenuous physical labor. We had drilled numerous protection bolts up this steep, virtually crackless wall of granite, while free climbing pitches as hard as 5.13d. The climb we had just completed was perhaps the most difficult first ascent ever done by a team of women. But beyond the climbing itself, I felt fortunate to be in this amazing wilderness with its abundance of unique plant and animal life, clear skies, and a community of native people that still maintain a close connection to the earth. As we shared the view of the great red orb of the sun setting over the arid landscape of the Andringitra Mountains, my thoughts wandered back in time to a climbing trip in Vietnam's Ha Long Bay three years earlier.

On one of our last days in Ha Long Bay, we visited residents of a small fishing village located in the Gulf of Tonkin. On their flotilla of thirty or so vessels, we found women cooking, older men repairing nets,

Striking a tai chi pose with new friends in Ha Long Bay. (BETH WALD)

and children hopping from deck to deck like the pirates who were said to still roam these waters. While touring one of these floating homes, our host showed us their Buddhist altars and explained how they performed ceremonial rituals and offerings as a means of showing respect for their ancestors and family heritage. Coming from America, a place that has become a fragmented mixture of so many different cultures, I was moved by their sense of loyalty for ancient family traditions, as well as their faith in defending their culture and freedom against the pressures of the modern world.

The contrast between our differing cultures was particularly evident when speaking with Nguyen Mien, one of the fisherman who had watched my companions and me going up and down several wildly sculpted limestone monoliths that jut out of the sea. Communicating through an interpreter, he asked me, "What are you looking for up there?"

We were the first rock climbers he had ever seen, and for a community of people whose lives were centered around fishing and a completely different way of life, our actions on the rock seemed incomprehensible.

"Nothing, really. I climb for fun. It's a kind of moving meditation similar to dance or martial arts," I explained, then I struck a tai chi pose, a physical and cultural statement that I thought he would understand. At this, we all laughed.

But deep down Nguyen's innocent question provoked me to consider the more profound meaning behind his words. Four decades earlier, a famous French alpinist named Lionel Terray had titled his memoir *Conquistadors of the Useless*. Climbers have commonly identified with the sentiment of that enigmatic title, which asks, "What do we conquer in a mountain?" Certainly we do not "conquer" anything by climbing to the top of a rock or peak. Perhaps forty or a hundred years ago getting to the top of a mountain and surviving the harsh conditions of the alpine environment was perceived as a triumph of man against nature. Today modern technology and extensive exploration of nearly every corner of the earth has changed our interaction with the world, but it seems that the spirit that drives us to search remains the same.

For me, climbing is a form of exploration that inspires me to confront my own inner nature within nature. It's a means of experiencing a state of consciousness where there are no distractions or expectations. This intuitive state of being is what allows me to experience moments of true freedom and harmony.

No matter where I am in the world or what summit I've attained, the greatest sense of fulfillment in my life is connected to people. I am fortunate to be part of a big international family bonded by a common passion. Throughout all my experiences over the years, the sheer joy of playing on the rocks with my friends has been the underlying inspiration for my love of climbing. What started out as a simple outing on a rocky outcrop in southern California twenty-six years ago has become a vehicle for evolving as a person, learning about the world, and sharing those experiences with others.